THE SOUTHERN PART OF HEAVEN

TOUJOURS PRET

THE Southern Part of Heaven

BY

WILLIAM MEADE PRINCE

WITH ILLUSTRATIONS
BY THE AUTHOR

The University of North Carolina Press
CHAPEL HILL

FOR LILLIAN

THE SOUTHERN PART OF HEAVEN

CHAPTER ONE

WE WERE at the dinner table, that calm summer midday—my father, who was on one of his rare visits home, and Mother and Grandpa, and my uncles, Mars' Phil and Mars' Pike.

North Carolina, in 1900, must have been one of the only thirteen places where uncles and other superior beings were called Mars'—that beloved Southern abbreviation for Master (broad a'd Master); the other twelve, naturally, being the remaining sovereign states of the greatest nation on which the sun ever shone—or set—the Confederate States of America. It was a term of high respect and affection, meaning everything from Sir to Boss Man. The best known of all the Mars'es, of course, was Mars' Robert—the name given Robert E. Lee by his devoted followers.

I called my two idolized uncles, Phil and Pike, Mars' Phil and Mars' Pike. I had always called them that; how and when it started I do not know. Probably they themselves instructed me so to do, humorously, and because it may have given them a slight feeling of distinction and power, they being somewhat youthful uncles and unused to deference.

They were my mother's brothers, junior to her by only a few years, and they were the bright stars around which my life revolved. They were prophets, oracles; whatever they did or said was gospel and not to be taken lightly (or "with a grain of salt," as I was sometimes told by my father, who did not share my idolatry). But I thought it ridiculous and terrible for my father or anybody else to think ill of them or question their shining integrity. Looking back, now, I am partly convinced that some of the things they told me may have been a little out of line, exaggerated, perhaps, but then no such suspicion worried me.

We were all having a fine time that day, and eating a lot —the dinner being extra special on account of Dad, the guest of honor. Dad was in high and expansive good humor and held our respectful attention as he recounted his adventures Out on the Road, since he was last at home. By the time we got to the watermelon, however, he was running down, dulled a little, probably, by all he had eaten. The pauses became longer, and it was during one of these that Mars' Phil brought up the matter of the pony. He didn't mention it to me, he mentioned it to Mars' Pike, and that's what made it doubly interesting and authentic. Mars' Pike was slightly the younger of the two, and might have been called Mars' Phil's stooge had there been such a word then.

Sort of idly and in a lowered voice, Mars' Phil said, "Pike, you saw that pony uptown, didn't you?"

I was eating the heart of my watermelon at the moment, having saved it for last, but I remember stopping with a big, juicy gob of it in my spoon, while my ears pricked forward.

Mars' Pike looked at his elder brother, and then said, calmly, "Yeah, I saw him; mighty pretty pony. Black, wasn't he?"

"Yeah, black," said Mars' Phil. "Prettiest pony I ever saw."

"What pony?" I asked, my heart beginning to thump a little.

Mars' Phil did not appear to have heard me. "Um-m-m," he said. "Bee-utiful. White feet."

"What pony?" I asked again, intensely.

"What did you say, son?" Mars' Phil asked, in the semi-annoyed tone one uses when interrupted in a private conversation.

"I said 'what pony?' " I repeated quickly. Then added "sir."

"Oh, just a pony I saw uptown," he said, kind of careless. "I meant to tell you about him. He was up in the telephone wires in front of Mr. Hoot Patterson's—"

"Up in the *telephone wires?*" I gasped.

Dad's expression had changed and he frowned a little. He cleared his throat. "Now, son—" he began.

"Yes, sir, up in the telephone wires," Mars' Phil said. "I don't know how he got there, but I heard somebody say that anybody who got him down could have him. It oughtn't to be such a hard job; he's not tangled up very bad."

"Now, look, Phil—" my father said.

"Mother, may I be excused?" I asked, jamming the piece of watermelon into my mouth.

"No, son, you sit still!" said Dad.

I had lost all interest in food. "How'd he get there," I demanded, "in the telephone wires?"

"Best thing about him was the saddle," Mars' Phil went on. "Prettiest saddle you ever saw—red saddle with fringe on it. And that bridle . . . !"

I was down from my chair by that time, and Dad turned on me. "Now you get back up there!" he ordered.

"But *Dad!*" I shouted.

Mother said, "Hush, son."

"There were a lot of people looking at him," Mars' Phil continued. "Somebody ought to get him down from there . . ."

"Now, Phil, you look here," Dad said, his voice rising. He was beginning to get red.

Grandpa hadn't said anything, he'd just been drinking his coffee, smiling a little, but now he said, "Son, I wouldn't—"

"Oh, *yes,* Grandpa!" I shouted. "I think—"

"Now, son, *stop it!*" Dad shouted, and grabbed at me—and upset his watermelon plate and the juice and seeds went all over the table cloth and the floor. Viola, our cook, came in, grumbling, and swabbed it up. I sat there, looking at Mars' Phil, and he grinned at me—very honest and affectionate, I thought.

"You think he's still there, Mars' Phil?" I asked, and my voice must have been trembling.

"Oh, I guess so," said Mars' Phil, carelessly. "Nobody seemed to want 'im."

"How high up is he?" I gasped.

Dad yanked me up, then, and he and Mother and I went out in the yard. Dad was really angry. He strode up and down and waved his arms while Mother said, "Now, Dad, don't get excited. The boys—"

"*The boys!*" Dad shouted. "How can you excuse this sort of thing? Here I come home, and what do I find? All this same, crazy monkey business going on! All these lies they fill him up with—"

"Now, Dad—" Mother would throw in.

"—It's a downright *shame* what Phil does! You oughtn't to allow it, Alice. You ought to put your foot down!"

I was standing off to one side, but I was shaking, and I kept thinking of the time going by, and that maybe somebody would come along who *did* want the pony . . . *maybe somebody had already gotten him* . . . !

"Dad," I implored, "c'n I go uptown?"

Dad turned on me then, and *"Hush!"* he yelled. *"Hush that!* There isn't any pony uptown, black or white!"

"There is so, Dad," I pleaded, rashly, for contradicting my father was something you did at your peril.

"Mars' Phil saw it! He said so!"

"God damn it!" Dad yelled, and Mother screamed.

He had got beet red as his rage increased—rage at me, at Mars' Phil, and at my mother, who was still trying to shush him. He was holding me firmly by one arm to prevent me taking off, and his grip hurt.

"No, Dad," I cried, as I twisted and squirmed with all my might. "He *saw* it—it's got white feet and a saddle on!"

Dad took a swipe at me then and Mother gave a sort of little yip and grabbed him. He shook her off and tightened his hold on me. "They've got to stop teasing him," he shouted. "All these *lies!"*

Mother winced at the brutal word "lies" and said faintly, "No, Dad, they're just teasing him. You oughtn't—"

"Yes, Dad," I screamed. "You oughtn't . . ."

That was the last straw, I guess, and while he shouted "So you're siding with them, Alice! You're as bad as they are!" he took it out on me, and I got a fine and fancy whipping, well rounded and complete. My anguish filled all that part of Chapel Hill. Mother cried, too. Duke, my dog, danced around yapping and barking and adding to the tumult. Grandpa came to the door of his study and looked out with mild interest.

Dad sat there, after the chastisement, glaring at me and chewing his mustache and breathing heavily and muttering threats and imprecations against my idols. "Looks as though you'd have more sense than to believe all the stuff they give you," he growled. "You're going on seven years old!" Blubbering, and holding my burning backsides, I gasped, "Yessuh. Mars' Phil said it was up in the telephone wires by Mr.

Patterson's store." The vision was unbearable, and I added, "It was the best chance I've ever had to get a pony."

It was, too. I never got one, for ponies cost a lot of money, and with that sole exception I have never known of a free pony hung up in the telephone wires. It took a long time for me to forget this near miss, and I could not understand why my father forced me to neglect such a golden opportunity.

He was a sort of stranger to me, though—my father. A mysterious, colorful stranger, a glamorous and affectionate Authority, who came at intervals from Out on the Road and spent a few days or a weekend and then disappeared again into the tremendous and exciting outside world. Always he brought me a present—a book, a pyrography set, a box of lead soldiers—and always he brought, for all of us, a big box of candy. He never failed. During the long periods when he was away he became almost unreal to me, a vague and faraway being I never tried very hard to picture. Sometimes people would ask me, "Where's your Daddy now?" and I would answer proudly, "He's Out on the Road." If they

had asked me, "What is he doing?" instead of, "Where is he?"
I don't know what I might have answered, for I did not
know just what his doings were. They were a vague com-
pound, in my mind, of meeting Consignees and Shippers,
whatever they were, of slaying dragons, and going to restau-
rants, and catching old 42 at Yemassee Junction—all smelling of Bay Rum under theatrical lighting. When he was
home, I listened spellbound, but only occasional words impressed themselves—block signal, Atlanta, broken rail, General
Beauregard Hotel, second section, gondola. . . . Ah, his was
a wonderful life of romance, and I have loved the faraway
whistle of a freight train ever since those days. Later I came
to know that he was a traveling claim agent for the Southern Railway. But I saw him then as the moving spirit, the
heart and core, the power behind the president's desk, of
the Southern's vast system, and to a certain extent I believe
he shared this belief. His honest and sincere enthusiasm for
his job, his loyalty and his deep pride in the Southern Railway, were very apparent. To his mind, it was the greatest
institution on earth, of which he was an indispensable part.
Perhaps he was, he and others like him. What they brought
to their jobs was never paid for in their meagre salaries.

Whenever there was a wreck anywhere on Dad's division,
which was pretty frequently, he was responsible for the
salvage of the freight, and he had to get there as quickly as
possible and by whatever means. I have even heard hand-
cars mentioned. In between wrecks he had to make Reports
(I imagined him standing in front of someone and saluting),
get the stuff to warehouses, and arrange sales. Sometimes he
brought home mysterious packages, which, he would explain, were items lost out of broken crates. ("There it was,
lying by the track! I could see it in the lantern light . . .")
A box of perfumed soap for my mother, a roll of player-

piano music, 'though we had no player piano, a complete
Shakespeare in one volume (I have it now). But most of
all when he came home he brought the freedom and excitement of the great, wide world with him, and all of us were
proud of him, and excited too. And then, after a day or so,
he'd go away again, Out on the Road.

I used to like to look at his passes, a thick stack of colored
and engraved cards he carried in a leather wallet. All the
railroads in the world, I thought! I was fascinated by the
names of all those railroads my Dad could ride *for nothing*. The fathers of most of my friends and contemporaries were
only professors, humdrum, so-so, and they had to live in Chapel
Hill. But not my father! Unfettered, he was a knight gone
forth to do battle in far places with foul and mysterious forces,
a Galahad on wheels, a great and important man. Look at his
passes!

When Dad came home I tried, hard, to be on my best behavior; Mother drilled this into me, and besides, of course,
I stood in great awe of him. He was the final and supreme
authority. When I drove Mother to the dread pronounce-
ment "I'll have to tell your father, when he comes home . . ."
it usually produced the desired result. My wholesome respect
was for him, but my blind devotion, I fear, was for my young
uncles, and my trust was theirs. I was dumb, and credulous,
and only six or seven—and I wanted very much to believe
everything they told me. I never doubted them. But Dad did,
and he used to say they made my life miserable. In this he
erred; they did no such thing; they made it beautiful and
full of color and enchantment, and, to say the least, they
stimulated my imagination. My occasional nightmares should
not be held against them, although this, too, my father did.
It was all very confusing. I do not blame my Dad, now, for
that, and other, lickings he gave me; the poor man was
doubtless driven to it, and after all he couldn't very well

beat up Mars' Phil, who laughed at him and weighed a hundred and ninety pounds and was strong as a bull—or Mars' Pike, either, for that matter. Only I was left. Dad used to say it hurt him worse than it did me, but of this I was extremely doubtful. I was no fool.

In this matter of making my life miserable, if you want to believe Dad, my two uncles usually worked together. What one didn't think of was bound to occur to the other. Like the time I grew a rabbit tail. That sounds foolish, I know, but such was the fact. It happened because of my inordinate appetite for rabbit, stewed, with thick gravy. Rabbits were very plentiful and cheap in Chapel Hill, and that I suppose is why we ate so many of them. I was a rather plumpish little boy, and it may be that the rabbits had something to do with it. I particularly enjoyed the firm, fully packed hind legs. Mars' Phil and Mars' Pike, I remember, used to tell me, laughing a great deal, that I'd grow a rabbit tail if I wasn't careful, but in this instance I didn't quite believe them, and I went right on eating rabbit. I didn't grow a tail, and the laugh was on them. And then, one night, or rather one morning, it happened. I waked, lying on my stomach, with my nightshirt around my shoulders, and as I reached around to pull it down my hand touched *it*. I know I must have given a violent start when my hand brushed the soft, furry ball on my rear, and I was a little frightened. But I grabbed the thing, backhanded, and pulled. Nothing happened. And then I was up with a bellow, and legging it for my mother's room, yelling, "Mother, I've got a tail!" Panic was upon me. But instantly the door opened, and there were my uncles. I don't know why they should have happened to be there just at that moment, but it seemed a lucky thing for me and I poured out my lamentations to them. I remember Mars' Pike tried to soothe me. "Don't worry," he said. "Your mother can cut a hole in the seat of your

pants, and pretty soon you'll hardly know you've got a tail."
They both laughed about it!

I guess I must have been in a pretty fine frenzy for a while,
for finally Mother (who had been doing some laughing herself) gave a yank and pulled the thing off. It had been stuck
to me with bicycle tape. Right there—and I am ashamed to
say it—I did suspect that my uncles had stuck it on while I
was helplessly asleep. But not for long. Mars' Phil explained
to me, gravely, that rabbits are one of the few animals with
no tails whatever of their own, and that Uncle Remus sticks
these round, white ones on the rabbits at night, so that they
may have something soft to sit down on. I thought this a
very good idea, for rabbits. I was a devout follower of Uncle
Remus, and Bre'r Rabbit and the Tar Baby, and I thought
of Uncle Remus as a sort of colored Deity. Mars' Phil said
he supposed Uncle Remus thought I was turning into a rabbit, and who could blame him when you considered the size
of my ears, and that Uncle Remus had likely thought it best to
go ahead with my tail. It all made sense, of course, and naturally I believed it. Even when I carefully examined a rabbit,
my faith was unshaken, and I figured that Uncle Remus had
done an extra good job on this particular rabbit, and that
the fur had grown over the bicycle tape.

Came the day, of course, when I knew I had been hoaxed,
and my mother, who was young, then, and pretty, and liked
a little fun, confessed that she had even held the lamp while
the dastard deed was done.

CHAPTER TWO

We had come to Chapel Hill when I was five years old, and I do not remember the details very clearly. This was just before the Century turned, and headed into trouble. I do recall, however, a lot of ladies bustling in with pies and cakes and loaves of bread; complete strangers who patted me on the head familiarly and asked, "And what's *your* name, little boy?" Grandpa was the new minister of the Chapel of the Cross, and everybody turned out to help us get settled into the rectory. I remember eagerly exploring the small, unfamiliar house—and a lot of boxes and confusion, and a colored man driving a big, white mule who brought our trunks on a wagon.

We had lived in Roanoke, where I was born, and when Grandpa answered the call to Chapel Hill, Mother came with him, and I, naturally, came along too. Dad being Out on the Road most of the time, it seemed best for Mother to stick with Grandpa and make a home for him. "He's as helpless as a baby," she would say. "I don't know how in the world he would get along." This used to puzzle me, as I thought Grandpa got along all right; he could dress himself and everything, and was by no means as helpless as a baby. Besides, he ate very little—"hardly enough to keep a bird alive," Mother said. But Mother fussed over him a great deal. It was Papa this and

13

Papa that. I am sure that the old gentleman must have had a very sweet and gentle nature to have accepted it all so placidly.

From the beginning, all of us loved Chapel Hill and the rectory. How long ago all that seems now. Even the little house has gone. The middle part, the original, was a log cabin of two rooms, and off this original center part had been built two wings of two rooms each, so that the house was a fat letter H shape. After you got the hang of it, you thought it was a wonderful little house, as it was, with a fireplace in each of its six rooms, and the well out back, a few yards from the back porch and the kitchen attached to it. There was a big woodhouse made of logs out by the well, and, behind that, the privy. I investigated that right away. Down in the lower corner of the back yard was a small barn and wagon shed. I was a little disappointed at not finding a horse inside, but I could see that this was a fine place for a rope trapeze and several other projects I had in mind. We never had a horse of our own, so later this was torn down. An apple tree hung over the well; I remember that apple tree with affection and sharp twinges in my stomach. There were two or three peach trees in the back yard, also. A line of fig bushes separated the back yard from the field behind it. The front yard, big and roomy, had six or eight big oaks, and a bird water dish of an old mill stone hollowed out by Indians, people said, and up by the street, in the left-hand corner, a huge water oak. When I came back to Chapel Hill, after thirty years away, the only way I could identify the spot where the rectory had been was by this tree, rugged and venerable. That, and the big magnolia next door where the Abernathys used to live.

In no time at all we were settled. The little boys in the neighborhood and I had looked each other over, cautiously, and I seemed to be accepted.

Grandpa's study, and behind it his bedroom, consti-

tuted one of the wings of the house. I wasn't allowed to
spend too much time in Grandpa's study, as he was generally
writing at his big, flat desk near the front windows which
were in a sort of bay, or reading in his old, beaten-up leather
chair (it was fine to have around you the furniture and things
you had grown up with in Roanoke; it took the strangeness
away from the new house, somehow, and made it friendly).
Grandpa's leather chair was over near the fireplace, and beside it the little round table with the big, silver-colored lamp
and his pipes and tobacco. He always smoked clay pipes with
a long stem. He cut these stems himself from fig bushes and
ran a hot wire through them to burn out the pith. By the fireplace, in addition to the box of paper lighters, there was a
bunch of stiff straw cleaners for his pipes. Mother used to
cut and fold these paper lighters from old copies of the Phila-
delphia *Public Ledger,* which came to Grandpa through the
mail. He wouldn't let her cut up old copies of *The Southern
Churchman* for lighters; said it didn't seem right.

There were bookcases on the side walls, theological
books, mostly, I guess; and there was an Encyclopedia in
green bindings which fascinated me because of the illustrations. There were two wooden chests, under the windows,
in which he kept his sermons. They were written on wonderful heavy white paper like parchment; there's no such thing
now. Sometimes he would give me some sheets of this paper,
and I would make drawings on them, Indians and soldiers.
And the scissors on his desk had snakes—"serpents," he
said—on the handles; I have them now.

But I see Grandpa most clearly from outside the study
windows, as I used to see him when I'd come home late on
a winter afternoon, maybe, when it was getting dark. The
blue smoke from the chimney drifted up, and the windows
would be warm and yellow, and Grandpa would be sitting
at his big desk, writing, the light from the student lamp

shining on his white hair. You never thought of closing shutters in Chapel Hill.

I don't remember any pictures in Grandpa's study except two, "The Last Supper" and a small engraving of General Lee, but in the dining room, one of the two rooms in the log cabin part of the house, there were four. Besides the portraits of Lee and Jackson, there was an enormous close-up picture of a hound in the door of his kennel, by Landseer, and a very exciting picture called "The Horse Fair," by Rosa Bonheur. These two probably influenced me, and I have always liked pictures of dogs and horses around.

The front room, which one entered from the small, recessed front porch which also contained an outside door to Grandpa's study (very handy when people, or students, came to see him on church matters, and a lot of them did) we called the hall, but it was really the sitting room. Mother's was the front room in the left hand wing, and behind that the room occupied by Mars' Phil and Mars' Pike when they came a little later. In between this wing and the log cabin part was a sort of passage, with a tiny room up front which was my own.

There we were, packed into that little cottage. There wasn't any bathroom, of course, but there were the washstands in all the bedrooms, with their big bowls and pitchers which had to be kept always full of fresh water from the well. I helped to tote this. Baths were had with the help of two big black kettles from the kitchen range, and a round zinc bath tub. (In the summer this tub did double duty, as we would fill it with cold water to cool off the watermelons.) I don't remember any icebox in those early days, but I do recall how butter and milk and meat and other things to be kept cold, in the summer, were put in buckets and tin pails and hung deep in the well. Of course we got ice occasionally from the icehouse uptown, but as this was a luxury, it wasn't often.

Practically always it was for ice cream. This spelled labor for me, but it was a happy labor, and always there was the reward of the dripping, heavy-laden dasher.

The big chunks of ice were put in sacks and Mars' Phil, if he were there, or Uncle John, would pound it up with the ax. If neither of them was around, Viola and I would do it, with Mother helping. Making ice cream was a family affair. Then we filled the wooden freezer bucket in which the ice cream container sat—a layer of ice, a layer of salt—and packed it down. Turning the crank was easy at first, but it got harder and harder to push around as the cream began to freeze. After a while you got a breathing spell while more ice was added—and then came the final heavy labor. When you couldn't turn the handle any more you called to Mother. She came and always asked skeptically, "Can't you turn it any more?" And you said, "No'm, not a bit," and you sat there and puffed while she unhooked the fastening and took off the top. It was always a thrill when she raised the lid and began pulling out the dasher. "Just right," she would always say. She scraped back the bulk of the rich, delicious mixture which hung on the dasher, but there was always still lots of it there (she didn't try to do a thorough job) and with your tongue you cleaned it off. Mother would get a spoon, and taste. "The very best I ever made," she'd say. "—Here," and she'd hold out a heaping spoonful. How wonderful it was, after your long, hard work! When the dripping dasher was relieved of all traces of ice cream you helped to pack the freezer full of ice again, and then it had to sit, for the ice cream to harden. After a while you had to go back and take off the sacks with which you had covered the top of the freezer, and pull the plug out from the side and tip the freezer over and let the water from the melted ice run out. Then you packed it up again, and waited for dinner time. We used to have a lot of peach ice cream. . . .

An added treat for Mother and Grandpa, when we made ice cream, was ice for their cold tea. Ordinarily this cold tea, which my mother said was very refreshing, was hung down the well along with the other stuff. It was always known as cold tea, never iced tea.

There was a long walk from the little front porch to the street, with borders of rose bushes. On one side there was a pile of big boulders sticking up, which helped to shelter a hammock slung behind them between two of the oaks. Grandpa's pet rosebushes, Talismans and Marshall Ney, were on the other side, and then the vegetable garden. Many of the best and hottest hours of my youth have been spent in that garden, and I have had a slight aversion to vegetables ever since. Also, the flavor of strawberries has always brought to mind the endless boy-hours necessary to keep them weeded. The little house was painted yellow and white, with green blinds, and under all those trees it must have looked very Currier & Ivesy, especially when a black man and a mule came along out front with a wagonload of canteloupes and watermelons.

There was a big field, usually planted in corn, beyond our vegetable garden, and on the other side a smaller vacant lot, and then the Abernathys' place, with it's "office" in the corner by the street. These "offices" were a sort of tradition in the South then, a carry-over from the plantation days when the planters of the "big houses" built and used them as real offices, or maybe schoolrooms. Anyhow, a lot of smaller, later houses, on village streets and little lots, had them, too, 'though there was no such use for them. The Abernathys rented theirs out.

The first house on the other side of us, beyond the cornfield, was a tall, bleak habitation known, for some obscure reason, as The Hoot Owl, and housing, in those early years, three pleasant and interesting young men. They were interesting because I heard my mother say they were Eligible Bachelors, and I figured this had to do with some secret, though commendable, activity they carried on at The Hoot Owl. In addition to being Eligible Bachelors, they were Instructors in the University. One of them, Mr. Ed Graham, was later a distinguished President of the University, while another, Mr. Will Coker, turned out to be the famous botanist for whom our beautiful Arboretum (now filled with courting couples and a wonderful collection of flora) is named. The third was Mr. Archibald Henderson, who, besides knowing more about mathematics, probably, than anybody else, wrote George Bernard Shaw's official and favorite biography. He still gets letters from Mr. Shaw, but then he was just an instructor with no idea of what a bright future was ahead of him. They all said "Hello," to me, and I said "Hello," to them when they passed by and I was out in our front yard.

Behind us lived one of my best friends, Wump Whitted. He was a gangly colored boy, black as the ace of spades, a few years my senior, and he lived with his mother in a little one-room cabin on the edge of the woods. Surely he couldn't have been christened Wump (or christened, for that matter), but Wump he was, and I never questioned it. He taught me many things, most of them good for me. Down the lane from his house stood another cabin, larger, which he swore was "ha'nted." It looked like it, all right, with its broken, sagging door, and it stood under a sinister-looking dead walnut tree with high weeds all around. We gave it a wide berth. Wump said they could hear the ha'nt at night, up at his house, amoanin' and agroanin' and arattlin' chains. This cabin was never occupied in all the years I lived in Chapel Hill.

New Hope Chapel, the little church which gave our town its name, has long since disappeared; even its exact location is uncertain. But the Hill itself is timeless, surrounded by the rolling country of the North Carolina Piedmont. The Chapel was standing, however, when William Davie, in April, 1787, tied his horse to a poplar tree a few hundred yards away, and said, "Here we shall build our University." There were giants in those days, and a few years later, in 1795, the institution opened its doors, the first State University in the nation. The handful of plain, ancient buildings is now the heart of the huge and sprawling modern school, and the drowsy village that my boyhood knew, more than a century later, is a far cry from the bustling, postwar college town, bursting at the seams, which we have become.

Trees everywhere. That is the feature of the town which first impresses the newcomer. And everywhere surrounding us in warm embrace are the woods. There are not so many trees now as I used to know, when the main street of the village lay under a leafy arch of oaks. No factories or industries, blowing whistles, belching smoke, despoiled the green and placid quiet of the town. Only birdsong and the soft note of the college bell in the cupola of Old South Building broke the stillness, and the church bells summoning the faith-

ful. Only the thin golden dust in the summers, and in the fall
the pungnent smoke of burning leaves, drifted through our
academic air.

It was a little town then, truly a village, and the student
body, most of it drawn from farms and other little towns
in the State, numbered around six hundred. The faculty and
townspeople could not have counted much more, I'm sure. We
seemed far removed from any United States Governmental
functions, except for the haphazard delivery of mail, and I
doubt that Uncle Sam bothered with any 1900 census of
Chapel Hill.

There were only two streets of much importance, which
we boys called Front Street and Back Street, although the
former was properly Franklin Street, and the quiet and narrow Back Street bore officially the poetic name of Rosemary
Lane. From these two thoroughfares there was a fringe of
lesser streets and some jagged roads jutting away from the
University. Most of the better homes, where the Faculty
members lived, and our more prosperous citizens, were on
Front Street, or Franklin. The rectory was on Rosemary.
The social status of our family was not impaired, however,
by the fact that we lived on the Back Street in a house which
was part log cabin; on the contrary, because my Grandfather
was the Episcopal rector he occupied an exalted position.
And anyway, Chapel Hill has ever stood for the things of the
spirit and the real virtues, with little emphasis on material
values and keeping up with the Joneses. Besides, we didn't
have any Joneses.

One of the most spacious and beautiful of our old places,
however, was on the Back Street, just beyond the Abernathys'.
It was the Mangum house, where a nephew, Charles, a con-
temporary of mine, used to come in the summers, from down
in the hot part of the State, to visit his kin. This old house,
architecturally, was typical North Carolina of a hundred years

ago, built of clapboard with a wide, deep porch across the
front of it, and the second story, where the bedrooms were,
only one room deep, so that the air went through. Nothing
fancy or elaborate about the house, and the doorway didn't
have any scrollwork or decoration—not even a carved pine-
apple over it. Tall chimneys at both ends. Viewed from the
side, it has always looked, with its sprawling downstairs base,
and the slender second story over it, like a slim young girl
in hoop skirts, sitting down. It sits far back from the Back
Street, behind and beneath huge trees which are a lot older
than any hundred years, and on one side there was a scuppernong arbor of noble proportions, a spot I knew well.
Charles liked to draw, too, and we were together a lot. When
I entered that old house again, after being so long away, it
was pretty much as it had been, but the most familiar thing
about it was the smell, the personal and particular fragrance
some old houses have and never lose—of leather-bound books
and linen packed away in lavender, and polished furniture
and woodsmoke—and, intangibly, the presence felt of people, young and old, long gone.

My friend Betty Smith abides there now. The Tree that
Grows in Brooklyn has borne such fruit that she has restored and garnished the old house and made of it a gracious
modern home. Still, though, like the hoop-skirted girl grown
old but dressed now for a party in brave new clothes, it
dozes in the dappled shade and smiles upon its past.

The trees and flowers of Chapel Hill are unforgettable.
The great, protective trees are everywhere—pine, hardwood,
evergreen—and make the village seem still a part of the
forest which once covered this whole section. And the flowers
—careless, extravagant—which deck the town are something
that a boy, kicking along the quiet street, may just accept and
take for granted, conscious only of their color and perfume.

But when he's been away a long, long time, and then comes
back, a boy no longer, he sees and recognizes them as loved
old friends who have been waiting for him all the while. He
feels like saying "Hello" to the yards and gardens, like bowing to the yellow jasmine and the intense violet-pink of the
redbud trees, because he realizes, with something tugging at
his heart, he knows them and they lived here long ago. And
he sees the whistling, white-bloused, knickerbockered boy,
bareheaded in the spring sunshine—a small, white dog at his
heels, perhaps—idling down the paths beside the low stone
walls. There are many of these low stone walls in Chapel
Hill. The custom of building them, it is supposed, originated
with one of the earliest professors, the celebrated scientist,
Dr. Elisha Mitchell, who may have been homesick for his
native Connecticut. They seem not designed to keep you out,
but to help you rest, and where not covered by ivy blankets
or climbing roses, afford fine seats for colored nursemaids
and other lazy pedestrians, the very old and the very young.
Young people with the world ahead sit upon them holding
hands.

You see the boy you were, scuffing at the dirt—and
watching a bird, perhaps, pass—all oblivious—great banks
of flaming pyrus japonica, and white-glowing hedges of spi-
rea, and the balconies and trees around him are draped in
wistaria's palest-purple splendor. Beside the boy are lilacs
and syringas and the drifting snow of dogwood. And way
back in your mind there is the tinkle of a little silver bell, and
something opens, like a secret inner door far back in the
closed and unused recesses of your memory, and suddenly you
want to rush up to the redbud and the forsythea and the dogwood, and the others, and say, "Why, I know *you!* You've
been here all the time! I didn't mean to pass you by, so long
ago. I guess I didn't see you then; you were just a part of
everything, and everything was beautiful." And perhaps you

pat a twisted, gnarled crepe myrtle, and you say, "Old Friend, a lot of water's gone down Battle's Branch, but I remember you."

Spring's beauty fades, just as you remember, but later on, when summer comes, the big white magnolia blossoms unfold, and myrtle's watermelon pink, and the feathery mimosa, and looking back you remember them, too, and want to put your arms around their trunks and say "Hello." Summer's beautiful, all right, but spring's the time, before the heat of June bears down—and spring comes early. Sometimes the jonquils and narcissus are blooming in the winds of February, and violets and hyacinths in gay profusion, with pear and peach and plum blossoms not far behind. And suddenly you remember—and your heart contracts a little—a time in early spring before you had your shoes off, when you didn't see and trampled some of Grandpa's bulbs just coming up. And you see the tiny, juicy little spears of green mashed down and broken, lying there, and you try to lift your clumsy feet away, and hope perhaps that Grandpa hasn't seen. But Grandpa saw, and you hear him say, with a rueful little smile, "Well . . . that's all right. Just watch out where you're going, next time."

CHAPTER THREE

THE AUTUMN of 1900 I became a wage earner. Up to that time I had been forced to depend upon largesse. Charity irked me, but that was the only way I got the stuff. In 1900 I was seven years old, and it must have been decided that I had reached an age of responsibility and discretion, so my name was put on the payroll. (Of course, even after this, I would receive occasional presents and benefactions in the way of hard cash, and at times I actually felt pretty well-to-do.)

Naturally, I started at the bottom of our organization, but the members of the family were very helpful in instructing me in my duties and making sure that I carried them all out in a creditable manner, and there were constant valuable suggestions and reminders such as, "Sonny, the wood box is empty," "Sonny, there are a lot of new suckers on the strawberry plants," "Sonny, Grandpa needs a basket of chips," or "Sonny, maybe you'd better gather the figs, so the new ones can get ripe; now don't eat any of them, they're for supper."

My salary was ten cents a week—my "allowance," it was called, but I thought of it as my salary and I was proud as only a man earning his money can be. Gradually I worked up, of course, and as time went on I was rewarded with substantial increases, so that by the time I put on long pants I was making fifty cents. But long pants were not put on too early then, and my rise to fortune was not as rapid as it sounds, and it was hard to put by anything. I never felt exactly, however, as though my labor around the garden and the woodpile and the well was being paid for by the hour or piece; rather, the undisputed fact was impressed upon me that *every*body had to work, everybody had his chores, and that doing these little things was only a slight way of showing your appreciation of your home, whether you got paid for it or not. In fact, Mother hinted strongly that it was my bounden duty so to do, and if I didn't, things might not be so well with me. But hers was really a velvet hand, and she hardly ever made good any of her threats.

Anyway, I didn't mind the work. All the boys had to work around their homes, just as soon as they were old enough; that was understood. One of the commonest answers to an invitation to go somewhere or do something was "Can't; got t'work." You heard it on all sides. My principal job (I'd never heard the word "chore") was, in cold weather, to bring in wood for our stoves and fireplaces. Viola brought in the wood for her kitchen range, but that was only a step from the woodhouse. It was hard to keep a wood fire overnight, so there had to be kindling, for which we used the chips which fell from Uncle John's ax (the woodhouse floor was deep in them), so as to get the fires going in the morning. The big woodbox on the back porch had to be filled every afternoon when I got home from school, before I could "go out." Sometimes, if there was something extra important afoot, the box seemed mighty big.

But I enjoyed the woodhouse the days Uncle John Atwater was out there chopping. He was not another real uncle, but the old colored man who did all sorts of things for us. He was one of the messiest tobacco-chewers I ever saw; the

juice would get all over his wrinkled, laughing old face and drop off his chin, because he had so few teeth, I reckon. He'd wipe the juice off with the back of his hand, and go on talking and chopping. He entertained me endlessly with fascinating stories of the time when he'd been a slave, and how, when he got E-mancipation, he'd gone off with the Yankees.

This business of E-mancipation was intriguing, and I pressed Uncle John for details.

"Well, I don' know," he'd say thoughtfully, scratching his head and leaning on his ax. "Hyah I wukin' f'Mist' Purefoy 'long time, an' den d'man say, 'You is E-mancipation'— and dere you is. Hit were like dat."

"What happened then?" I'd ask.

"Hit were a mighty fine time," said Uncle John. "Mist' Purefoy he come an' say, 'John, you is E-mancipation.' Den me an' Mist' Purefoy we shake han's and he say, 'G'bye, John,' an' I goes in d'town an' dey was jes' a singin' an' dancin' an' carr'in' on. But byen'bye I goes back out tudda farm an' Mist' Purefoy he say, 'Howdy, John. Ain't you E-mancipation? You don't hafta wuk no' mo' . . .' Das d'way hit were."

This explanation did not satisfy me. "But how . . . ?" I asked, "*Every*body's got to work!"

Uncle John smiled wryly and spat a rich stream. "Ya'ah," he said, and chuckled. "'At a fac'. I fin' hit out." He left me with the impression that E-mancipation was something you had to look out for.

Seeking light on the subject, I even inquired of Grandpa. "Grandpa," I asked, "is Uncle John E-mancipation?"

"That's what they say," said Grandpa.

Anyway, Uncle John went off trailing the Yankee Army. He went clear up in Virginia. But he didn't like Yankees, he said, so after a while he got back to Chapel Hill, and he'd been doing a "li'l u'dis an' a li'l u'dat" ever since.

Sometimes I almost enjoyed working in the garden too
—in the summer—for often Grandpa came out and worked
along with me. I wouldn't say that he did it because he
thought best to make sure I was doing it right, but maybe that
entered into it. He was a wiry little old man, for all his
frailty, and he knew his way around with a hoe. Sometimes he
would open up and talk, too, and I liked to listen as I pulled
weeds or picked off potato bugs, but his stories were never
as exciting as Uncle John's. Of course Grandpa could answer
most of your questions and Uncle John could not, but after
all, anybody who had done as adventurous and daring a thing
as to go off with the Yankees was in a class apart.

I remember that first payday, and the bright little dime
Mother gave me. "Here's your allowance," she said. "What
are you going to do with it?" (I knew, but I wasn't telling.)

"Don't look like much to me," said Mars' Phil, when I
showed it to him. "Wait a minute." From somewhere he
dug up a lot of pennies and poured them into my hand and
took the dime.

"Now you've really got a pocketful of money," he said.

I counted the pennies, and there were nine. "Where's
my other penny?" I demanded.

Mars' Phil laughed and handed it to me. "That's the
stuff, Buster," he said. "Don't ever let anybody put anything over on you—and don't try to put too much over on
anybody else!"

With that in mind, and the pennies jingling in my pocket,
I started on the long and tiresome trek uptown, to Dr.
Kluttz's store. Only, it didn't seem long that day, or tiresome;
there was money in my pocket, and merchandise to buy. Fine,
what a strong and independent feeling cash in hand can give.

Our uptown, or marts of trade area, whither I was

bound, was a long block on the Front Street, which lay wide and shady under its big trees. There were several homes along there, too, and the Methodist Church, relieving the commercial aspect, in between the business establishments. A pump and a watering trough were near the middle of the block, and some of the stores had hitching rails out front. As progress brought the water pipes, a couple of fire hydrants were put in, and telephone and electric wires thrust their way along, and some of the big trees suffered. The sidewalks, like the street itself, were sandy gravel and clay, in wet weather full of rivulets and mud puddles. This matter of the dirt sidewalks is sort of an institution in Chapel Hill, along with the stone walls, and to a large extent persists to this day—a great irritation to newcomers who do not realize the relief afforded from Pavement Feet suffered by less fortunate city dwellers. Of course cement sidewalks uptown, and on the Campus some brick, have long since come into being, but in those days there was no thought of wasting concrete underfoot, and I joyously kicked up the dust as I went along.

I passed Mrs. MacRae's weather-beaten old house under the cedar trees (which the colored people said was bad luck) and the A.T.O. house where some A.T.O.'s sat with their feet on the rail of the porch, and the livery stable and the Presbyterian Church, with a colored man already beginning to rake leaves in the yard. Old Tom Dunstan's barbershop was next door to the church. He was working on my cowlick at this period. ("No use letting it grow that way," my mother said, "the sooner we get at it the better.") Adjoining the barbershop was the grocery and general merchandise establishment of Mr. Hoot Patterson. I stopped to look in the window, but nothing appealed. All the things seemed either canned or dried or in need of cooking, and didn't stack up very well with Dr. Kluttz's candy counter.

Mr. Patterson's real name was Mr. H. H. Patterson, but

I never heard of him as other than Mr. Hoot. I wondered if
he had had any connection with the Hoot Owl. His was a
high class and dignified store, patronized by the better element
—the sort of store where the clientele is not watched—and
often while my mother did her marketing (I having been
brought along to help carry the stuff home) I was left to
my own devices and made the trip worth while by filling my
pockets with dried apples and lumps of brown sugar from
the barrels which stood conveniently to hand near the front
door. The black molasses I loved came from Mr. Patterson's,
and the salt roe herring which my grandfather ate every
morning for his breakfast. Candles and kerosene came from
there, and wicks and chimneys. There were black stockings, and bolts of calico and ginghams and dress goods, and
there was a spool case full of beautiful colored silks where my
mother chose the materials for her embroidery, of which she
did a great deal. Mr. Fred Patterson, Mr. Hoot's son, was a
friend of Mars' Phil's, which may be a reason he never
seemed to see me hanging around the dried apple barrel.

The north end of the University Campus was across the
street, stretching away under its great trees, and flanked by
two sprawling and even then dilapidated frame "hotels,"
Williamson's and Mr. Pickard's University Inn. The small
wooden building next to the Williamson Hotel served as the
town hall, and I could see the fat figures of "Judge" Brockwell and Sheriff Suggs, the local representatives of law and
order, tipped back in their chairs, asleep, outside in the October sun. Next to the town hall was the Methodist Church,
and beyond was the Barbees' house. Miss Nellie Barbee, who
was very pretty, I thought, sang in our choir. But time was
a-wasting, I realized, while I dallied before Mr. Patterson's
unappetizing window, and I pushed on.

Beyond the cross street was the McNider cottage, almost lost behind heavy vines and shrubs. George McNider,

the younger son of the family, had a wonderful collection of bird eggs. Every boy collected bird eggs, but his collection was by far the best in town. He was a grown man—that is he wore long pants—but he was very nice about showing the bird eggs to me when I went to his house with my mother. The thought came to me, then, that I might go in and ask Mrs. McNider, or George, if he was home, if he could sell me some real *good* bird eggs for ten cents, but on second thought I discarded the idea, and kept my money. Maybe, next time I came, he'd *give* me some, as he had once before. He had put them in a box with cotton, and I had carefully carried them home and transferred them to the old spool case where I kept my own. I cut a card and printed a label, along the lines of displays I had seen, saying From the Collection of George McNider.

Abutting the McNider yard was the dingy little post office, with its rows of boxes inside, if you didn't want to get your mail at General Delivery (when I first heard of General Delivery I expected to have a general in a flashing uniform hand you your mail), and splintery wooden steps across the front, usually covered by lounging students waiting for the window to open. But the mail had evidently come, and the steps were empty except for a couple of dogs. I went inside, and at the window which I could look over by h'isting up a little, asked Mr. Rob McRae, the postmaster, if there was any mail for me. Sometimes I got mail—a birthday greeting from one of my aunts, or a picture postcard from Dad— and once or twice there had been a real letter from Dad, addressed to me; so whenever I passed the post office I always went in and asked Mr. McRae. He was very nice about it, and would look all through the M's and P's. Today he put several letters and Grandpa's paper down on the shelf in front of him before he said "Nothing today, Your Royal High-

ness. But here's things you can take home, Stick-in-the-Mud."
(That was another name he called me which he thought was
funny.) "No. Phil'll be coming by soon; you might lose 'em."

I left the post office, letterless, but with the feeling of
importance you always have when inquiring for your mail.
Past Old Mrs. Tankersley's house, and I faced the hurdle of
Eubanks' Drug Store. Eubanks' Drug Store—and ten cents!
My mouth began to water a little. Inside, behind the big red
and blue and green urns in the window, was the shining soda
fountain, where soda water and grape juice and cherry phosphate, limeade and Moxie, with shaved ice, awaited to thrill
your palate, provided you had the necessary nickel. (It is
extraordinary how well Southerners of that day got along
without Coca Cola.) On occasion, when Mother treated me,
she'd take a Cherry phosphate, but almost always she said she
didn't really want a thing— "Oh, well, maybe just a glass of
soda water, Mr. Eubanks; it's so refreshing." "Yes, Ma'am,"
Mr. Eubanks would say, smiling, and he'd bring her the soda
water along with my grape juice or strawberry soda, and
never charge her a thing for it.

The results of the few occasions on which my own financial condition forced me, when Mother or some other
benefactor wasn't along, to "charge" my purchases to her
or to my grandfather, were definite and discouraging. However, sometimes resources were pooled if an impecunious
friend and I went in together, and two straws (real straws,
too; none of your modern paper affairs) or two spoons were
provided at no extra cost. This resulted in an argument as
to who got the most. You always tried to.

But my mind was set, that day, and I did not weaken,
even though Mr. Eubanks waved at me from behind the soda
fountain, and I never even slackened pace on my trudge to
Dr. Kluttz's. People hailed me and dogs I knew came up and

sniffed, but my objective lay before me, and I did not turn aside.

Dr. Kluttz's store was much more than that. It was a solid, rock-ribbed institution in Chapel Hill, like the stone walls. It was a club, a headquarters, a Mecca for everybody. It occupied an imposing two-story red-brick building in the heart of town, in the middle of the long block on Franklin Street. (Dr. Kluttz built the building, and you can still decipher his name across the front of it; he rented the rooms upstairs to students, pressing clubs, etc.) I am sure that had we had other roads of any importance they would all have led to Dr. Kluttz's. The bank was next door to Dr. Kluttz's, and I think the bank people must have put it there for the feeling of security and stability it gave them.

I pushed open the screen door and went inside. This screen door hung there, winter and summer, and the ravages of time had done it no good. It didn't keep the flies out in summer, but for some unaccountable reason, and regardless of its gaping holes, it helped to keep them in.

It was darkish inside, but knowing the exact location of the candy, I didn't wait for my eyes to become accustomed to the gloom, but pushed boldly forward. The store was very cluttered, filled with heavy-loaded tables and counters over which a junior customer could hardly see. But the dusty candy showcase was near the door. It displayed enticing if perhaps stale sweetmeats in great variety.

The accompanying advertisement from the college year book will give you a pretty fair idea of the nature of the establishment. Dr. Kluttz used exactly this same advertisement year after year with never a change. It must have cost him a great effort to assemble it in the first place, and he let it lie. Also, he may have been pioneering in the principle of repetition in advertising, although this was long before L.S./M.F.T., or any other of the maddening jargon you

can't get away from nowadays. Anyway, I think it is a fine, dignified ad, and it certainly gives you a lot of information. That last line, too, inspires supreme confidence.

The A.A. stood for Adam Alexander—a beautiful name, I thought. His family must have gone back a long, long way. He sold everything from textbooks for the students to patent medicines and bicycle tubes. How he ever kept up with his stock beats me. He sold things, that is, when it pleased him. One of the many stories told of him has to do with an occasion on which he was quietly playing checkers with a crony, as he so often did, in the dim recess back by the stove. A customer entered, up front, and prowled around. Dr. Kluttz's attention was finally called to this prospective source of revenue by his friend.

"Sh-h-h," whispered the Doctor. "Be still, and maybe he'll go away."

I stood before the candy showcase that day, and counted my money. My present business with Dr. Kluttz was no light affair, nothing that you ought to plunge right into; it demanded thought and care. Money did not grow on trees, my father said, and here I had *ten cents* to be invested wisely and well. Dr. Kluttz, who had silently materialized out of the murk, waited patiently while I wrestled with my problem. He was a large man, very deliberate, with a droopy mustache and a warm-looking nose. " 'Evenin', suh," he said. "G'd-evenin', Dr. Kluttz, suh," I said. We were always very polite to each other. I appreciated his courtesy, for he was a man of consequence and standing. We always said "G'dmawnin'n, suh," or "G'devenin', suh," whenever we met. You always said "Good evening," at any time after the middle of the day; there was no such term as "afternoon;" because from dinner-time on it was evening.

I wanted five cents worth of jelly beans, that I knew. This would make a wonderful big bag, and a fine backlog

which I fully intended keeping until next week and stringing out as far as it would go. Of course I could have done for five cents' worth of jelly beans in no time, had I a mind to, but I figured I still had five cents with which to satisfy the needs of the moment, and as Dad said you always ought to have something for a rainy day, I thought I'd save the jelly beans, and it might rain next week.

Marshmellers were four for a cent. I liked the ones Dr. Kluttz had, they seemed a little tougher than most, and didn't dissolve so quickly. I decided on two cents' worth. Then, one cent for sour balls, one for a stick of licorice, and the last penny for caramels, my favorite. They were four for a penny,

too—dark brown or light brown chewy, each one wrapped in
a separate piece of paper. They were fine eating. Usually,
when maybe I had only a penny to spend, I bought caramels
because they lasted longer, but today—with ten cents—I
thought I'd branch out.

I gave my order, and Dr. Kluttz began putting the things
into separate little bags. "Will you take 'em with you, suh,"
he asked in his drawly voice, "or do you want 'em sent?"

"Uh, I'll take 'em," I said.

I had noticed, with sudden exultation, that Dr. Kluttz
had dropped *five* caramels into the caramel bag! just as he had
on some previous occasions. The only way I can explain it is
that he was getting old, then, and careless.

"Thank you, suh," I said, grabbing my five little sacks,
and I beat it for the door before Dr. Kluttz could discover his
mistake. Outside I opened the caramel bag and counted them
again. Yes, that was right; he had given me five. I took the
paper off one and put it in my mouth. It made a fine lump in
the side of your jaw, while the syrup oozed down your throat,
and every now and then you'd shift it with your tongue and
give it a couple of chews.

I saw Bruce Strowd on the sidewalk as I passed his
father's store.

"What you got there?" he demanded accusingly, indicating the sacks.

"Nothin'," I said. "Somethin' for my mother." It wasn't
for my mother, but I didn't want Bruce Strowd's heavy hand
in my candy.

After the first one was gone, I unwrapped and popped in
another; the first was "velvet," anyhow, and I had plenty. By
the time I got home there was only one left. Oh, well, I
thought. I took it out, and crumpled up the bag and threw it
in the scrap basket.

I don't know anything that ever gave me more trouble,

for a while, than that caramel. I looked at it, and delayed eating it. It began to seem as though it was not only the fifth caramel; it was actually *the* extra one Dr. Kluttz had dropped in the bag. What's the matter with you? I thought: if Dr. Kluttz is all that careless . . . ! But somehow I didn't want to eat it, just then. Yes, I did want it, too, and I started to take the paper off, but folded it back on. And then I thought of what Mars' Phil had said: *"Don't try to put too much over on anybody else."*

Was this putting something over on Dr. Kluttz? Was one caramel "too much?" I was in an agony of conscience.

I sat there looking at the caramel, and it came to me that I was *cheating* Dr. Kluttz, and cheating was stealing, Grandpa said. He had given me the caramel, but it was by mistake, and it didn't belong to me, it belonged to Dr. Kluttz. Keeping it was stealing it. I thought of the convicts I had seen, once, working on the road while a man with a gun watched them. I pictured myself among them. I thought of Sheriff Suggs, with a pistol in one hand and handcuffs in the other. I heard his measured, fateful footfalls coming down our walk. I heard him knocking at the door. I heard him ask, "Is Willie Meade Prince here?" My breath stopped coming as I thought of all the *other* extra caramels Dr. Kluttz had given me, and that, any time, he might count his caramels and try to match them up with the money he had taken in, and think of *me!* And clutching the caramel in my hand I took out again for uptown, as hard as I could go.

When I entered the store I was puffing, and even though it was October I was hot. Dr. Kluttz was reading a newspaper, his feet on one of the tables. (So he hadn't discovered the loss!) "What's matter?" he asked.

In overwhelming confusion, but relief, I held out the caramel.

"You gave me five," I said.

Dr. Kluttz looked at me over his spectacles, then he put down his paper and took his feet off the table.

"Well, I be dog gone!" he said. "Did I?"

"Yessuh," I gasped, still extending the piece of candy.

"Well, now, thank you, suh," he said. He took the caramel, which had got kind of squshed, and looked at it, then he gave it back to me. "I tell you," he said "you just keep it. I guess a man ought to have to pay for his mistakes. . . . Here, hold on, that one ain't much good, I'll give you another one for it. Oh, just keep the two of 'em!"

Didn't Wordsworth say "That best portion of a good man's life,—his little, nameless, unremembered acts of kindness and of love"?

CHAPTER FOUR

DR. KLUTTZ died with a clear picture of Heaven in his mind.

He was never much of a psalm-singing churchman, but he did a lot of work in the Lord's vineyard, and he loved people and flowers. He was everybody's friend. I have heard that he was a real Doctor of Medicine, but gave it up because it interfered with his rest and other nocturnal activities. Whether or not this is true, he was called Doctor, but in a community where Ph.D.'s are the rule almost anybody who could claim respect was called Doctor. My grandfather was a Doctor, too, and I remember inquiring about the D.D. after his name. I was told that he was a Doctor, all right, of Divinity (there was an extremely succulent candy of the period called divinity, and this made an impression on me) and that he prescribed remedies for the immortal soul. I didn't follow that.

Dr. Kluttz's final illness, however, was mortal, and it was Mr. Moss, the Presbyterian minister, who gave him cheer and courage at the end.

On the winter day on which he passed on to even better things, a thin sheath of ice lay over the village and the leaves of the magnolia outside his window made a little dry crackling in the wind. Mr. Moss sat by his bed, thinking he was asleep. There had been a long silence, when Dr. Kluttz—who may or may not have thought about it before—asked, "Mr. Moss, do you think I'll go to Heaven?" (Anyway, that's the way the story is.)

"Yes, Dr. Kluttz," said Mr. Moss, "I think you will."

Dr. Kluttz smiled a little, and there was another long pause. Then, "Mr. Moss, what do you think Heaven is like?" he asked.

Mr. Moss took his time on that one, and finally he said, "Dr. Kluttz, I believe Heaven must be a lot like Chapel Hill in the spring."

"That's good," said Dr. Kluttz—and he started on his journey.

This idea of Heaven is generally accepted by people who lived in Chapel Hill a long time ago.

CHAPTER FIVE

An old resident was recently asked how long one must live here to qualify as a real Chapel Hillian. "It isn't a matter of years, at all," he replied. "It's whether you lived here before the First World War." He knew what he was talking about. Nineteen-seventeen must have been the time when the modern influence crept in and we began to be a part of the worried, hurried U.S.A.

Back before that, in the infant days of the new century, our only link with the outside world was ten miles of rusty rails which wound through the woods and the scrubby farm lands to University Station. University Station was a stop, consisting mostly of a water tank and a dreary general store, on the Main Line of the Southern Railway. At least I thought of it as the Main Line because on my many trips there the mighty locomotives and the big, dusty coaches, full of people you never saw before, with sometimes a mysterious Pullman on the end of the train, were very impressive alongside our train, the Whooper, small and humble on the siding. I used to look at the Whooper, as I sat on the high, car-level floor of the loading platform and swung my feet, and feel a little apologetic for it; but everybody loved the Whooper and called it a unique little train. The big trains on the Main Line were not so hot, either, for all their noise and smoke and arrogance, for

it was not the Main Line at all, I found out later. It was only
an insignificant little offshoot of the Southern, and went only
as far as Goldsboro, or somewhere, and the real Main Line
came through at Greensboro, fifty miles away. Greensboro
was Bagdad, to me. I went to Greensboro for the first time
when I was about eight years old, I guess. There, hard by the
station, there was a small, red-brick hotel which had a big
dining room window where one sat and watched switch engines and the *real* Main Line trains come through, and—
attended by a colored waiter in a white coat—ate all the buckwheat cakes and maple syrup one wanted. There was too
much silver on the table, I remember; there were several forks
and spoons by my plate, and I called this to the waiter's attention. "Cert'ny, suh," he said, and bowed—and took away the
extra things. We never had maple syrup at our house, or big,
thick buckwheat cakes. Indigestible, Mother said. So Greensboro has always represented this epicurean delight to me.

Twice a day the Whooper puffed and groaned to and
from University Station. It was made up, ordinarily, of Mr.
Nesbit's ancient engine and a combination passenger and
baggage car, under the charge of fiercely mustachioed Captain
Smith, the conductor, who was also flagman, brakeman and
crew. He was a little man of great importance, but kindly
withal, cracking jokes and bounding about on his spindly
legs. He let the small fry ride to and from University Station
whenever they wanted.

We would go out to the depot, Collier Cobb and I, or
some other boon companion, by whatever means available—
"shanks' mare," as Mars' Phil called it, being the most usual
means of locomotion. The Chapel Hill depot was not actually
in Chapel Hill; it was a long, long mile (a "country mile,"
maybe) from uptown, and it was really in a little place called
Carrboro, alongside a brick cotton mill and some drab-looking
warehouses and stores and sheds. Our station, or the depot,

as it was called, wasn't much to look at, either, but it had two
waiting rooms, one for white people and one for colored people, with a stove in each one, and the ticket office was between
the two waiting rooms with a window opening into each one.
We never had to pay to go to University Station, and I wondered how much it cost if you just went up to the window and
said, "University Station, please," and bought a ticket.

While they were loading freight and things, and the
Whooper was getting ready, Collier and I would begin to get
ready, too, to ask Captain Smith if we could go. "You ask
him," I'd say. "No, siree! *You* ask him!" Collier would say.
"You're the oldest." This matter of seniority was tough; the
elders always had to shoulder the responsibility and do the
unpleasant things. This was even true of the Venable twins,
and Manning Venable, who was a couple of hours younger
than his brother, Charles, would shove the burdens onto
Charles's shoulders.

Not that we had any doubts about Captain Smith's letting us go, but having to come right out and *ask* him, that way,
was a little humbling to your pride. While we argued, Captain
Smith would come along.

"Hi, there, young men!" he'd say. "Want to take a trip?
Want to go to *University Station?*" He always said *"University Station"* as if he were offering you a trip to New York
and a weekend at the Waldorf, all expenses paid.

"Yessuh!" we'd both yell.

"Git aboard," he'd say. "You c'nride in the baggage car
if you want; just behave yourse'f."

It was fine, looking out the open door of the baggage car,
and waving to the people on the porches of the sad little houses
which looked so forlorn out there in the country. The people
would wave back, mostly, and the men in the fields always
waved.

There wasn't much to do at University Station, of course.

You sat on the platform, and watched a long freight train, maybe, crawl by, while you waited for the train the Whooper had come to meet. One of the two of you usually had some money with him—not much, but enough for a box of Zu Zus, and you'd go over to the store and look around a long time before you bought the Zu Zus. The store didn't have much in it but cans which seemed to be mostly pork and beans, or tomatoes, and hams hanging up, and rope and lanterns and oil lamps and washtubs and shovels and things like that. After you went back to the platform and ate the Zu Zus, you'd drop down and walk down the track on the rails, a little way, to the water tank and get a drink of water from the barrel there. It was always cool and wet under the mossy water tank, with the water dripping all around. Way off down the track, then, you'd hear the train whistle, and you'd say to each other, excited, "Here she comes!"

When she came, a few people would get off, those who were going to Chapel Hill, and you always knew some of them. You'd stand there with your hands in your pockets and grin, and they'd see you and say, "Hey, what you doing here?"

"Oh, I don't know," you'd say.

There would be another long wait while the Whooper wheezed up from the siding and took on the peoples' trunks and the other baggage, and then finally Captain Smith would go down to the end of the train and climb up on the step and look up and down the track and swing a lantern, (though it was broad daylight) and yell, "All-l-l aboar-r-d!" and with a jerk you'd start for Chapel Hill.

Sometimes a boxcar or a flat would be added—and at times of heavy traffic, like in September, when college opened, or at Commencement, there would be another coach—and the Whooper looked more like a train.

A few miles out from the village, off through the woods from the railroad tracks, there was an old, abandoned iron mine (silver, somebody told us, and of course we eagerly believed it) and there we often hiked against parental orders, to climb down the crumbling ladders and feel around in the darkness for silver. Of course we never found any, but we were sure it was there, and sometimes we'd find stones we felt certain were chunks of pure silver until we got them up to the light and saw they were only stones. But it was a sort of challenge, looking for the silver. One day when we went out there, the top ladder was broken and fallen off into the mine. It sure was a good thing, we felt, that we hadn't been climbing down it when it broke. So, we were never able to make really sure that there wasn't any silver in the mine.

After these unsuccessful searches at the bottom of the shaft, we'd walk back through the woods to the railroad track, and, sitting on the rails in the shank of the afternoon, await the Whooper to take us home. You'd see its plume of smoke above the trees, and hear it coming, long before it came. Upon its sometimes delayed arrival at the spot where we stood waving, Mr. Nesbit would bring his clanking engine to a standstill, with a fine hissing of steam, and we would clamber aboard with him, up in the cab. There was a colored fireman who would always grin at us. Fine old man, Mr. Nesbit, with his mane of snowy hair sticking out from under his blue-striped engineer's cap, and his white mustache beautifully tinted with tobacco juice. Great sport, too, riding the engine into Chapel Hill (even though the depot was in Carrboro the sign on it said Chapel Hill), and as we came to the trestle approaching the station, he would let us clang the bell in fine, excited clamor.

At the station waited the "hacks," varied vehicles, from the livery stables uptown. They stood in a close line, with barely room between the hubs for people to get to the doors. There were Victorias of a vanished vintage, one or two closed cabs, a sort of big buggy with seats across (I think they called it a carryall) and a strange and very swank contrivance called a landau with a kind of divided top, so that if a rain came up suddenly you could just switch over to the covered part, and keep dry. This last was the pride of Mr. George Pickard's Livery Stable. (Mr. Pickard's publicity claimed "New and Up-to-date Rubber-tire Buggies and Carriages. Fast and Stylish Horses. Prompt attention to business. Always Clever and Accommodating to Customers." He was clever, all right, Dad said: clever at charging you!)

It was a fine fleet of conveyances, and before the train got in they had all been turned around and backed into line, and stood waiting like a bunch of runners toeing the mark.

The hacks were drawn by lackadaisical and decrepit horses of all ages. However, we were not horseflesh experts, and to us they seemed satisfactorily spirited steeds. They'd do a little shuffling and prancing as the train came in, held in check by their colored drivers. The best known of these chari-oteers was a bony black man of uncertain age named Poor Dave. Poor Dave drove for Mr. Tank Hunter, the owner of another of our higher-class liveries. "Hyah Po' Dave, Boss! Yassuh, Boss! Hyah Po' Dave!" I can hear him yell, as a great hubbub was raised by all the drivers, with an extrava-gant brandishing of whips, in loud and keen competition for the alighting passengers.

I would always make a beeline for Poor Dave's carriage. He was my friend. He drove one of the Victorias. As he stood up there waving and yelling, I would climb up on the wheel and grab his leg and shout, "Dave, c'n I . . . ?" and he'd glance down and shout an injected, "*Sho'* you kin!" into his sales argument of "Hyah Po' Dave, Boss—hyah Po' Dave!" and he'd reach down and hook a horny hand into me some-where and hoist me swiftly to the box beside him. "Git off hyah, Useless!" he'd say to some colored boy alongside him, making his point clear with a mighty sweep of his arm, "Mist'

Willie want t'ride!" And Dave and I would have the box to
ourselves.

Turmoil raged and swelled around us. Passengers
clutched at their bags and carriage handles and struggled into
the hacks. Horses reared, wheels locked, men swore and sometimes ladies screamed, if there were ladies. The drivers fought
for position, as the hacks got away.

"Look out, you Jeeter! I'm comin' th'u!" Dave would
roar, giving his bays their heads and their backs his whip,
and off we shot. I hung on tight to the little rail on the side of
the box as the carriage careened away from the depot, and
"Ya-a-a!" I'd whoop, as we passed somebody. "Yaa!" the
driver would yell back, but his tone held no triumphant note,
and he knew that all the way into town he'd take our dust.
Collier would be hanging onto one of the other boxes, too,
and each of us hoped he'd be the one to say "We beat!" when
we got uptown!

It was as fine a race as you could want to see. I think
perhaps the expression "Don't spare the horses!" originated in
Chapel Hill at this time. Maybe the driver of the winning
team expected some small token of appreciation from his paying passengers if he won and kept them free from the clouds
of yellow dust which engulfed the also-rans, or maybe there
was nothing commercial in the drivers' point of view and they
were strictly amateurs racing for the love of sport. I don't
know. But anyway, they made the race fine and stirring.

Some of the hacks might get left at the post, as it were, if
they had the bad luck to take aboard sedate old ladies or professors who took too long to dispose themselves and their
baggage; and these wallowed along far back in the wake of the
leaders, but usually the field was pretty well bunched as you
swung the big S curve through Sunset, which was the colored
residential district, and passed the Potters' Field, where the
Potters lay. (The people buried there, I knew, were bums, and

destitute, but I never understood why their resting place was known as Potters' Field until I heard Dad, once, describe such a person as having "gone to pot." Ever after that I thought of a human derelict, as Grandpa called them—as a potter. We had very few of these in Chapel Hill, and there wasn't more than a handful of bare and shabby graves in Potters' Field.)

You swung around the sunny bend into the long, tree-shrouded straightaway of Franklin Street, and the drivers went to the whip, for here you might get passed, and that was a disgrace. Pickaninnies playing in the gutter straightened up and waved and danced as you pounded past, and some of them ran frenziedly along the sidewalk trying to keep abreast of the flying carriages. Black faces in the doors of little Negro stores flashed toothy grins at you as you hurtled by, and there was always shouting and the barking of the running dogs you'd picked up all along the way. You thundered on, and the field began to string out behind as the real class of man and horse began to show. The rigs back in the ruck, without a chance, pulled up and trotted through the dust.

I wished the drivers could have been dressed in bright-hued silks and racing boots and jaunty caps tied with a ribbon in front, like the jockeys I had seen at the big State Fair. Anyway I always thought of them as jockeys, and of Dave as the greatest, smartest jockey of them all. He seldom lost, and then through no fault of his own. When one of his passengers delayed him, " 'At ole gemman, 'Fessor Toy!" he'd grumble, "he a fine man, but he sho is slow-movin'."

But Dave usually spread the field, and we pulled up in front of Dr. Kluttz's (which was the accepted finish line) with a handsome lead, our horses lathered and panting. The thankful, shaken people in the hacks climbed out in great relief.

"*Thank* you, Dave," I'd say gratefully, as I dropped down off the box, and he'd smile a mighty, gold-toothed smile back at me and say, "Yas*suh*, Mist' Willie!"

Why he was called Poor Dave I do not know. He had a limp, but then he seldom walked. Of course the term may have been related to money matters, or his home life, but I never felt that Dave deserved much sympathy, only admiration.

CHAPTER SIX

Long before the Whooper's rails were laid our little town attracted visitors, and some of them were quite distinguished. But Southern hospitality has its limits, and not always have these unbidden guests been welcome.

Many years ago, along the old post road from Pittsboro, to the south of us, came the coach of Lord Cornwallis, lurching over the stumps and the red clay ruts, as he made his arrogant, ill-fated way north toward his appointment at Yorktown. If he was a God-fearing man, as many good commanders are, it is likely that he bade his driver stop and went into the Chapel for a passing prayer for victory over the rebel upstart Washington, whom he would corner and destroy. His glittering staff disposed themselves beneath the oaks and sent out foragers for cattle, suckling pigs and meal, and scarlet-coated soldiers eased their packs and stacked their arms and rested here, and sang "God Save the King." The cavalry raiders of Bloody Tarleton, in their forest green, must have paused in Chapel Hill to water their mounts and inquire for friends of the Crown, and pick up horses. Later on came General Sherman.

From the east—past the old Indian Camping Ground, and the country where we hunted arrowheads—the Yankees

came, fresh from the Battle of Bentonville, and hard on the
heels of General Joseph E. Johnston. It is said by some histori-
ans that the final battle of the war was planned for Chapel
Hill. It seemed the place to make a stand—its heights domi-
nating the approaches—but this scheme failed. At any rate, the
worn-out boys in gray dug trenches along the old stagecoach
road from Raleigh, now scarcely more than an overgrown
trail through the pines. You can still trace the dim line of the
rifle pits, close by the modern highway along which the solid
stream of motors thunder nowadays into Chapel Hill for the
football games. It was still a road, however, when we boys
went there through the tangled woods and climbed the old,
vine-covered breastworks and looked for Minie balls. All was
peace and quiet and shifting shade, but one could almost feel
the ghosts in ragged butternut by one's side and see Yankee-
blue shadows and the glitter of approaching bayonets creeping
forward through the pine trees. You always talked in lowered
voices. You thought of the thousands of dusty men, in gray
and blue, who jammed that narrow, rutty road once—and the
horses and guns and creaking wagons—as the Yankees
pressed the beaten foe ahead of them, and just before the final
rendezvous near Durham, twelve miles away. There, a few
days after Appomattox, tired Joe Johnston gave his sword to
Sherman.

Many of the older people in Chapel Hill remembered
those terrible days very clearly, and old ladies told me, while
I listened goggle-eyed, about burying their treasures, and
carrying food and coffee, or what passed for coffee, to the gray
soldiers in those trenches.

One such old lady was Miss Hattie Cole. She lived in a
house set back from Franklin Street, with a big wistaria vine
on the pillars of the porch. Mother used to go to see her sometimes, and I went along. We would sit down in the parlor, and
Mother and Miss Hattie would have tea, which Miss Hattie

poured from a big, fancy china teapot, with bright flowers painted on it. She told me it was an heirloom. She always had some lemonade for me. There was a sturdy Windsor chair she always made me sit in. I think it was Mr. Jim Taylor's chair —her brother-in-law who ran the bank. They must have been very rich, with all that money, but some of their chairs were very wobbly, and, I thought, unsafe.

Mother went to see Miss Hattie to talk about church or Women's Auxiliary matters, but I went to hear Miss Hattie talk about the Yankees. She was gray-haired and stout and wore glasses, but she had been just a young girl, she said, when the Yankees came.

She and Mother talked a long time, and I drank my lemonade and wished Miss Hattie had made a little more of it.

"Keep still, now," Mother would say to me.

After a while Miss Hattie would smile at me, and say "Well."

And I'd say, "Miss Hattie, would you tell me about the time the Yankees stole the horse?" or "the time the Yankee soldier helped you across the street?"

Miss Hattie would sit back and look off in the corner, and say, "Well, now, let me see . . ."

She'd tell me about the time—"the last ninety days," she called it—when they hadn't had much to eat for a long time ("and *no* lemonade!") and she and her mother had spun and woven the cloth for their own clothes, and people were very sad. But this didn't interest me so much, and I wanted her to hurry and get to the part where the Yankees were really here, on Franklin Street, in Chapel Hill! "They did look mighty fine," she said, "their horses were so fat . . . Some of them were real nice." I wondered if she meant the horses or the Yankees, but I didn't want to interrupt her.

The people didn't get worried, much, she said, until they heard about Bentonville, and Raleigh, and then the war, they

knew, was coming to Chapel Hill. There was some more fighting at Morrisville, this side of Raleigh, and then some more—
"the last skirmish," she said—at New Hope Creek, which was
just a few miles out of town. Everybody began to run around
and wonder what they were going to do, and they rang the
bell in South Building, and people wrapped up their silver and
buried it in the back yard and dragged trash over the place,
and the stores were locked up, even though there was hardly
anything in them, and the colored people led the horses and
mules off into the woods and hid them.

"Yessum," I'd say, when she stopped.

"Well, our men got here first," she said. "The Yankees
were chasing them. . . . General Wheeler's cavalry—they
were a sight! They were mighty hungry, and the cavalry didn't
have shoes, all the shoes went to the men who had to walk.
They had no wounded with them, as they had no medicines
and no way to look after them, and they'd had to leave them
for the Yankees to take care of."

She said that the people in Chapel Hill were even worried
about General Wheeler's cavalry soldiers. It seems they had
acquired the reputation of picking up whatever they wanted—
"not that they couldn't have had it, and welcome," Miss Hattie said. "They didn't take much," she added. The Confederates couldn't rest, the Yankees were so close, and they had to
dig trenches and get ready to try to stop them before they got
into the town. This was along in April, in 1865, Miss Hattie
said. The very next day, they got the news of General Lee's
surrender, up in Virginia. It was a *time,* she said. I'd sit still
and wait, for Miss Hattie always paused there.

"The streets got full of people," she said. "It was awful.
Some of General Wheeler's men *cried.* They knew the war
was just about over, and they didn't know where to go or what
to do. They didn't have any money, or homes, any more."

"Yessum," I said. "The Yankees . . . ?"

"The Yankees got here next day," she said, still looking in the corner.

She told me about the terror and the stillness when the last Confederates had left them, and how the people gathered in the churches or locked the doors of their homes, and while they waited, prayed. And then Kilpatrick's Cavalry rode in, with jingling spurs and shining sabres, and they were captured. The inhabitants saw the Stars and Stripes for the first time in years, and the Yankees rode around and gave orders.

"Sit back in your chair," Mother said.

"They were cert'ny a fine-looking lot," Miss Hattie said, "but of course nobody had anything to do with them." I could just see our people turning up their noses at the Yankees.

Chapel Hill had a hard time after that, Miss Hattie said. The Northern Army occupied the town and the surrounding countryside, and stripped it of everything they could carry away, and left as a guard a detachment of Michigan troopers who stabled their horses in the old and lovely library. This old library is the most beautiful of all the buildings on the campus, (it's the theatre now)—a Grecian templelike structure erected in the gracious days of the beginning of the nineteenth century, as a ball room. This seems to have been the only concession to art and beauty, and the only departure from the strictly utilitarian, on the part of the early builders. Perhaps it appealed to the Yankee cavalrymen on account of its book stalls (I wonder what became of the books?) and because they could lounge on its portico and lean against its graceful Grecian columns.

Afterward came the Scalawags and the Carpetbaggers, and the University had to close its doors. The village was policed by Negro soldiers and the inhabitants looked out through shuttered windows, and the long, lean years of Reconstruction dragged along.

There had been a Yankee officer who helped her across

the street, once, Miss Hattie said. It was raining and the street was full of puddles, and he came up behind her and took her arm. "I didn't know what in the world to do," she said. "But he was a real pleasant young man. He asked me, when we got across the street, if he could see me home, but I said, 'No, I thank you, Sir. . . .' I've sometimes wondered whatever became of him."

There was another Yankee officer, handsome and dashing, who was quite irresistible to another of the Chapel Hill girls, however, and the result caused a great furore in the village. This turned out to be one of the happier consequences of the War. Mrs. McNider told me the story.

This officer was none other than General Smith Atkins, who commanded the Northern troops stationed in Chapel Hill. She said he was "a fine-looking man of around thirty." He made a prompt call at the home of the University President, Governor Swain (so called because he had been a former Governor of the State), to pay his respects. Miss Ellie Swain, the Governor's beautiful daughter, just happened along while he was there, and she fell for the good-looking Yankee, good and hard. It was just scandalous, Mrs. McNider said; love at first sight, on both sides. As befitted a gallant cavalryman, the General dashed into his courtship hell-for-leather, and brooked no opposition. It was a very open and energetic wooing, Mrs. McNider said.

Every evening the Yankee band came and played on the Swain lawn—sentimental ballads as well as martial marches —and you could hear it all over the village. In addition to the serenades, the General presented his ladylove with a fine and spirited saddle horse, and the two of them often rode out together on the country lanes. It was rumored that the horse was one of the blooded Southern mounts which had somehow found its way into the Yankee Army. The village was shocked and indignant. "The War is done," was General Atkins's sentiment; "let's let bygones be bygones and love one another." But the village could not quite bring itself to share this magnanimous attitude. Governor and Mrs. Swain were greatly embarrassed and distressed, but helpless in the face of their willful daughter's determination.

When the wedding invitations went around, the town almost blew up! A few people tried to be nice about it, but most

of them were mighty angry, Mrs. McNider said. However, there was nothing they could do about it, what with General Atkins's four thousand Yankee soldiers behind him, and the happy couple were married in the little church which later became my grandfather's. I was mighty glad that Grandpa wasn't in the pulpit then and had to marry that Yankee General to Miss Ellie Swain! But of course I am old enough now to realize that even war can't do anything to break up a case of true love. The couple lived happily ever after in Michigan, Mrs. McNider said.

Dad, too, told me a lot about the Civil War. He had been a little boy then, and he remembered. Grandpa, who had been a chaplain, didn't talk much about it, although sometimes he would say something about Jeb Stuart, or what General Jackson said. Mother wasn't born until after the War, so of course she didn't know a thing. My favorite story was the one in which Dad was captured by the Yankees. His father was with a Virginia regiment, somewhere near Petersburg, where the family lived, and Dad got on a freight train to go down to visit him. This was when the war was almost over. He went to sleep in the boxcar and apparently went by the place where he should have got off. When he waked up some Yankee soldiers were standing in the empty boxcar, looking at him. Dad said he thought his time had come.

The Yankees laughed at him and asked him where he thought he was going. When he told them about his father they said he was probably back aways where the Rebels were; that they had captured the train, but that they would try to get him back to his father. They took him to where some Yankee officers were, and they asked him a lot of questions, most of which Dad didn't know the answers to, and then he was put up on a horse behind a Yankee. They rode and rode, Dad holding on to the Yankee, and finally they came to a bridge where the Yankee told Dad to get down and go across the bridge and keep on walking down the road. He told Dad to make as much noise as he could, to whistle and to yell, which Dad did to the limit of his lungs. After a long time some Confederate soldiers came along and picked him up, and then he rode behind one of the Confederate soldiers. They came to a place where there was a wagon, and Dad was put in that and he rode a long way in the wagon. He didn't remember much about that part of it, except that that night he found his father. The Yankees had let him keep a package of food he had

brought for his father, too, so I don't believe they could have
been quite so bad as people said. Dad avowed they were pretty
bad, however.

Very soon after the War, both Dad's father and mother
died. He was only about twelve years old, and he had had little
schooling, but he had to go to work in a tobacco factory near
Petersburg to help support his two younger sisters. They had
a hard time, Dad said, but he never "took anything off a Yankee." I am sure he lives very happily now in the southern part
of Heaven.

I was brought up in the more or less unreconstructed
atmosphere then general in the South. Erring children were
told that the Yankees would get them, rather than the goblins,
and it was a terrifying prospect. Quiet mourning for the Lost
Cause, and veneration for its leaders, was almost a religion. In
fact, in one instance I remember, it came right out in church.
*"The God of Abraham, Isaac and Jacob, Stonewall Jackson
and Robert E. Lee,"* was a phrase proudly hurled from the
pulpit by Dr. Jones, the Baptist minister. Dr. Jones was a
grand old man, and an orator in the old tradition. He had been
a chaplain on Lee's staff, and sometimes we went to hear him
preach.

In all the homes, and public buildings, too, there were
pictures of Lee and Stonewall Jackson. Our picture of General
Lee, one of them, was magnificent, a life-size steel engraving,
in a heavy gold frame, which hung over the sideboard in our
modest dining room, and I remember often gazing at his grave
and noble face. Our picture of Stonewall Jackson, across the
room, was almost as imposing. Neither of these mighty warriors looked at you. This gave you a chance to study them un-
observed, as it were. Both seemed to gaze afar off, past the
fighting and the failure, perhaps, and down the golden aisles
of history. Just a few years ago, when I came back to Chapel

Hill after my long absence, I went one day to the elementary school, and there, in the auditorium, flanking the stage—the only pictures in the room—were portraits of this immortal pair.

The University had its own particular heroes, too. Pettigrew's Tar Heels made up a large part of Pickett's Charge at Gettysburg, and in Memorial Hall are tall marble tablets with the names of hundreds of alumni from U.N.C. and students who did not come back to finish their schooling.

Many of the Faculty had been in the Army, and I remember distinctly Major Cain. Accompanied by his old bird dog, Nellie, he thumped along the street with a stick which I imagined as a sword. And Major Patterson, white haired and handsome, who had lost a leg, romantic on his crutches.

Decoration Day, or Memorial Day as it is called in the South, comes early, varying in the different States as the flowers reach their peak. In North Carolina it is May 10th, and this was always a great and thrilling day. The village would be full of people from the countryside. There was always speech-making on the Campus, by the Confederate Monument, and the little college band played "The Bonnie Blue Flag," and "Dixie." The boys and dogs ran around and shouted and barked and rolled on the grass, while the old men got together in groups and brandished their canes and drew diagrams on the ground, and the ladies bustled about getting ready for the dinner served the veterans on long trestle tables under the trees. This came after the dusty pilgrimage to the Cemetery, with the band leading the way and playing "Onward, Christian Soldiers," and the banking of flowers on the many soldier graves. The quiet little graveyard is now surrounded on three sides by the buildings and playing fields of the University, but still it blossoms out each Tenth of May with brilliant little Confederate battle flags flying once again over those unforgotten heroes.

My first commercial art enterprise, I believe, was painting, in water color, Confederate flags, rippling gallantly in
the breeze, with golden tassels flying, and *C.S.A.*, with curli-
cues, underneath. These I peddled around for twenty-five
cents, and while, looking back, I am afraid that most of my
customers were friends of the family and therefore did not
buy solely because they were overpowered by the excellence of
the art work, it was a very profitable project. Artists, however,
are notoriously loose with their money, and Dr. Kluttz and
Mr. Eubanks eventually got the most of it.

A pair of these little flags, beautifully framed, hangs in
my home here now. In a heart-warming gesture, Dr. Will
McNider presented them to me. His mother had bought them
from me, many years ago. His mother was one of the girls
who carried the sweet potato "coffee" on those April days in
1865 to the men in the trenches along the Raleigh Road.

CHAPTER SEVEN

As far back as I can remember, I liked to draw. In fact, Mars' Phil used to say I was born with a pencil in my hand, but this seems exaggerated. Certain it must be, however, to hear the family tell it, that almost as soon as I could hold a pencil or a crayon I was marking things up. I have ruined many a good surface in my time. I preferred to draw lying flat on my stomach; this may indicate that I started drawing before I could walk.

But other hands than mine had a part in my drawing and the shaping of my destiny, and in those formative years were the guiding force in my life, I believe, which boldly led me toward my fate, that of becoming an illustrator. One of these hands was Satan's, which, holding a pitchfork, reached out and grabbed me from the pages of a large copy of Dante's *Inferno* which was in my grandfather's study. Gustave Doré's illustrations of His Satanic Majesty, and the dark angels, and the fires of hell affected me greatly. I have never tried to draw a picture of Satan, but I could; I know just what he looks like.

The other—even firmer, more authoritative—belonged to General George A. Custer. Neither Satan nor General Custer was actually present in the flesh, of course, but their forceful spirits were with me, and very influential. I first met General Custer when I was very young—in that blood-curdling lithograph put out, I think, by the Anheuser-Busch people in the nineties—showing the gallant and intrepid Yellow Hair with upraised sabre, his last cartridge gone, standing alone among his fallen men, and surrounded by the yelling redskins. This is literally the first picture I ever remember seeing. I am on the track of one now, and I hope to secure it and hang it across from my bed, so that it may also be the last.

This copy of "Custer's Last Stand" hung in the Richmond office which was Dad's headquarters just before and just after we came to Chapel Hill. Once or twice during that time Mother and I went to Richmond to be with him, while an aunt or a cousin came to Chapel Hill and looked after Grandpa. This period is naturally a bit hazy in my mind as I was only five or six years old at the time, but there is nothing hazy about my recollection of Custer. Several things about Richmond stand out in my memory, but Custer is clearest of all. I used to beg Dad to take me to the office on Sundays so that I could look at the picture. That's what I called it, The Picture.

"Don't you ever get tired of that picture?" Dad would ask.

"No, sir," I would say, with relish.

Mother would get me into my Sunday suit, a check affair with a blue vest and a big sailor collar and many buttons on the jacket. The pants were very short and tight. It was quite a snappy outfit, topped off by a wing collar and a bow tie and my soldier cap with its strip of gold cord on the visor. When I was thus arrayed I was a pretty arresting, if small, sight.

"We'll be back in time for dinner, Patty," Dad would say to my aunt, and off we would go, I trying to match Dad's steps and not look too dressed up but nonchalant and easy like Dad, and as though I wore gorgeous raiment like that every day.

The Picture always moved me profoundly. It hung, in a dirty, chipped gold frame, in the empty Claim Department

office, over a roll-top desk which of course was always closed
on Sundays. I don't see how the clerks ever did any work with
that picture hanging there. Dad would hold me up so that my
feet rested on the slanting, corrugated surface of the desk top,
and I could get very close to it and study it. Every gory detail
of The Picture is indeliby etched on my memory. I remember
the design of the war paint on the Indians, the blood on a
scalped skull, the curling wisp of smoke from Custer's empty
pistol. I know now that other and better Custers have been
painted, but still the lurid lithograph of Anheuser-Busch re-
presents, for me, the final frightful moments of the gallant, if
foolhardy, general and his equally gallant troopers.

In Richmond we visited my Uncle Norman, who had a
haberdashery store there, and lived downtown in a little house
on lower Main Street. Uncle Norman was fattish and very
laughing and jolly. His dark hair was parted in the middle
(practically everybody's hair was parted in the middle; you
looked like a dude if your hair was parted on the side, Dad
said) and he had a mustache, an even better one than Dad's.
He wore gay and arresting neckties, sort of advertising his
business, I suppose. My Aunt Patty was Dad's youngest sister,
and she was jolly, also, and very pretty. Dad's other sister, my
Aunt Elizabeth, (Aunt Lizzie, we called her) lived over in
Petersburg, close by, and she would come over and join us.

The house had a narrow front porch or piazza right on
the sidewalk. There was no yard at all. You sat on the step
and your feet were on the pavement, and people passing could
have stepped on your feet, if they had wanted to. Late on the
summer afternoons I was made to clean up and Mother and
my aunts would come downstairs in fresh, ruffly dresses, and
Aunt Patty would bring out a pitcher of lemonade and we
would sit on the porch and watch the people and the trolley
cars go by.

I remember feeding the squirrels in Capitol Square—

and the great statue of George Washington, on his horse, which is there. And I remember finding and keeping a bag of marbles which belonged to a neighbor boy. Mother cried, when discovery was made, for she thought surely I would grow up to be a thief, and then she gave me a real and spirited licking. She used a hairbrush. I remember this so well because the necessary punishments administered by my mother hardly ever took the form of physical violence.

There was a Carnival, or maybe it was Chautauqua, and there was a balloon ascension. It was quite an occasion, and everybody went. It was at the Fair Grounds, I think. I remember that they were blowing the balloon up, and then a terrible black cloud came in the sky and people began rushing home or for shelter. We all saw it suddenly, low in the sky behind us, and everybody was surprised, for it was a sunny day. I remember Dad hurrying us to the street cars.

"Come on, come on!" Dad cried. "there's going to be a *cyclone!*" (He had been to Texas when he was a young man, and he knew a cyclone when he saw one, or thought he did.) I remember his picking me up as we pushed among the people trying to get on the street car, and over his shoulder I saw the cloud, black and funnel-shaped. We got home all right, and there *was* a violent wind storm, a sort of minor tornado, and we learned later that the balloon broke loose and went flying off and was wrecked.

And I remember that one Sunday Dad took me down to the James River Bridge, where, on a fish trap, or weir, almost under the bridge, there lay a huge shad. A crowd of people were on the bridge, and men were dangling lines over and trying to catch a hook in the shad's side or gills. Finally one of them succeeded and began carefully pulling the big fish up to the bridge, and the people cheered and crowded around. Dad held me up on the parapet so that I could see. The man got the shad almost up to the bridge rail, when it fell off the hook and down into the river. Everybody said "Oh-h-h!" when it fell, and I remember the splash the big fish made when it hit the water.

So many exciting things happened in Richmond, usually on Sunday. I suppose this was because we didn't go to church. Dad said this was the only day he could be with us, and that he'd be dog gone if we were going to spend it in church; that we had to go to church in Chapel Hill, plenty. Also, it was because my father was a very exciting man, and I knew that always on Sunday when he took me out something would happen.

One of the more stimulating of these Sunday excursions was the trip to the near-by firehouse. Dad was on friendly terms with the firemen, which confirmed my feeling that he was a truly great and distinguished man. I was allowed to climb up on the engine, a glorious vehicle, and to put on a fireman's helmet. Behind the engine and the hose reel, (the hook and ladder was at another station; we visited that, too) was a row of stalls for the horses, four wonderful big beasts— a pair of white horses and a pair of dappled gray—and the firemen kept them as clean and polished as they kept the engine and the trucks. The horses just stood there quietly, chewing on hay, until the alarm sounded from the big shining gong up front by the desk, and then the check reins which held them dropped away and they rushed up to the vehicles and into their places, and the harness, collars and all, which always hung suspended there, dropped down onto them. A click here, a snap there, and they were ready to go before you could say Jack Robinson. The men would come sliding down a polished pole from the second floor where they lived. A drill was held every day to perfect and shorten this operation, and this is what we would go to see. One day, just as we got to the engine house, a real alarm came in and the whole outfit dashed off to a bona fide fire. This was one of the most excit-

ing moments of my life, with the big doors swinging open and
the get-out-of-the-way bells jangling on the fire wagons and
the horses snorting and plunging and striking sparks from the
cobblestones as they got under way. The ultimate in delight at
the firehouse, however, was when a fireman would take me
upstairs and slide with me down the polished pole. The firemen had a tortoise-shell cat which they had taught to slide
down the pole, too, all by himself.

On our trips down Main Street we always stopped to
look at the great, grim-visaged wooden Indian guarding the
door of the tobacconist's where Dad bought his cigarettes,
Home Runs and Picayunes. The Indian held a tomahawk in
one hand and in the other a package of wooden cigars. This
bothered me, as I supposed Indians smoked only peace pipes.

"I don't know," said Dad. "Maybe his peace pipe is too
big to carry around and he leaves it in his wigwam."

But it didn't seem just right to me, an Indian smoking a
cigar when he was away from home and on the warpath,
maybe—as denoted by the upraised tomahawk. . . . I asked
Mr. Fitzhugh, the man who ran the tobacco shop, what the
Indian's name was, and he said his name was Charley.

Another very fine and inspiring experience in Richmond
was an occasional parade by the Richmond Light Infantry
Blues. Somehow, in those early years of the century, there
seemed always to be time and place in the scheme of things
for parades. Even a circus parade, nowadays, is a rarity, and
modern life is the poorer.

The Blues constitute one of the very oldest military or-
ganizations in all the land, and Richmond has always been
very proud of them. When they stepped out for our benefit
they were a dazzling spectacle in their magnificent dress uniforms, patterned after the War of 1812 model. Of course the
uniforms were blue, but that was the least of it. The tight-
fitting jackets, which had white epaulettes on the shoulders,

were cut away at the waist and fell in a fine tail down to the
knees at the back. They wore white fronts, or dickies, with a
row of shining silver buttons up each side, and a broad white
stripe down the trouser legs. Their hands were in the cleanest
white gloves you ever saw, and they wore tall and shining
shakos topped with flying feathers of white. The heavy metal
chin-straps were hooked under their lower lips and you could
hardly see their eyes for the broad, flat visors of the shakos
which came down over them. It was a fine and breath-taking
sight to see the Blues swing down the street, their tall white
plumes filling the street from curb to curb. And they were
wonderful to draw. I always put them in these uniforms, even
in battle.

We also went to Richmond to visit my Great-aunt Ed-

monia, who lived uptown in a big house, very dark and full of
things. It contained, also, my Great-uncle George, a large and
pleasant Englishman who smoked a carved meerschaum pipe
of a British sailor's head, and loved creamed sturgeon. Uncle
George was the first Englishman of my acquaintance, and I
often sniffed him surreptitously and with curiosity because of
"Fee, fi, fo, fum." He was portly and sandy-colored, and had
a rather high voice. I had great difficulty in understanding
him at times, because, being a foreigner, he spoke very poor
English. But Mother said it was his "accent," and that he
really spoke all right. He had a tiny, narrow office on one side
of the entrance hall, where he sat at a high secretary and
smoked the meerschaum pipe and shuffled papers. He was an
importer, but what he imported is lost to me now. He had a
long, blond mustache, and in summer he wore a pith helmet.

A peculiar thing about Uncle George was that he ate his
meals one thing at a time. He never liked to have but one kind
of food on his plate, and when he'd finish his hominy he'd
have some snap beans and eat them all, and then his eggplant,
maybe, and then the creamed sturgeon or roast beef. I thought
it was a good idea, and that maybe he had picked it up in
England. I wanted to eat my meals that way, but Mother
said No.

"But why?" I asked. "Uncle George—"

"Uncle George is grown up," said Mother. "When you
are grown up you can do whatever you want to." How wonderful, I thought.

The house at 509 Grace Street held many memories for
me. There are smart shoppes there now, and sleek motors
line the curb where once the carriage blocks stood and the
little nigger-boy hitching post before Uncle George's door.

The street was quiet and dignified and Victorian. Trees
stood along the sidewalk, and the clop-clopping of the carriage

horses made a pleasant sound (you didn't hear horses much in
Chapel Hill because our streets weren't paved).

The houses rested beam to beam. If you were a trades-
man you reached the back door through a dark tunnel from
the street. The houses all had basement rooms, and the first
floor and the front door were at the top of a flight of steps
from the sidewalk. There was a long, narrow veranda at Uncle
George's, on which people never sat, covered and upheld by a
lot of fancy ironwork. The hall inside was dark as pitch except
for the gaslight which was always burning, and the light in
the big rooms came only from front or back as there were of
course no windows on the sides. On the marble mantel in the
parlor there was a clock under a glass cover; you could see
the works moving. I remember best the basement area, however, and the dining room, downstairs and in the rear, which
looked out onto a big brick-paved and walled back yard or
court. This yard contained the kitchen above which lived Cora,
the most wonderful of colored cooks and the kindest of women.
At the end of the brick court, which was dampish and mossy,
there was a heavy door giving on to the alley, which was off
limits for me. There was a wicket in the door, and I'd climb
up and look out this wicket at the colored men who came along
the alley to get the garbage and the trash. When one of them
came to the door to deliver something he would pull the bell
cord and Cora would come and unlock the door and let him in.

On the far corner down the street was the beautiful old
Westmoreland Club, not only Richmond's swankiest, but the
hotbed of ex-Confederate officers and unreconstructed rebels.
Richmond was, and is, the most Southern of cities. Oh, yes, I
know about Charleston and Mobile and New Orleans and
Natchez, but if there is any Bonnie Blue Flag-waving to be
done, I'll take Richmond. Uncle George, as a full-blooded
Englishman (fee, fi, fo, fum!) must have felt very lonely in
this atmosphere, but he bore up bravely, and in at least one

instance, which affected me, gallantly carried on the Southern
tradition.

Just two doors down the street from us, on the near corner across from the Westmoreland Club, lived Dr. Hunter
McGuire, famous medic and even more famous Confederate
Army officer and surgeon. He was even then a sort of living
legend. I always hoped he would wear his gray uniform some-
time, but I never saw him do it. Many men removed their hats
when greeting Dr. McGuire, and the ladies took on over him
very much. He was tall and straight and distinguished looking, with his gray hair and grave eyes, and always carried
himself like a soldier. I wondered about him, and I always
took my hat off, too, when he came by Uncle George's. He
noticed me do this one day and he laughed and said, "Hello,
there."

Of necessity Uncle George was calling on him one evening after supper, and my Great-aunt Edmonia suggested
that he take me along to meet the famous man. The proposal
came suddenly and it gave me a shivery but delightful shock.
"It will be a fine thing for him to be able to say that he met Dr.
McGuire," she said. Of course this introduction would enable
me not only to meet Dr. McGuire himself, but it would also
be for the sake of enabling me to "shake the hand that shook
the hand of John L. Sullivan," as it were. (Mr. Sullivan was
in no way involved, of course; I only use this as a simile.)

"Right," said Uncle George. "I'll be very happy to intro-
duce the—ah—nipper to the Doctah."

Mother hurriedly spruced me up, and brushed my hair.
"Now leave it alone," she said. "I want you to look nice when
you meet Dr. McGuire."

Uncle George and I went outside and down our steps, I
holding his hand in the dark. "Well, my boy," he said, as we
walked down the brick sidewalk, "be on your best behavior
now. Just speak right up to the Doctah." We went up Dr.

McGuire's steps and Uncle George pulled the bell handle and I heard the bell jangle inside. A colored girl in a white apron and cap came to the door and took Uncle George's helmet and stick and showed us into the front room where there was a desk with a green-shaded lamp on it. I looked around hopefully for swords and guns, but the room seemed empty of them and I found nothing to interest me. Uncle George sat down on the sofa and crossed his knees and I climbed up on a stiff, brocaded chair, and we waited for Dr. McGuire. I was nervous, while we waited. I thought of all I had heard about Dr. McGuire, how fearless he was under fire—and the terrible Time, and the dark days that came after it—and I swung my feet and plucked at the brocade.

"It's quite all right," said Uncle George. "Don't fidget."

We waited a long time, it seemed to me, and I began to hope that Dr. McGuire had heard that we were there and was putting on his uniform. But at last when he came in he was just wearing clothes, like Uncle George. We stood up. Dr. McGuire and Uncle George shook hands, and Uncle George motioned toward me. "Dr. McGuire, Sir," he said, "I should like to present my nephew. He's an admirer—" and Dr. McGuire turned and greeted me gravely and with dignity, and held out his hand and I took it. "How are you, young man?" he asked.

"Yes, Sir. All right, Sir," I mumbled, "I hope that you are well." I tried to speak up, as Uncle George had said, but my words came out awkwardly and I felt hot and embarrassed. He understood me, though.

"Yes, thank you," he said. "Are you my patient?"

I started to speak again and tell him no, that I—but Uncle George cut in and said, "Oh, no, he's very well indeed. I am your patient." Anyway, it was a wonderful conversation, Dr. McGuire looking at me, and all, but I felt glad it was over.

After that he and Uncle George began to talk and I listened expectantly. To my disappointment, almost to my distress, Dr. McGuire did not speak of battles or of glory, of powder smoke or bullet-riddled flags, but only of my Uncle George's asthma. Then he sat down and wrote out a prescription and handed it to Uncle George. They talked a little while longer and then Uncle George and I stood up and told Dr. McGuire good night and went home. Anyway, I met him, and I shook the hand that closed the eyes of Stonewall Jackson.

CHAPTER EIGHT

I HAD typhoid fever in the house on Grace Street, when I was about eight years old. We had gone there in the early summer, to visit my Uncle and Aunt, and I got sick. After a little Aunt "Monie," as we called her, and Uncle George had to go off to Greenwood, where their summer place was, up in the mountains, and Mother and I were left in the big house to ourselves, except when Dad was there. But we had Cora, who couldn't leave on account of her children or something, and of course we couldn't have stayed there without Cora to help Mother. Cora was a tower of strength, Mother said, but after a while we had to get a nurse, too.

They moved me down into Aunt Monie's and Uncle George's big bedroom behind the parlor. It was the coolest room in the house and opened onto a back porch overlooking the brick courtyard. I used to lie in the big double bed and watch the sun on the walls of the yard, and the sparrows. There were a lot of sparrows around, building nests, and there was a nest at the corner of the porch, high up. Sometimes a rat would run along the top of the wall.

A young, red-haired Dr. Fisher "pulled me through," Dad said, "by the skin of my teeth." I remember Dr. Fisher, and how cheerful he was. He used to bring me presents sometimes, a little toy or a puzzle, and once he brought me a picture an artist had drawn for the paper, of the Richmond Blues. I liked to try to work the puzzles, and when I got tired of that I could count the prisms in the big chandelier which hung down from the ceiling. The room had been the back parlor, I guess, with big double doors into the front parlor, until they made it into a bedroom. But the shiny glass prisms were hard to count; you got mixed up and never came out twice with the same number. After I began to get well they'd move me out in a chair on the porch and then I could see the back yard better and hear people in the alley. Mother used to read to me a lot, stories from *St. Nicholas Magazine,* and sometimes the Alger books, and Dad, after supper would read and tell me the Uncle Remus stories, which he knew by heart, he'd read them to me so often. When I got strong enough I had to learn to walk all over again. I remember Dad holding out his arms, and I'd stumble into them, like a baby. He and mother would count my steps. "Five!" Mother would say.

"No, six!" Dad would shout. "It was *six!* That's the stuff, Buster!"

But I was hungry all the time. All I had to eat for a long while, when I could have anything, was "slip," a loathsome, gelatinlike substance, quite tasteless. Those were the days when medical method, as applied to typhoid, was to starve you back to health and strength. I'd lie there in the heat and think of good things to eat—cool watermelons and ice cream —and beg Mother for them. Finally, they put a little sugar in the slip, and from that I progressd to one small, wafer-thin battercake. By the time I could be got back to Chapel Hill (and how happy my Great-aunt Edmonia and my Great-uncle George must have been) I was still a sorry sight, thin and white as a ghost, everybody said.

I don't remember the trip home, but I do remember going out in the kitchen, as soon as we got there, and telling our cook Viola (a wonderful woman, butterscotch-colored) about the one battercake I could have for my supper, and asking her to make the very *biggest* battercake she had ever made, and she promised. I thought about it all afternoon, and I could hardly wait for suppertime. At last it came and Mother tinkled her little bell and everybody came, and after Grandpa had said grace, we all sat down and everybody began to eat, "while it's hot," Mother said. All but me, waiting for my battercake. I almost drooled, anticipating it, and when it came it was all I'd hoped—it was a masterpiece; Viola had outdone herself! How she ever made and turned it over I don't know. She came in grinning broadly and proudly bearing my banquet, with a great hunk of golden butter in the middle, and all conversation stopped. Just one it was, but what a battercake! It was golden to dark brown and fluffy, and its crisp edges literally hung over the sides of the plate and hid Viola's hands. I yelled, I think, and grabbed for it, but Mother's hand was quicker.

"Why, *Viola!*" she said. "He can't have that; he's on a *diet!*"

"He say . . ." began Viola, looking at me accusingly. But Mother fixed her with her eye, and she saw it was no use and stopped. My hungry wails and tears and entreaties followed, but Mother stood firm. "No, *Sir!*" she said. "You can have one battercake, but not one like *that!*" She would only let me have one small fragment of that beautiful creation, and I have never forgotten the famished anguish of that night, or the waste of good Viola's masterpiece.

CHAPTER NINE

Travel always broadens one,
there's no disputing that, but it can also play hob with one's
career—slows you up: and trips away (and of course getting sick) sadly restricted my artistic output. However, those
early expeditions to Richmond proved invaluable in the way
of providing material, and after I was home again I piled
right into making pictures of the balloon ascension, the Blues,
the Richmond Fire Department (with fires)—all the colorful subjects with which I had become familiar. I drew Uncle
George in his pith helmet, trailing great clouds of smoke from
his sailor-head pipe, and instead of a cat sliding down the pole
at the firehouse I drew a lion. The shad I drew was the biggest shad ever taken from the James River, and Dr. McGuire
was in his Confederate uniform. I was on my way toward becoming an illustrator.

There was one subject, though, on which I failed, and that
was Charley. I could draw him, after a fashion, but the real
Charley eluded me; I could not seem to get his haughty,
wooden dignity, his hawklike chiseled features, his cold, contemptuous eye. I wished I had a real wooden Indian of my
own. But no one had one, not even Dr. Kluttz or Mr. Eubanks;
that was one great lack in Chapel Hill.

In toy stores, then, along with decalcomania pictures, if

you liked them which I didn't, wonderful paper soldiers could be had. They came on a long heavy cardboard sheet, maybe a dozen in a row, and you cut them out and bent back the ends of the base and they stood up. There were many kinds in many uniforms. The most common were French Zouaves and American soldiers in dress uniforms of the Spanish War period with horsehair plumes on their spiked helmets, and Rough Riders all looking like Teddy Roosevelt (without horses). There were Britishers in red coats and big bear-skin Busbees, and German soldiers in little flat caps, and Arabs and Moors in long robes and carrying strange-looking guns and great curved swords. You couldn't get them in Chapel Hill, as there were no toy stores, but people would send the soldiers to us from away and Dad usually brought some when he came. (I had some lead soldiers, too, Christmas presents, a set of Americans in campaign hats and blue uniforms, and a wonderful set of cavalry on prancing horses; they wore little square-topped helmets and carried lances with little flags on them, like the Light Brigade.) But the paper soldiers were larger and made the better showing. Once we got the idea we went ahead and created others, Billy Cobb and I, and Charles Mangum. Pasteboard was at a premium around our houses. The store-bought ones never included any Confederates, but that presented no difficulty and we made some fine, fierce ones. We never wasted our time making Yankee soldiers. My first really serious work, however, of which I have any definite recollection—and the only one of that era which has survived—was a portrait of the greatest soldier and Confederate of them all, General Lee. It is dated 1901. Just why I located the General at Fredericksburg I do not know. Fredericksburg was a great victory for Southern arms, whereas in my portrait the General looks peculiarly battered and discouraged.

The Cobb boys' father's library included a couple of

Charles Dana Gibson books, and sometimes we copied these
drawings. Better artists than we have done this, before and
since. Mostly, though, we just looked at the pictures and wished
to goodness we could draw like that.

My first formal instruction in the unalterable rules of
drawing came along a year or so later. At least the rules
were unalterable then. Now, of course, everybody makes his
own rules, but then the code was pretty tight. Hanging in
my studio today is a fine drawing by H. T. Webster, the
original of one of his famous and penetrating cartoons, which
depicts a small boy of my vintage gazing spellbound at a
Frederick Remington painting of a mounted Comanche scout.
On the wall beside it are indicated other pictures with immortal signatures, C. D. Gibson and A. B. Frost and How-
ard Pyle. The caption says "The Good Old Days,—when
artists made Indians look like Indians, and not like something drawn by a subnormal child." That's the way it was
then; you tried to make things look like what they were. You

could never mistake a Frederick Remington Indian for a bowl of pansies or a Young Woman Drying Her Hair.

However, with the idea that my interpretation of art lacked something, and feeling that I had better be got busy and taught some fundamentals, my mother enrolled me in an art class in the University's Summer School. I still have my entrance card, and proudly show it if anybody asks me if I am a University man.

This class was taught by a Mr. Bentime, a fat gentleman with a thick German or catarrhal accent. Anyway, I could never understand much of what he said, and neither could I enjoy very much the work I had to do. I remember the first time I went to his class. Mother had made me take some of my soldiers and Indians and circus scenes to show Mr. Bentime. The classroom, instead of being an artist's studio full of glamour, was a dreary place on the top floor of one of the University buildings with one-arm writing seats around and blackboards on the wall. I thought Mr. Bentime looked pretty dreary, too. He was sort of rumpled and wheezy, with buttons missing. He looked at my pictures and smiled and rubbed his stubbly chin. "So," he said. "You vish to be an artist, yes? Vell, vell, vell. Ve shall see. It may take time: You know von does not dance before von valks." I had not the slightest idea what he was talking about. What had dancing to do with it? I was there to learn how to *draw* better.

"Don't be hasty," Mr. Bentime would admonish. "Take your time. The race is not alvays to the svift."

How he made us work. Every morning for two long hours we did his bidding. There were only two or three other students, grown people, and I believe they enjoyed it as little as I did. Mr. Bentime would stand at the blackboard and draw boxes and pyramids and cones. Form, he called it. We copied these forms. Then he would tell us what to do

—say, draw a box tipped up against the wall, or a ball with a foreshortened circle around it, or a pyramid with the top broken off and lying over on its side beside it. Strangely enough, however, some of the perspective he taught us stuck with me, maybe because he insisted that everything had to have a "wanishing point." "If it iss in perspectiff," he would say, "it iss good drawink."

But it was dull stuff for one straining to give birth to fire engines and football players and cavalry charges. It was my first encounter with discipline, other than the strictly personal variety I met with at home, and it wasn't easy to take. But I drew away at my spheres and cubes, and sometimes Mr. Bentime would look at my struggles and beam at me through his thick glasses and say, "Dot's right. Keep trying. You are doing vell." Not that I needed encouragement; anybody could draw the boxes and the balls. All I needed, I thought, was to get away from Mr. Bentime and give my creative instincts a chance! But I never got beyond the "form" with Mr. Bentime. "Do not be discourached," he would say, his finger on his big red nose. "What I giff you you vill find most waluable, some day." I am inclined to think that he was right.

The tinsel and the color of the world of action drew me, though. A circus was a rare and great event, and then only the little one-ring wagon shows that sometimes came to Durham or to Hillsboro. There has always been an attempt to shield the students here from tawdry, evil influence, and thumbs were down on circuses, poolrooms or saloons, so we missed much. The best part of the circuses which came as near as possible, however, (that is if you couldn't see them, which we very rarely could) was the publicity beforehand. I recall no billboard advertising, no gaudy posters of any kind. Advance information about the show was contained in hand-circulated sheets, or "throw-aways." Only, we didn't throw them away! They were among the things you held most dear. Sometimes these small sheets were followed by larger folders of several pages containing drawings which left no doubt whatever that this particular greatest show on earth had begun where Barnum left off, and they were really treasures. The ladies in tights were always incredibly beautiful, the plumed and caparisoned horses always unbelievably spirited, and the great herd of elephants always gigantic. An enormous parade, filled with bands and glittering wagons and cages stretched clear away over the far horizon, and the Brothers who owned the circus, riding in an opulent open carriage at the head of the parade, always looked benign and philanthropic in their tall silk hats. The Congress of Ferocious Wild Beasts was always the greatest menagerie ever assembled on earth, and the high diver always made his death-defying leap from a height greater than man had ever attained before (and into only three feet of water). These circus sheets were prized possessions, and much branch water went under the bridge while I copied and embellished the pictures and under their inspiration created others.

The life of an artist is necessarily full of ups and downs, and my first fall in connection with my art was a very disconcerting experience. On a wet and windy day I had collected an armful of these throw-aways, advertising a coming show, and was hurrying along Rosemary with a big umbrella which was keeping me and my pictures dry. There used to be a deep ditch in front of the old Baptist Church, four or five feet lower than the sidewalk, and for some reason I was making my way along the very edge of the retaining wall above this ditch, inspired by the daredeviltry of the circus performers and imagining, no doubt, that I was a tightrope walker. Anyway, a sudden gust of wind got under the umbrella, and blew me off into the ditch. I would probably have been all right had I held onto the umbrella and parachuted to a landing, but I let go. Down I plopped into mud and water, my throwaways flying in all directions. I must have let out an awful bellow, for men came running from Mr. Frank Pickard's Livery Stable, over on the other corner, and picked me up and retrieved my umbrella, which was wrong-side out. I was unhurt, only very wet and muddy, but my circus pictures were gone or ruined, and my sorrow was loud and genuine. I viewed their loss as irreplaceable, and I gathered up what I could of the torn and muddy sheets and carried them tenderly home and spread them out to dry. The ink must have been very poor, however, for it ran, and the sheets were not much good after that. Grandpa had his lighter moments, and while he was sympathetic, he said it was very appropriate that this ducking happened in front of the Baptist Church.

Before I forget, I'd like to tell you one of Grandpa's favorite stories. He didn't tell many, but this one he always enjoyed, and he would slip it in if the occasion seemed right. There was an old colored man, he said, coming home from the millpond with a string of fish he had caught. An interested stranger asked him about the varities of the fish.

"Well, suh," he answered, "dis hyah a brim, an' dis'un a yeller-belly perch, an' hyah a catfish, and dis'n a Baptist—"

"Why do you call him a Baptist?" the man asked.

"Well, suh," the old colored man said, "we calls him a Baptist 'cause he *sp'ile* so soon after y'git him out'a de water!"

Strangely enough, Grandpa was always very interested and helpful in my efforts at drawing, and never criticized my subject matter, some of which was pretty lurid.

There were no regular art classes in the public schools then, but following my studies with Mr. Bentime I had another teacher. This was an enthusiastic, understanding lady named Mrs. Wardlaw, who painted flowers and landscapes. Very well, too, as I recall. However, these subjects appealed

to me little more than those of Mr. Bentime's class, and I am
afraid my heart was not in it.

Funny thing, but what I remember most clearly about
Mrs. Wardlaw is her husband. He was a young instructor
in the University and had come here from some Eastern
school where he had become something of an expert swordsman. So, on the side, he taught fencing to interested students. After some of his pupils had attained a certain skill he
would stage exhibitions, in Gerard Hall, and these matches
were thrilling. Mother, and the other ladies, said it seemed
very dangerous, though, even with the padded vests and the
big wire basket masks the fencers used. The word "dangerous" of course made it doubly attractive to us small fry. From
somewhere I got hold of a couple of old, worthless foils, and
hung them on the wall in my room, crossed, with a Carolina
pennant underneath. I thought Mr. Wardlaw the greatest
swordsman in the world, and a dangerous fellow who would
slit your gullet just like that! I would go around with a
stick (as I wasn't allowed to take the foils off the wall) imi-
tating his poses, to the peril of bystanders' eyes. Because of
my studies with his wife, I suppose, Mr. Wardlaw was always
very nice to me, and I felt fairly safe with him.

This little room of mine, at the front end of the little
passage between Mother's and Mars' Phil's rooms and the
"hall," as so many people called their living room then
(maybe it was some sort of baronial hangover from the ancient days of manor houses and castles where the general
meeting place was called the hall) was my refuge, my re-
treat, my inviolate ivory tower. It was referred to by everybody except Mars' Phil as my Sanctum Sanctorum, whatever that meant, but Mars' Phil said it looked like an over-
stocked museum to him. Anyway, it was a wonderful little
room, and in it I was lord.

"Put it in your room," Mother said of any of my traps.

And in the room it would go, and the things got deeper and deeper.

The room, Mother guessed, must have been a place for plants, or even chickens, once, for there was a solid row of sunny windows across the front, facing south across the front yard to the street, high-up windows touching the low ceiling, and a big, broad shelf under them, all the way across the room. "A fine place for seedlings," Grandpa said once, speculatively, but he never pressed the matter. I had to stand up to look out the windows, but this was good because when I was sitting down or squatting it gave you a fine sense of privacy and nobody could look in on you from outside. It was a very small room, hardly more than a cubbyhole, you might say, and there was no fireplace in it, which of course made it a little chilly in the wintertime. The walls were not finished off with plaster like the other rooms, but were just plain boards, which, however, were painted a light blue, and I liked this feature because the U.N.C. colors were light blue and white. A narrow iron bed, painted white, took up most of one wall, and against the other was my chest of drawers with the mirror on top in front of which I could pose and grimace when alone. There was the spool case for my bird eggs in a corner, and under the row of windows a kitchen chair and a large unstable table piled high with my trophies and other valuable matter. In the corner by the door was my sporting paraphernalia, baseball bats, my tennis racket, in which there seemed to be always a couple of busted strings, an old, hard-used football, my mitt and mask, my Beebee gun (and later my .22) and other items appropriate for outdoor activity. There was no closet in the room, of course (none of our rooms had closets) and no room for a wardrobe, so the corner on the other side of the door from my athletic stuff had a curtain across it and hooks and nails on the wall for my clothes. Mother always picked them up and

hung them there and pulled the curtain back across, which
was a little inconvenient when I was in a hurry for something.

The decoration of my walls was very pleasing. In the
big space over the bed I had the fencing foils and the large
Carolina banner; but I had other pennants, too. I had an old
Episcopal High School one of Mars' Phil's, and a red and
white A. & M. one, a dark blue and white Trinity pennant,
and—my pride—a gorgeous Princeton pennant of orange
and black. (You could buy pennants of other colleges at Mr.
Neville's store—he had a lot of them—but they really ran
into money.) I had a wire rack which hung on the wall and
held picture postcards, and another for mounted kodak snapshots. I had fine collections of both. I had a Frederick Remington print (framed) called "The Attack on the Stagecoach," and a large drawing which I myself had made of a
football player. I thought it almost as good as the Remington,
but then it was not exactly mine, either, being a copy I had
made of a figure in a football picture by Charles Dana Gibson.
This football player was running toward you, and his very
long hair was blowing around. He wore a canvas jacket, and
one of his stockings was coming down. He held his straight-
arm straight out before him. It was very realistic. Those who
think Charles Dana Gibson was a sissy and drew only girls
are very much mistaken; he drew football players, too. In
the other corners, and under my bed and under the table, and,
I'm afraid, underfoot also, were my *things*. Stamp albums,
boxes of arrowheads, a couple of stuffed birds, my collection
of tobacco tags, my drawing and painting tools, books and
magazines and pictures, my pyrography set, the rabbit trap
I might be working on at the moment, a small sculptured
group of iron horses which used to be on top of a clock we
had once which got broken, my box of carpenter tools, the
'coon skin Uncle John Atwater had given me, and of course

stuff like string and wire and pieces of wood, and all, and a few other things like that. Things I liked to have around, handy. Of course there wasn't much room to move around, unless you did it carefully, and I doubt that it would have been large enough for a man, say, as big as Mars' Phil. My bed was covered with a bright striped blanket whose origin I do not know, but it was a good thing to use as an Indian. However, Duke, my dog, was practically always lying on the bed when I was in the room, and I disturbed him only when absolutely necessary. He didn't disturb easily, either, and I could pile a lot of stuff on him when I had to. On the bed, too—my pride and joy, my Kohinoor—rested, with its beautiful purple ruffle Mother had made, my Pillow.

This pillow, upon which no human head had ever rested, was made of beautiful and exquisite little college seals of silk, in all their authentic colors and detail, close set and chain-stitched by my Mother. The seals were the prizes, the little extra something (like the actresses of the Nineties, and the baseball players later on), which some of the cigarette manu-facturers baited you with. These seals came in—I wish I could remember. I lie awake at night groping for that brand of cigarettes. It was a fancy and superior brand, costing more than ordinary cigarettes like Sweet Caporals or Piedmonts or Home Runs, and was in the class of Richmond Straight Cuts or Melachrinos. Could it have been the oldtime Fatima? Or Turkish Trophies? I don't know now, but Fatima always comes to mind. Anyway, Mr. Neville's high class Athletic Goods and Ice Cream, across from Dr. Kluttz's, was the only store in town which sold them, and then only rarely to stu-dents who were flush. They were very, very rare. The lit-tle seals inside, just the size of the package, were thrilling to pull out, and you never knew. But sometimes you were disappointed. *"Harvard!"* you would sneer, "they're *com-mon;* I've got three of *them!"* But usually you gasped for

joy. *"Yale . . . !"* you breathed in an awestruck tone. Or
you might extract a strange insignia of red and gold and
smooth its silky face and laboriously turn the seal and spell
out M-i-n-n-e-s-o-t-a, "Minnesota! *Wheeeee!"*

That pillow top spelled achievement; it was the culmi-
nation and the climax of collection, when I had enough to
make the top complete. It represented endless hours of waiting and of search, of begging and of trading, and at last I
had them all. . . . No antiquer, having found the final chair
of a Chippendale dining room set, was ever more proud. The
value of my pillow was beyond all calculation.

Mr. Neville helped me get the seals. He would ask the
students if they wanted them, and while most did, sometimes
they'd give them to him. He was my friend. His was a
fascinating establishment, with pictures of the Teams around
the walls, and pennants and big college seals, and the first
drugstore chairs and tables I ever saw. Footballs and tennis
rackets and baseball equipment were in the showcases. Mr.
Neville had greenish-blue hair, on one side—the result, I was
told, of an explosion when he was fiddling with some sort of
chemical experiment. Because of this blue hair Mr. Neville
was a very striking looking man. It used to be one of my
ambitions to grow up to look like Mr. Neville, and own a
Sporting Goods and Ice Cream.

Collecting, and interior decoration, were only sidelines,
after all; my real love was Art, and artistic success awaited
me. In the red letter year of 1906 my work saw printer's ink!

The year book of the University has always gloried in
the name of *Yackety Yack.* Strangers are apt to start and
say "How's that?" when you mention the *Yackety Yack.* The
University has a yell which begins "Yackety Yack, 'Ray!
'Ray!" but even so this is hardly an adequate excuse for giving
the annual such a name. Its publication was one of the major

events of the local year and its preparation, for the staff, took up most of it. It was probably much like other college annuals of that time, with individual photographs of the Senior Class, accompanied by quotations and prophecies, also pictures of the Faculty looking extremely intellectual, and group pictures of the other classes and the fraternities and the athletic teams, with lists of names and records and dates. But there were also many drawings and cartoons, headings for departments and activities. There was an occasional color page, a rather sad affair in reproduction. One of these, usually, was a general title page for the Athletics section of the book, and almost invariably showed a pompadoured and lifeless-faced young woman wearing a huge white chrysanthemum and waving a Carolina banner. I didn't aspire to anything like this, but kept my drawings on a pen and ink basis. It was considered quite an accomplishment, artistically speaking, to have a drawing accepted by the *Yackety Yack,* which was a sort of Chapel Hill Salon, and the Art Editor, like most Art Editors everywhere, was swamped with contributions most of which he had to turn down. In 1906 the book carried three of my pictures, all of them having to do with the glories of our football and baseball teams; the cultural aspects of our institution meaning little or nothing to me. It was a proud day when I saw my drawings printed in the *Yackety Yack,* with my name beneath them.

This was perhaps the beginning of my so-called commercial point of view. Up to that time, except for the matter of the Confederate flags, my work had been purely for Art's sake, but the *Yackety Yack* opened for me a new and wide horizon. Not only was I doing what I enjoyed and wanted to do more than anything else in the world, and getting it printed but, incredibly, I was being *paid* for it. Not that the *Yackety Yack* put out cold cash for their pictures; you took it out in trade, so to speak, and the remuneration, or emolument, as we say in academic circles, consisted of a copy of the book, all wrapped up in tissue paper and absolutely free, gratis, for nothing! Inasmuch as the book cost two dollars and a half if you bought it, which of course you couldn't, this seemed extravagantly high pay.

I continued to work for the *Yackety Yack,* and the 1910 book (published after I had said good-bye to Chapel Hill) contained sixteen of my pictures. It was about that time, I guess, that I began to think about going into business for myself.

A small and youthful, smiling student named Frank Graham was Art Editor of the *Yackety Yack.* He has since become President of the University, an internationally known and respected educator and mediator, a famous humanitarian and statesman, and as much saint as man. He is now North Carolina's great contribution to the United States Senate. This just goes to prove that an Art Editor, no matter how difficult and distasteful his work, need not necessarily feel discouraged about his future.

Chapter Ten

Two highly important influences upon my early youth were Wump, my colored friend and neighbor, and my dog, Duke. (At the present time it would be worth your life, or that of the dog, to name a Chapel Hill dog "Duke." Old Trinity College, over in Durham, has grown since the old days—and with the help of Bull Durham millions—into lordly Duke University and become our deadly athletic scourge and rival. *"Beat Duke!"* is chanted around these parts with fervor and sincerity. Duke is a mighty factor in football, and in other phases of education, too, but smugly, over here, we let Duke count its money, and we tend our ivy vines. No man with proper instincts and the finer feelings could even conceive of naming a Chapel Hill dog Duke nowadays; that would be unthinkable. But my Duke was given his name when Trinity College was poor and still Trinity. Mars' Phil named him, I think—or could it have been Miss Alice Jones?—because the combination of "Duke Prince" sounded euphonious and regal. Miss Alice, by the way, was one of those rare beings, a coed, and lived with us one winter when we first came to Chapel Hill, in the room later occupied by Mars' Phil. She was a gay and sentimental young lady with a flair for naming things; it was she who poetically dubbed the rectory Jonquil Cottage on Rosemary Lane.

95

Dogs have always been important to me, and beginning with Duke (and before him, in Roanoke, Dad's big red setter, Rab, who is one of my earliest dim memories) there has been a long and almost unbroken parade of unforgettable dogs, large and small, rough and smooth, but all with hearts of gold. Wump had a golden heart, too. I wish there might also have been a long string of Wumps in my life, but he was the only one of his kind.

I do not remember where Duke came from or when I got him, but it must have been after we came to Chapel Hill. It seemed as though I had always had him. He was my constant companion, day and night, a fine dog, a great dog, self-made, as his antecedents were nothing to boast of. He resembled most a stocky Fox Terrier, so a Fox Terrier I called him. A definite breed has been developed here, over generations, which is recognized by canine connoisseurs as The Chapel Hill Dog. The Chapel Hill Dog varies in size from the standard (very large) to the miniature, and in coloration there is no set rule. The chief identifying characteristics of the breed are a sunny disposition and an extra long, curling tail. I believe Duke to be one of the progenitors of this breed. He got around a lot. I have no knowledge of his tail, he having been relieved of it when he was small.

Duke's personality was easy-going and admirable in every way. He was an adaptable dog, and he put up uncomplainingly with many indignities and inconveniences, such as being thrown in the creek or the briar patch by the Venable boys, having rocks chunked at him, the "lessons" given him with turpentine by the irate owners of his girl friends, the semiannual baths, with soap, insisted upon by my mother, and occasional applications of Glover's Mange Cure in the hotter months. And there was the terrible dosing with whiskey administered by the local horse doctor, the time he was bitten by a copperhead. He was one of the first inebriates I ever saw, or carried home and put to bed, and I remember that before he passed out he fell off the veterinarian's side porch. Next day, however, he was all right except for a bad hangover indicated by his ill humor and thirst. I have never doubted, since, the efficacy of whiskey as a snakebite remedy.

I remember very vividly the time the copperhead bit Duke, and that except for Wump he might have bitten *me*. We were snooping around the Gimghoul Hall that day. Gimghoul Hall was the stronghold of a secret order or society in the University, called Gimghoul. (Somebody else with imagination was responsible for that name.) Their meeting place was a fearsome, spooky building way down at the end of Rosemary in the woods. Things seem overlarge to children—buildings, people, even furniture, because they are viewed from such a low perspective—and Gimghoul Hall as I remember it was enormous. It was the most ominous and forbidding house I think I ever saw. It was built of logs, the bark hanging in shreds and tatters on the outside, and the roof swept up to a high, sharp peak and down, low, over a porch around three sides. The porch made a good place to run around, when you felt brave. The windows had great heavy solid shutters, always closed, and the door was secured by a rusty padlock and a chain. In the half-gloom of the cedar trees around it, it looked ghostly and deserted. But we knew that things went on in there, when the Gimghouls were in session, and we thought that the Gimghouls were probably like Ku Kluxers and wore masks and long white robes and had chains and wracks and wheels and other implements of torture in the Hall, and smoking pots of boiling oil, and such. "Dey is bats in dere, too," said Wump, though how he knew this I do not know, as he never saw inside. He wasn't any too enthusiastic about going around the place.

That day, however, we were up on the porch among the

trash and twigs and fallen leaves, feeling at the windows as
we often did in the hope that a shutter might be loose and
we could open it and peer within, but everything was closed
up tight, as usual. "Dey's nailed," said Wump. "Dem Gimghouls [he pronounced it "Jimghouls"] don' want *no*body
see what dey got in dere."

   You always felt a little apprehensive, leaving the sinister
and scary place, and instinctively you glanced behind as you
retreated. I think I must have done that then, as we started
toward the littered steps. I felt a violent blow, and landed
on my face among the weeds. "Git 'way fum hyah! *Snake!*"
Wump screamed. He had shoved me off the porch just as
the reptile, coiled—unseen—beside a post, had struck.
Wump's sharp eyes had caught him, and his reaction was
immediate and definite. I scrambled to my feet, while Wump
—like lightning—grabbed a heavy stick and struck the snake
which was slithering away. "Kill him, kill him!" we both
shouted, and I got a club, too, and joined Wump in the battle. The snake writhed and thrashed and squirmed and struck,
and tried to get away. And then, before either of us could
prevent, old Duke joined in. He leaped and tried to grab the
copperhead, and Wump belted him with his stick, and Duke
yelped and jumped away and I grabbed and held him, for the
snake was almost done and Wump was finishing him. But a
snake dies slowly, and he lay and twitched. "Keep away fum
'im," Wump warned. "He ain't dead. A high lan' moccasin
kin bite yuh wid his tail jes lak his head!" (Copperhead may
have been technically correct, but we always called them high
land moccasins.) I held Duke by his collar, and he struggled,
but when I let him go, and threatened him and yelled, "Go
'way from here!" he subsided and went off on one side and
lay down, panting. We squatted on our haunches and watched
the snake. I can see him now, the thick, tawny body shuddering, the moving, blunted tail, blood on his head where

Wump had banged a heavy stone, but his eyes still glittering and the deadly fangs licking from his jaws. Slowly he relaxed as we watched. "He a'mos' dead," said Wump. Wump began to look around him. "When y'kill a snake," he said, "d'other snake come. Hit his wife. She git to lukkin' f'im, an' ef y'don' look peert she sneak up behin' yeh an' bite yeh. Da's the way de lady snake do."

"Suppose you kill the lady snake first?" I asked him. "What does the other snake do?—the husband snake?"

Wump scratched his head. This was a new idea. "I don' know," he said, after he had thought it over. "Maybe don' *nothin'* happen . . . but I think dis hyah de man snake, he look s'big an' mean."

We both felt uncomfortable, with the idea of the lady snake sneaking up on us from behind, and I suggested we leave there and go on home. Wump gingerly picked up the snake on his stick and carried him over to the porch and slid him off under the steps. "We come back an' look at 'im t'morrer," he said.

Only then did we notice Duke. He was lying off a little way, licking and biting at his front foot. "Come on," I called him, but he didn't get up, just raised his head and panted. Then he bit his paw again. We went over to him and Wump took the leg and looked at it. Just above the paw there were two tiny bluish holes, and the foot and leg were swollen a little. "He done got bit," said Wump, and he picked Duke up in his arms and we started running. We had to stop and rest often, for Duke was heavy, and by the time we got him home the swelling was much worse and Duke was shivering and his eyes looked funny. He couldn't stand up. Grandpa looked at him, and then we put him in my wagon (*"Hurry,"* said Grandpa) and ran up to Dr. Merritt's, and I prayed hard, all the way, that he wouldn't die.

Dr. Merritt took one look at him when we carried him

in, and then he went to work. First he opened Duke's mouth and poured some whiskey in. Duke coughed and sputtered, but the whiskey went down. "To stimulate his heart," Dr. Merritt said. Then he cut the leg open a little, so that it would bleed, and began rubbing and massaging Duke, working away from his heart. Every now and then he'd stop and give Duke another shot of whiskey. After a while he put a bandage on the leg but he didn't stop giving him drinks. Duke would try to get up, and fall over. Dr. Merritt would laugh and say, "He's drunk as a coot." We watched him a while, and he went to sleep. The whiskey bottle was almost empty, so Dr. Merritt tipped it up and drank the rest. "Whiskey is a mighty fine thing," he said, "if rightly used. A man never knows when he might get snakebit."

We wrapped Duke up in an old piece of blanket of Dr. Merritt's.

"Keep him warm," he said. "I think maybe he'll be all right," and we picked Duke up and put him back in the wagon and pulled him home. We got a box and placed him in it, right by my bed, and I stayed awake and watched him, that night, as long as I could. Mother said she would watch him after that. He snored and snored. When I waked up it was morning, and Duke was still snoring and the swelling had gone down. "It would take more than a high land moccasin to kill Duke," Mars' Phil said, and I said, "Yes Siree!"

That morning Wump and I went back to Gimghoul Hall, and our copperhead was quite, quite dead. We brought him back to Wump's house and Wump showed me how to skin him. We stretched the ugly, mottled skin on a board and hung it up.

Duke was patient and forgiving when I pushed or kicked him out of bed. This usually happened on summer nights when the warmth of his proximity made me restless. He just bided his time until he could get back in. In the winter he was comfortingly hot as only a smooth coated dog under numerous blankets and quilts can be. Stamina and an iron constitution saved him from smothering. Like a camel which can go indefinitely without water, Duke seemed to be able to get along all right without air.

At times, when I could think of nothing better to do, I would daub some thick black molasses on his tail, or a piece of sticky candy which he dearly loved, just to watch him endlessly whirl around chasing it. His tail had been docked very short, was hardly more than a nubbin or a bump on his posterior, and he could never quite reach the candy. Finally he got so dizzy he would stagger around and fall over. He would lie there panting and looking at me with eyes slightly out of focus until his head cleared and he felt strong enough to get up and resume the hopeless chase.

Like all Chapel Hill dogs of the period, he could sleep in the soft, warm dust of the sunny streets, had he a mind to. Automobiles were neither a danger nor a disturbance, and of course horses will never step on sleeping dogs. Sometimes, too, he and Malachi, our old Maltese cat, napped back to back. They always ate together from the same dish. He and Malachi had been brought up together and were on good terms, Malachi having taught him the amenities when he was a puppy, but to all other cats he was poison. Whenever I missed him I knew he was absent on business of his own, some cat matter or other. Many's the time he came home chewed up and bloody, but always he licked his wounds with a gleam of triumph and satisfaction in his eye and wagged his stump of a tail. If I was with him when a cat was sighted, I of course gave him such aid as I could.

He was a jaunty little dog, with a swagger and a roving eye, and he moved with a bouncy half-trot, his cocked ears flopping a little. His ears were brown, and his body white all over except for one small brown spot by his tail. I taught him several tricks—simple things like catching a ball and jumping through my arms and sitting up. I would balance a tidbit or a piece of candy on the tip of his nose and he'd sit there rigid, trying to look at the candy only an inch or so away and achieving a comical cross-eyed effect. On the signal he'd toss the candy in the air and catch it. His best trick was one I had seen in a trained dog act. As I walked, slowly and lifting my knees high, he would weave in and out, back and forth, between my feet. It was a difficult trick to master, as I often stepped on him and he would upset me just as frequently. However, once he got the hang of it he liked it and enjoyed his performance. Got so he couldn't bear to see anyone walking slowly without joining in. Grandpa was the gentlest, most deliberate old gentleman I ever saw, and on that day he was stepping quietly down our front walk on his way uptown, Duke trotting happily along with him. And then suddenly, senselessly, Duke decided to do his stuff . . . Grandpa's feet went up, his stick flew off in one direction and his hat in another. I was in the front yard and saw it all. As Grandpa landed, all sprawled out, after hanging an interminable time in mid-air, it seemed to me, I let out a bellow for Mother. When we reached him he was lying quietly on his back. He had sense enough to stay down and take the full count. Duke was prancing around and after I aimed a kick at him he retired behind the Sweet Breath of Spring bush. Mother and I got Grandpa up, which wasn't difficult because he weighed so little (less than ever with the breath knocked out of him), and got him to a chair on the porch. Mother brought her smelling salts and felt his joints and stuffed pillows behind him. Finally he said, "Well, I declare." That was as far as he went toward raising a rumpus, and after a while when she was sure he wasn't maimed or crippled, Mother let him up and after I collected his hat and stick and glasses he continued his walk uptown. But ever after that I noticed he was careful of his footwork when Duke came around.

That was the end of Duke's best trick; at Mother's behest I labored to undo my teaching, and every time it occurred to Duke to do his specialty I forcibly discouraged him. I believe he understood, in a measure, that he had committed the ultimate sin, that of upsetting Grandpa, and for a while he seemed a meeker dog.

But nothing could make him meek or apologetic about cats. He was born into the world to keep cats in their place, he thought, and this he did to the utmost of his powers. The worst licking I ever got was because of a cat, or rather because I helped him corner a cat under circumstances and at a time that called for more than a licking. I should have been strung up by the thumbs, then drawn and quartered. Mother was terribly ill one autumn with typhoid, so ill that it was touch and go. Dr. Manning took care of her and did a heroic job but there was a time when it semed as though that were not enough. Dad gave up his job and came home to help nurse her. We had a day nurse for Mother and Dad sat up nights. Strict orders were for quiet during the day, not only for poor mother's sake but so that Dad, too, could get the rest he so sorely needed. Everybody tiptoed around and whispered.

To my shame, Duke and I chased a cat under the house. There was no basement, only a shallow air space, in places only a few inches. Both Duke and the cat got stuck, and there they stayed for hours, Duke barking savagely. Dad, of course, was fit to be tied, and when I finally dragged Duke out, and the cat escaped, and I had admitted my part in the sorry business, he rolled up his sleeves and really laid it on. The fact that he didn't just kill me outright speaks for his kindness and mercy.

Even Wump, my yes man, gave me a blistering tongue-

lashing, and that hurt even more than the licking. "Ef Miss
Alice die," Wump said grimly, "you de cause uh it, you'n 'at
Dook!" I prayed for forgiveness that night when I went to
bed supperless—and Mother didn't die.

The rear half of our lot, between us and Wump's house,
was a sun-baked red clay cornfield. Every spring Uncle John
Atwater plowed and planted it in field corn, which miraculously grew, and as the various plantings matured we ate what
we could and the rest was taken by Wump and me to the
mill to be ground into meal for the pone and corn muffins
I loved. Those trips were great events. Wump had certain
rights in an old, blind mule; at least he could borrow the mule
when necessary from a friend who lived nearby. This mule,
whose name was Sam, had an unlovable disposition, and
when approached from the rear, if he heard you coming, was
apt to lash out in a mighty kick. Wump said he had killed a
man, wunst. "Yassuh, 'at ole mule he kill him dead as a do'
nail. I dunno d'man's name, but 'at's what dey tell me fer a
fac'. Ole Sam he kick 'im so hard d'man's head go flyin' off
one way and d'res' uv'im de yuther. Aftuh while dey fin' d'res'
uv'im over in d'bushes but dey ain't never fin' d'head. Some
folk say hit fall in d'mill pond and some folks say hit go
kerplunk down a ole well. Dey had t'give up lookin' fer hit
so's dey could bury d'man, wha's lef' uv'im. So dey has
d'funeral and den dey hitch up ole Sam and Sam he haul de
remains to d'graveyard. Reckon could dey fin' d'head dey'd
have 'nother funeral. Da's whut my Unc' Will say, and my
Unc' Apex, too. Dey warn't dere when hit happen, but folks
tell 'em."

I always enjoyed this story, and whenever Wump told
it, which was fairly often, he embellished it a little.

"But why didn't they do something to Sam?" I asked,
horrified, the first time I heard it. "Gee whillikens—*killing*
a man! The Bible says an eye for an eye, a tooth for a

tooth . . ." (I was showing off my knowledge of Scripture, at that time extensive.)

Wump laughed. "Ole Sam ain't got no eye and he ain't got no teeth," he said, "and I reckon he more useful 'live den dead."

I had to agree. Old Sam was useful to us, and many's the sack of our corn his bony back has borne to the mill. Wump would lead him over with a rope bridle tied to the halter, and we would load him up and mount. I sat behind, holding onto Wump, my legs spread wide by the grain sacks, and off we would go, Sam slowly picking his way down Windy Hill to Mr. Durham's mill on the Hillsboro Road. This mill was something out of a fairy story to us, with everything including Mr. Durham covered with meal, and the great, mossy millwheel turning slowly and dripping water, which came down the "race" from the millpond above.

It was an all-day operation; we saw to that. In addition to something to eat we always carried fishing poles, and after we left our corn with Mr. Durham we hurried to the millpond for bream, or to the creek below the mill for perch and catfish. The creek had a high bank on one side, and it was pleasant to sit on it and hang your feet over and watch the water below and haul up the little fish. Sam we had pastured in a fenced field by the mill. There was a big locust tree near the mill, and we would always get a lot of the fallen black-purple pods from this tree and break them and eat the thick, brownish, sickly-sweet stuff which oozed out, before we turned our attention to fishing. Very tasty, locusts, when you're hungry. Grown people made locust beer. When the sun dipped down and we had our fill of fishing, we got our meal from Mr. Durham and caught Sam and loaded up, and with our strings of fish, rode slowly up the hill and home.

It was Wump who, when I was only about seven years old, helped me build my first rabbit gum, and if you don't

understand the thrill that goes with that, you're no woodsman.
A rabbit gum follows a basic pattern adopted by some hairy,
prehistoric man to catch the first rabbit, for everywhere they
are the same. Men are born with the knowledge of the exact
construction of a rabbit gum.

The box itself is longer than a rabbit, but not so long or
heavy as to prevent you moving it around with ease. The trigger is a long stick, or sweep, to which at one end the door is
loosely tied with string, and on the other end is tied a lighter,
shorter stick which goes down through a large hole in the top
of the rear end of the gum. To this little stick the bait is
fastened. The stick has a little notch in it which rests on the
edge of the hole. Setting the trap is a delicate business as the
weight of the raised door is held and balanced on the notch of
the little stick. The door moves up and down in a sliding track
or groove and the long sweep rests in a notched upright set
midway of the box. When a hungry, foolish rabbit enters and
investigates the inviting lure at the far end, he dislodges the
little stick so delicately resting on the edge of the hole, and

bingo! down behind him falls the door. This takes care of the opening direction in the recipe for stewed rabbit which reads "First catch your rabbit."

We made ours, back of Wump's house, from some old boards rotting in the grass and a plank or two we pulled from his back stoop, for the lumber should look old and weathered.

" 'At's a fine gum," Wump said with satisfaction, after it was finished and we had repeatedly set the trigger and tripped it with a stick, making the door fall with a pleasing thump. "We go'n ketch d'bigges' ole rabbit on d'whole Back Street. You wait'n see! C'mon, les tote hit over hyar'n d'brush." We baited it with a cabbage from Wump's mother's larder, and I said, "Eerum, eyerum, ohrum" over it—which is a fine charm and usually gets you what you want.

The next morning I was up in the cold November dawn and excitedly stumbling across the back lot toward the thicket where lay my rabbit gum. I remember creeping up on it, peering over a bush, and standing breathless when I saw it. It was sprung, and the door was down! Having been in on similar occasions at the traps of other and older boys, I knew just what to do, i. e., look through the empty trigger hole at my rabbit. Only this was not a rabbit; even in my inexperience I could see that. But Ah, I knew what it was; it was a guinea pig! That beady, baleful little black eye shining up at me belonged to no rabbit, and the Cobb boys, who lived nearby, had guinea pigs. Doubtless this was one of theirs, escaped and gone astray. How fortunate for the Cobb boys!

I was right in assuming it was no rabbit, but wrong on the second assumption, as I discovered when I upended the gum and thrust my arm down through the door to grasp and bring forth my prize. Sharp teeth made a life scar on my right hand, and I abandoned my plan with a yell of surprise and pain. Wrapping my wounded hand in my stocking cap, I hoisted gum and occupant to my shoulder and floundered off across the field toward home, shouting for Wump (who came running through the weeds), Mars' Phil, Grandpa, or anybody. Arrived at the house, winded, I got a box, with Wump's help, and we dumped our prisoner in. He was a fine, fat 'possum.

Following the proper and proud display to our neighbors of both my 'possum and my bandaged hand, we presented the 'possum to Uncle John Atwater. Somehow he did not appeal to me as a pet. It is a good bet the 'possum ended his career, and achieved his destiny, on Uncle John's Thanksgiving board, surrounded by sweet potatoes and drooling little Atwaters.

CHAPTER ELEVEN

Wump's language, while direct and explicit, was not dirty. Well, not very dirty. Most of the first ten four-letter words I was taught at school, not by the regularly commissioned instructors, of course, but as extracurricular items by older and better educated boys. Language—that is popular and really expressive language—was denied me, I being a preacher's grandson, and at home and around the family I had to watch my step. Even with clean but unrefined words I had difficulty. Such a word, for example, was belly. Mother frowned upon belly; stomach, she said, was so much nicer. I quoted the Bible and reminded her of Jonah's experience, but she said that was different. When I was quite small, however, Dad (who was more unconventional) and I had a game we called Shocking Mother. I am sure that Mother was not so shocked as she appeared to be, but the playing of the game made you feel rough and tough and masculine. I would crouch down and put my face in the grass and call to Dad. "Hey, Dad," I would yell, "how low am I?"

"Well, I declare," Dad would say, in mock amazement, "you're as low as a snake's belly! Yes siree, you're just as low as a striped-tailed snake's belly!" Then we would both laugh and laugh and I would roll over and over on the grass and shout "I'm low as a snake's belly!" and Mother would look horrified and cluck "Tch-ch-ch-ch."

But it wasn't just Mother, it was the stiff and super refinement of the times, that era when ladies' legs were never mentioned and limbs only when unavoidable. A bitch was "a female dog;" grave consequences would have ensued had any of the ladies ever been exposed to bitch. Stink, of course, was not mentioned in polite society other than as a bad smell. I remember that when it became necessary to convey my meaning referring to it as "that word." A bastard was "an illegitimate child, poor thing"—mentioned, when imperative, in a low voice, with lifted eyebrows. I was quite a big boy before I ever heard the bald and naked word sex, now one of our most popular terms.

Of course, hell and damn were words only common people used, and never, even by them, in the presence of ladies. (This, of course, did not apply to Dad, because he was a railroad man, and sometimes when something upset him, like bad news or running into a door in the dark, he might say something before he thought, but he was sorry for it immediately. "Excuse me, Alice," he would say. And Mother would look a little shocked and pained, and say, "It's those *men* you're thrown with . . ." Then Dad would stiffen up and say, "What's the matter with those men, I'd like to know? They're a fine lot of men, let me tell you—yes, sir, a *fine* lot of men!" But Mother would sniff. I thought they were a fine lot of men, too, from what Dad had said about them, and I knew they had a fine time, riding around on trains so much.)

Being what I was unfortunately born, I couldn't even say "Gosh," or "Golly Moses," and when "Ye Gods!" came into vogue, later on, Mother frowned on that, too. I remember that my fiercest oath, that is whenever any of my elders was around, was Jiminy Chris'mus! Puke, of course, was an invaluable term, and with so many little boys and dogs around

could be used quite often, but this, too, was discouraged. I was
held to "spit up." Vomit, disgorge or spew might have been
all right, but they seemed affected, and up-chuck—the gay,
modern term—had not been thought of then. The handicap,
not of choosing the right word but of being able to use it, has
hindered me all my life.

Wump gave me a lot of detailed information concerning
the activities of the birds and bees, scientific data in which most
boys are deeply interested, and a certain amount of voodoo,
some of which I have found helpful to this day.

One of Wump's accomplishments that I envied him was
chewing tobacco (at this I was a miserable and nauseated
failure) and when somebody gave him a chew he was very
happy. He was an expert expectorator and could sometimes
score bull's-eyes on things like bumblebees and lizards. He
taught me the therapeutic value of tobacco juice, and many's
the cut and abrasion he has treated with the healing, stinging
liquid. (In cases where he happened to be chewless and juice-
less, he would run and borrow some.) A certain clay was good
for black eyes, he said, and if you could get a toad to pee on
your wart it was sure to disappear. Sheep droppings, boiled
into a tea, were quite effective in bringing on the measles, he
claimed, and while I did not relish the idea it was a good thing
to know. Wump said he never touched the stuff, himself, but
it was most efficacious in case your brother had a rising. He
taught me how to kill a rabbit, instantly and painlessly, by
holding the rabbit up by the ears and then with the knuckle
of your forefinger hitting him a sharp, swift rap at the base of
the skull. He knew how to make a mud turtle let go at once,
which ordinarily does not occur until it thunders. He gave me
a demonstration of this one day, when I doubted his statement.
He certainly proved his point.

Mars' Phil and Wump and I had been fishing in Strowd's

Creek, and Mars' Phil's line, we thought, had gotten hung up
on the bottom, caught on a log or something. He pulled and
pulled, and said maybe he'd have to cut his line. Then he felt
a tug and said, "No, sir, it's a *fish!* I've caught a whale." After
a lot of careful pulling so as not to break the line, and during
which Mars' Phil could feel the fish fighting, he said, he pulled
up an enormous mud or "snapping" turtle! He was big as a
dinner plate. He had swallowed the hook, poor turtle, with
the worm on it, so Mars' Phil cut his line off and we carried
him home by the end of the string. He would make fine soup,
Mars' Phil said. But Mother said she wasn't going to ask
Viola to cut him up and make soup of him, and that we ought
to give him to Wump. Wump was agreeable, and we carried
him over to his house and put him in a pen Wump got together, and got him some water and put some cold biscuits in
the pen for him to eat. He got on well, too, until one day we
went to look at him, and he had dug out under the side of the
pen, and gone. We never knew what became of him. At any
rate, Wump showed me how he could make him turn loose.
We stuck a stick at him until he snapped at it and caught it in
his jaws and held on. You couldn't pull the stick away from
him, even by dragging him around. "I told you so," I said, "he
won't let go 'til it thunders."

"I kin, so, make 'im," said Wump, and he went and got
an old lard can and put some rocks in it and shook it in front
of the turtle. It made an awful racket. "Thunder," said Wump.

"It don't sound much like thunder to me," I said.

"'A's a'right," said Wump. "Hit soun' lak thunder
t'him. Tu'tles can't tell d'diff'nce."

But the turtle didn't let go. He just sat there holding the
stick in his mouth.

"Hit take a little time," Wump said. "He got t'think
about hit. C'mon, go 'way an' leave 'im alone."

So we did, and after a while we went back, and sure enough—just as Wump said—the turtle had turned loose the stick.

Wump was an artist at blowing birds' eggs, an operation requiring delicacy and finesse. He had a sixth sense when it came to a bird's nest (he'd point to a patch of weeds or high grass and say, "Dey's a part'idge nes' dere, I betcha," and we'd look and there it would be, the fifteen or twenty white eggs on the ground) and I had Wump to thank for many of the rarest items in my bird egg collection. He climbed like a monkey, and to places from which I would have fallen and broken my neck. He was openhanded and generous. Always when we snitched figs or other fruit he insisted that I have the biggest and best, and if he ever told me a lie I never knew it. Once, when I was little and too frightened to be of any use, I saw him take a beating from another and older, bigger colored boy, and then get up off the floor, as it were, and give the other boy, in turn, an even worse battering. The fight occurred because the other boy had made a sassy remark about *me,* and shied a rock at Duke. When the other boy finally ran, I helped the bruised and bloody Wump throw rocks after him, and Wump never once reproved me for failing to jump in and help him in the fight.

Before I left Chapel Hill I had attained the insufferable and snobbish age where palling with colored boys seemed not quite the thing, and Wump and I had drifted apart. I think he understood the inevitability of this, and in the sad way of the black man accepted it and loved me none the less. Pondering him, I love him all the more as time goes by. Hail, Wump, wherever you are. Good luck—and thanks.

Chapter Twelve

To us boys, especially when we were very small, Battle's Park seemed a perfect and well-balanced combination of the Garden of Eden, the Forest Primeval and the Happy Hunting Ground. It was a great and beautiful tract of rolling woodland lying to the east and south of the village at the edge of the almost unbroken woods which surrounded us. Battle's Park was not a park in the accepted sense of the word, neither was it similar in all details to the Forest Primeval, as it was bisected and crisscrossed by paths and trails through the trees. Some of these were old Indian trails, we were told—the same holding true of most of our old-time roads which followed their course according to the lay of the land and brought you to your destination comfortably if in a somewhat circuitious fashion. Our mothers never worried about us when we went to Battle's Park, for they knew that if we got lost all we had to do was pick up and follow a path which was bound to bring us out *some*where. Even though we might feel at times, in the depths of the park, that we were explorers on safari in the jungle, there were landmarks aplenty by which we could make our way back to civilization.

The trees in Battle's Park are for the most part oaks, of great variety, and of all sizes and ages and shapes. But hickory and maple and ash and poplar and birch and beech abound, and dogwood and sweet gum and cottonwood and sycamore. In the spring the tender leaves of the tall and pointed sweet gum are so many golden stars, and those of the dogwood like slim young hearts or butterfly wings. And mighty pines are here and there, bowing and whispering to each other in the wind and towering over the mournful cedars underneath. The pine-needle covered earth may be milky with bluets, or gold with yellow primroses, or blue with periwinkle flowers.

These woods represent the life and love and labor of a man who is a legend here to most, but to some of us an unforgettable living character full of good works. Old Dr. Kemp Battle was a venerable gentleman even when I knew him, as a little shaver, a chin-whiskered, sturdy old man with snowy hair. It was he who opened up the thickets, cut the paths and built the seats and benches, made the picnic spots, and damned and channeled the little brook and built the bridges. He planted the flowers and cultivated the banks of laurel and rhododendron and azaleas which bloom thick on the hillsides. Whether or not these woods ever legally belonged to him, or whether they have always been part of the far-flung University property, I do not know. But Dr. Battle, I am sure, felt that the University belonged to him, or he to it, and actual ownership and title made little difference. Perhaps he gave it to the college; at any rate it has always been known as Battle's Park, and now it is, as it was in my day, a place restricted by the law where nothing ever can be built. Always it shall be a place of peace and shadowed trails and purling waters, where boys and dogs and sweethearts can wander to their hearts' content.

Old Dr. Battle was here when war swirled about us and the Yankees came. When the University shut down and life was hard and empty he had nothing much to do, and maybe that is when he began to seek from nature solace for his

soul, and started working in his woods. The whole community was dependent on the University, and when that gave
up the useless struggle, in the Reconstruction time, and
closed its doors, Dr. Battle made good use of unemployment.
Perhaps then, too—when the weather was bad—he began his
writing of his famous history. Whenever a point of the past is
disputed around here, people always say, "Well, look at Dr.
Battle's *History of the University.*" There were five long and
dreary years in there, and finally in 1875 the State scraped
together enough money to stake the University to a new start,
and the old doors on their broken hinges were pulled open.
Mrs. McNider told me about it. She said that when the news
came from Raleigh, Dr. Battle and Mrs. Spencer, a famous
lady then in Chapel Hill, went up to the dilapidated, shuttered
college, where grass grew in the paths and cobwebs hung in
the empty classrooms, and the two of them pulled the tattered
rope and rang the bell in the Old South Building. For a solid
hour they rang it, laughing and crying, and the whole town
heard the joyous peals and knew that the good days had come
again. What a time of deep rejoicing that must have been!
From that time on and for many years Dr. Battle was President—"Old Pres" the boys would call him.

He lived in a very beautiful old house on the edge of his
woods, a house set far back under the trees across an emerald
lawn. There was a recessed porch across the central unit of the
house, and wings extending on each side. Everywhere were
birdhouses, and drinking and bathing stones and dishes, big
feeding boards, and apples and suet hung in the trees. It was
a real bird sanctuary, and well the birds knew it. I have heard
about flocks of birds lighting on certain people, but I have
never actually seen it happen except in the case of Dr. Battle.
In the late afternoon, as the hour approached at which he usually fed them, the birds began to gather. They came in droves
—the trees and lawn were full of them. I have a clear picture

in my memory of Dr. Battle as he came out on the steps of his front porch, feed in hand, and the birds flying down and lighting on his shoulders and arms and head. They swarmed and fluttered all around him, on his hands, his face. Flashes of color they were, bluebirds, "redbirds," as we called the cardinals, and orange orioles and yellow warblers. I think the birds must have passed the word along to their young as soon as they were hatched. "Look," they would say to their fledglings, "the world is a very dangerous place, but you won't find it that way around Dr. Battle's; he's your friend, you can depend on him." He said he had listed seventy-five kinds of birds around his place. Whenever I see a picture or a statue of St. Francis, I think of Dr. Battle. As befits its heritage, the park is now a wild-life refuge, and in walking there you hear the unending songs of happy birds and the movements of small animals in the underbrush.

The branch was full of crawfish, which you'd find by turning over stones. You grabbed them quickly, careful of their claws, before they could burrow into the sand and hide. Battle's Park abounded in box turtles, those strange creatures who retire within themselves. "High land terrapins," we called them. They were absolutely harmless, with no thought of biting you, and no relation whatever of the "high land moccasin." Their rounded shells are beautifully designed in black and brown and yellow, and when you pick one up he offers no resistance but just withdraws and shuts his doors. After a long time he may slowly open up a little, to see if you are there, and if you are he gently pulls the portal tight again. Some of the boys would try to carve their initials on the flinty shells, and sometimes you would find a turtle thus inscribed. Of course we'd take one home with us every now and then, for all of us had zoos and we were zealous of our stock. Nowadays I see a poor box turtle on the dangerous highway, lumbering slowly across the pavement, and I want to say, "Hurry,

chum!" and I think of the carefree, secure turtles of Battle's
Park. The same thing, of course, applies to boys and other
animals.

Dr. Battle had a little, lily-filled pond below and behind
his house, down in the woods, and there we would catch tadpoles, all we wanted, with tails or without. He had a shower
bath there, too, which we boys delighted in using. It was in a
little shack, and consisted only of an open pipe above your
head, fed by gravity from the stream which dropped down
just above, and its water seemed as cold as ice, even on the
hottest days. The water ran off through a hole in the floor and
into the lilypond. You couldn't use soap there, as soap would
have done the lilies and the tadpoles and the bullfrogs no good.
You just dashed into the frigid stream and out again. You
squealed and pranced, and then, because it was deep in the
woods, you ran around outside naked in the sun to dry and
warm yourself. There were real shower baths up at the University, in the rear and basement of the Library, the only
shower baths then, I'm told, the college had. (Later on, of
course, the Gym was built, with many more, and it's wonderful
little tiled swimming pool) but the Library showers, even
though you could turn them off and on, had only cold water,
too, and the floors were very wet and slippery with soap.
You much preferred Dr. Battle's primitive one.

The students went to and from these Library showers in
scant attire or with only bath towels wrapped modestly around
them, and sometimes the shout of *"Woman on the Campus!"*
would go up, and dormitory windows would be thrown wide
and heads emerge, and the warning *"Woman on the Campus!"* would echo back and forth between the buildings as the
cry was taken up. These women, these intruders, were the
rare and strange coeds, looking neither to right nor left,
dragging their heavy skirts behind them in the dust, weird
hats atop mountainous pompadours, proceeding decorously

about their business. But it was the accepted duty of every
male, when one of these oddities hove in sight, to sound the
alarm with haste and volume, and the bathers would streak
for home, their bare legs flashing and their towels or bath-
robes standing out behind them as they ran.

The uses to which Battle's Park was put varied greatly.
Of course I did not know for sure what went on there at night,
but sometimes you would hear great shouting and laughter,
and screams or ghostly moans, and I knew that some poor
Freshman, all alone and far from home, was getting his. For
this was the period when hazing was in flower, and Battle's
Park offered an ideal and sequestered setting for the infliction
of discomforture and mental anguish upon the hapless First
Year Men. In a student body as small as ours, where everybody knew every face, Freshmen were marked men, of course,
and their way was hard and their lot unhappy. Hazing ran
the gamut from whistling the "Freshman Song," to which
the Freshman had to keep step as he walked along before the
whistlers, to the shaving of his head and the painting of his
body, or to the locking of a terrified yearling in the Stiff
House, which was the descriptive name given the lonely,

depressed-looking wooden building, smelling strongly of
formaldehyde, and located in the deep woods on the other side
of the Campus from Battle's Park, and which housed the dis-
secting laboratory of the University's medical school. There
the gibbering Freshman would be left among the corpses in
the dark, his tormentors meanwhile giving vent to appropriate
unearthly noises in the woods surrounding. These were no
ordinary corpses, either, as they consisted mostly of unfor-
tunate individuals who had been hanged in the State
Penitentiary in Raleigh for some transgression or other. I
remember once going to the Stiff House (it drew us irresist-
ibly) and viewing a cadaver whose rope burn on the neck
was quite apparent. But for the most part hazing was good,
clean fun, and the Freshmen, even though their year was a
time of tribulation and uncertainty, were always comforted by
the thought of what they, as Sophomores, could do to their
successors.

One of the more harmless pastimes, though not conducive to tranquillity, was a snipe hunt in Battle's Park.
These snipe hunts were arranged by charitable upperclassmen
for the benefit and entertainment of newly arrived Freshmen
who might be lonely and at loose ends. Kindly, gracious
Sophomores would issue the invitations, which were usually
eagerly accepted. On the first dark night (utter darkness is
best suited to snipe hunting) the Freshman and his new friends
would repair to Battle's Park, and after the entertainment
committee had walked the victim around in circles for a while
and gotten him completely confused and pretty badly scratched
up by briars and branches, they would come to Piney Prospect,
that romantic and legendary spot whereon the Bloody Stone
is lying, and suggest that he rest there while they go on and
beat the bushes and locate the elusive snipes. They would leave
him there with many a friendly slap on the back and cheerful
directions to be sure to hold the mouth of the bag, with which

they had provided him, wide open, so that they might round up and drive the snipes, skulking in the near-by underbrush, within. So off they'd go, leaving the Freshman alone in the darkness, holding open the bag. Eventually, of course, he would find his way back to the questionable safety of his room, in the wee sma' hours, saddened by the hoax put upon him.

Piney Prospect is a clearing in the far reaches of the park, and its chief feature is the Bloody Stone which stands there on the summit of the ridge. It can be a beautiful though ghostly spot at night, in the silence and darkness of the woods, with the moonlight mysterious over the vast valley spread below. In the daytime a great panorama stretches away before you; on a clear day you can see the smoke of Raleigh, thirty miles away, and Durham, twelve miles distant across the ridges, seems just next door. As space is measured now, Piney Prospect isn't far from the Campus, but in my day a journey there seemed an endless expedition through a far and fearsome forest. What interested us at Piney Prospect, however, was not the view. It was the Bloody Stone.

Dr. Battle told me the story of the duel there, one day as we sat and looked across the valley. Seems it happened 'way back in 1831, he said, and the names and dates were true. There was a student named Peter Dromgoole, not a legendary personage, but a real live student, who lived in a certain room in the Old South Building. He was a very handsome, brilliant young man, Dr. Battle said, but he had a fierce and fiery temper. This fierce and fiery temper led to a challenge to his best friend, one "Louis," whose last name seems to have got lost in the mists of time, because of an argument concerning priority rights and privileges in the hand of a lady, fair and frail. After everything was arranged, the rivals, with their seconds, repaired to lonely Piney Prospect, and there the duel was fought to its tragic end. "Louis" was the one who got plugged by the dueling pistol in the hand of Peter Dromgoole, and "Louis" fell and died across the stone which stands there still, the dark stains of his blood upon it all these years. Peter Dromgoole dropped his gun and drew his Inverness across his face, and then he mounted a fast horse and went away from there and disappeared into the great unknown, and nothing was ever heard of him from that day to this.

The story was one of the most delightful I have ever heard, and while Dr. Battle said he would not vouch for the authenticity of all its details, still it had a certain basis in fact. I believe every bit of it, however. So do, or did, the colored folk in Chapel Hill, who swore that the cloaked figure of Peter Dromgoole still stalked the woods on stormy nights, and none of them for love or money would approach the Bloody Stone.

"Taking a Walk in Battle's Park" was one of the things you did. Everybody did. Of an afternoon, especially on Sunday, you would meet groups of students, well behaved, sauntering the shady paths. And you—and students by the hundreds, nay, the thousands—carved names and initials in the soft, smooth skin of the beechtree boles, and on the seats and backs of the benches. My W.M.P. was on many trees in Battle's Park, despite what my elders had to say about "fools' names—like their faces," but since coming back I have never found a set. Time and bark have almost obliterated most of the older carvings, some of them undecipherable now as the trees have grown, and even though I have identified certain of the beeches as trees I cut upon, I have never found my name. The great, good days of Battle's Park are gone, I fear, for now beer cans and discarded comic books are found beside the sylvan paths, and snipe hunting and dueling have been long abandoned.

Zoology was an absorbing interest, and at one time my back yard presented an interesting spectacle. I had built a chicken-wire-covered aviary, with Mars' Phil's help, in the corner made by the back porch and the rear of the house, and in it I had several nondescript pigeons who made soothing pigeon noises. (I wasn't allowed to keep songbirds in captivity, even though we had much fun catching them. This was accomplished by means of a trap built of lengths of old lath, one square on another, gradually decreasing into a sort of pyramid. One side of the trap was upheld by a delicately set, figure-four trigger. The birds would hop on this trigger, set an inch off the ground, when they came after the breadcrumbs scattered there, and down would fall the trap. Through the openwork of the lath strips you could see the birds and study them before you let them go. All of us had these traps and kept count of the birds we caught.) There was a rabbit hutch made of a big box and a wire pen outside, in which I kept a pair of Belgian Hares secured for me somewhere by Mars' Phil. The idea was not only that you could enjoy very much looking at the Belgian Hares, but also that there was a lot of money to be made raising them. This didn't pan out, for oddly enough these Belgian Hares never had any young. Mars' Phil said he suspected they were both males, or that if they were a real married couple they didn't like each other. In the spring, of course, you always caught a lot of baby rabbits. You usually carried one around with you, in your pocket or inside your blouse, and these sometimes lived to a good size before they got away or something happened. I had a turtle pen, both mud and high land, and a bucket of tadpoles. It was fun to watch the tadpoles turn into frogs. The Cobb boys, besides their guinea pigs, had a pair of squirrels in a cage with a big wire cylinder or wheel which the squirrels got on and rode. I had a box of snakes, harmless ones, of course, like black, or "green," as we called grass snakes, and pretty little garter snakes. Nobody around our house seemed to enjoy them except myself. Then we had mice and white rats and an occasional "ground squirrel" or chipmunk. We caught moles, but moles did not thrive.

At the time we had our circus (all this happened at the time I was seven or eight years old, I guess) our various zoos were at their high-water mark, and the menagerie would be one of the chief attractions, we thought. The circus itself was to be held in the Bruners' barn, which was fairly large and had cross timbers ideal for trapezes and swinging rings, and plenty of hay to fall on. We practised up on acrobatic and tumbling acts; for weeks our rehearsals were of prime importance. Duke, of course, was to be put through his tricks in the center of the ring, and Billy Cobb had a wonderful act where he lay down and his white rats would run around over him and crawl up his sleeves. Proper circus costumes worried us and gave us grave concern, but the matter of tights we took care of easily by wearing our winter union suits with pieces of bright colored stuffs around the middle, like trunks. But I am not going to bore you with details of our circus, because everybody in the world has taken part in a kids' circus and knows all about it. What practically none of you has ever done, however, is to arrange and execute a circus parade on Rosemary Street, and this I will tell you of. It was really a very colorful and impressive parade, and would, we felt sure, create something of a furore on Rosemary. It did, but not the sort we anticipated.

The parade assembled right after breakfast, at the Cobbs' pony stable. There was a lot of inevitable confusion, and as Grand Marshal I had my hands full. Arguments ensued as to who should be a horse and who a performer. Delays occurred. Dogs fought. Paraders had to go to the bathroom, or get a drink of water. Disputes as to precedence had to be settled. Even so, we were all ready to go long before the zero hour which has been set at eleven o'clock, the traditional hour for circus parades. After consulting with my assistants, it was decided to move, the logical argument for the affirmative being that the sooner we got going the greater would be the number of people who would hear about the parade and lay their plans to attend the performance. We had ropes stretched outside the Bruner barn so as to control the public in case of a stampede to get in. Also, it seemed wise to get the parade over before the day got too hot. In addition, as somebody pointed out, the early hour would give us opportunity to parade a second or third time, if that seemed advisable. Final orders were shouted, banners unfurled, a stirring fanfare sounded from the band, and we moved off.

First came Billy Cobb, riding on his pony, Dan, and carrying a large American flag, the property of his father. Billy wore his Indian suit and we had stuck feathers, too, in the browband of Dan's bridle. I accompanied Billy, on foot, in my capacity of ringmaster, with a fine long buggy whip in my hand, but my costume was disappointing. I had on my blue serge (Sunday) suit, and a broad red ribbon filched from my mother across my chest, but instead of a silk hat I had one made of cardboard and painted black, a real silk hat being unavailable at the moment. Behind us were as many musicians as could be got aboard an express wagon, playing on combs with tissue paper, and beating drums. Our cages, as well as this band wagon, had to be pulled by hand, of course, as we had no horses, but the boys doing the pulling tried to look and act like horses, whinnying and prancing. The cages were all right—boxes with lath bars nailed on—reposing on other express wagons. In the first of these rode our old gray Maltese cat, Malachi. His cage was labeled African Lion. In front of the string of cages walked little Frank Herty carrying a sign which said Menagerie. This was superfluous, of course, but it helped decorate the parade. Other of our choicest animals and reptiles occupied the other cages; one cage labeled Tiger

contained a mother cat and a litter of kittens. My Belgian
Hares had changed their identity to Belgian Kangaroos. Our
dogs had ribbons tied on them, and we led or dragged them
along on strings. It was a very zoological parade, but we did
have somebody's little sister, wrapped up in another American
flag, and carrying a parasol, riding in another of the wagons
which was marked Queen. In order to keep little Arthur
Bruner still (he was never much use to us; we used to make
him play right field on the baseball team), we had stuffed
wads of hay and newspaper inside his union suit at strategic
points and designated him Strong Man, and he rode in one of
the wagons. Willis Bruner, because he was fat, we allowed to
be clown, and he cavorted up and down the line. We of course
all had mustaches painted on, and wore whatever bits of
decorative or unusual clothing we could find. The band was
playing gaily and we proceeded down the sidewalk calling out
the attractions and features of our show which was about to
begin in Bruners' barn. Our sidewalk audience was very
limited, of course, due no doubt to the early hour, but we were
sure that when word got around the crowds would gather. We
had gotten halfway down the long block when Mrs. Horace
Williams appeared on the horizon.

Collier Cobb and I had recently gone through an unpleasant experience at the hands of Dr. Williams, her husband. He lived in a low, rambling house off the end of Rosemary, not far from the Gimghoul Hall, and down in one
corner of his lot in a grove of trees he kept pigs, of which he
was very proud. He made Collier and me a business proposition; he entered into a gentleman's agreement with us
whereby we were to gather acorns for his gluttonous pigs,
and he was to pay us five cents a bushel therefor. There is
many an acorn to the bushel, as you know if you have ever
picked them up, but we measured them conscientiously and
put them in croker sacks and lugged them to Dr. Williams'

pigpen. I hate to say it, of course, but Dr. Williams did not do us right about those acorns. He said they were not prime, or first grade, and that we would have to bring him others, as these were very poor acorns, hardly any good at all, and certainly not worth more than four cents a bushel. Then he took the sacks and dumped the acorns out—into his pigpen! He was an eminent and distinguished philosopher, Dr. Williams, but he was a sharp trader, and he skinned us. There has been talk of recent years by his many and devoted students of making his old home into a sort of shrine sacred to his memory and high ideals, but I, myself, passing it, never feel any reverence, only rage.

But what he did to us was as nothing compared to the havoc Mrs. Williams wrought. She was a tall, austere lady of grim and despondent mien, who it was said, played the violin and painted at odd times when she was not helping Dr. Williams with the pigs. It may be that she put him up to the business of the acorns. Eccentric, my mother called her, and as eccentric was she regarded throughout the village. She was an animal lover, but then, who wasn't? This seemed no basis for the charge of eccentricity. She took in strange stray cats, her place crawled with them. And I had reason to know she hated Duke, and Wump had told me I had best look out or Miz Williams might poison him. But she had always been most polite—or at least not insulting—until that day of the parade.

I can see her now, bearing down upon us like a berserk camel. She had on a long, camel-colored suit with two or three capes of different sizes flapping from the shoulders. The suit was trimmed in heavy brown braid. A little cloud of dust followed her as her long skirt dragged. Her hat was a bit askew and her hair blew around. In her hand was a large umbrella. She had spied the animals in the cages, and on deliverance was she bent! She was crying out imprecations and "For shames!" as she approached, brandishing the umbrella like a battle-ax, and some of the more timid members of our cortege began to run. She saw old Malachi stretched out on his side and peacefully dozing, enjoying the ride he was getting, and she upset the wagon and began tearing at the bars to set him free. She made a hash of that cage in no time. "Shoo! Scat!" she screamed, as she dragged him from the wreckage. "It's shameful, you torturing these poor dumb animals like this!" she shouted, then another cage she tore asunder, then another. The street seemed full of flying cats, with dogs broken loose from all restraint in hot pursuit. Turtles and terrapins lumbered away and rabbits hightailed it for the bushes and snakes crawled out and into the grass along the ditch. Pandemonium reigned while she swung that umbrella and ripped apart the cages—and the American flag was trampled in the dust. In less time than it takes to tell it, our circus was a heap of ruins, a forgotten thing, and even the bravest of us took to our heels and ran for cover. The acrobats in union suits seemed the most distressed of all.

After a while the noise subsided, and our angry tears had ceased to flow. We came from hiding and looked at the shambles of our show . . . There was no sound but the far-away barking of the dogs.

CHAPTER THIRTEEN

UNFORTUNATELY, I have always had a criminal streak, and despite such instances of righteousness as the case of Dr. Kluttz and the fifth caramel, it has got me in trouble more than once. I do not like to think that my criminal streak was larger than that of most little boys: I believe I was about average in resistance to temptation, but little boys, I feel, are born into this tempting world under a great handicap, that of arriving here already little thugs and potential burglars. I have no explanation to offer as to why these evil tendencies are peculiar to my sex; perhaps little girls have them, too, but if so they conceal or stifle them better than little boys. I agree whole heartedly with that part of the old nursery rhyme which claims that little girls are constructed of sugar and spice, et al, but I go even farther than the jingle in my analysis of the ingredients of little boys. Little boys are public enemies and dangers to the community.

The first overt act of my criminal career, insofar as I can recollect (it even antedated the purloining of my friend's marbles, in Richmond), occurred in the somewhat opaque days before we came to Chapel Hill, when we lived in Roanoke and my chief interest in life was Dad's red setter, Rab. In fact, it is one of the only three things of that hazy period which I clearly remember. I remember Rab's silky, sanguine coat and his magnificent head and drooling jaws, and a night Dad took me out on a back porch somewhere (it must have belonged to the house in which we lived, though I have no recollection of the house) while he called and whistled to Rab, who was hidden from sight out in the impenetrable and mysterious darkness. I remember being a little afraid of the black void and imagining the sinister things which might be out there where Rab was.

The second of these three memories is Miss Daisy Wills. I remember her house, all right; it had a lot of gingerbread and jigsaw cornices on it, and a round, towerlike projection with a cupola which hung over the street below, and was a part of Miss Daisy's boudoir. And I remember vividly that Mother took me with her, calling on Miss Daisy, because they were great friends, and Miss Daisy, being not quite dressed, called down to us to come up to her room with the round alcove . . . and Miss Daisy was in her unimagined undergarments. What struck me forcibly and made a lasting and indelible impression upon my youthful consciousness was Miss Daisy's drawers—voluminous affairs of white with ruffles on the bottom. Miss Daisy walked around the room in them, her midriff and superstructure (which was really super) enclosed in a long laced corset, which was just as novel and interesting an article to me as the drawers. I had never seen, and never did see, my mother thus arrayed. This was the important moment in my life when I became aware of the hitherto unsuspected fact that ladies have legs. Miss Daisy was not brazen or even immodest in this display before a gentleman; she just failed to realize the powers of perception and the deep appreciation of the gentleman. I couldn't have been much more than three years old, an age at which children are not supposed to see things, or if they do, remember them. But somehow in bold relief, and starched ruffle detail, the picture formed upon my infant brain, and there it has stuck for more than half a century. I have never before told anyone about Miss Daisy Wills' drawers.

Third, and clearest of all these three Roanoke recollections, is my stealing of the candy—the first indication I believe I could have given of the evil impulses which dominated me. I said I could remember nothing of the house in which we must have lived, but this is not altogether true: I do remember a fireplace, in awful detail. The mantel was an awesome thing of filigree and gingerbread, with several shelves and levels and projections, and the hearth below it was laid with small and glistening tiles of a green-and-brownish mottled, or curdled, design, quite horrible. These tiles were very slick and smooth and gleaming, baked enamel, probably. Anyway they were hideous things. These nauseating tiles continued up the sides and across the top of the fireplace opening, framed by the malignant mantel. Close on each side of the fireplace sat a light and fragile gilt chair which appeared to be constructed of small golden balls, backed against the mantel frame, purely for decorative purposes and not under any conditions for use, as one was fairly sturdy and the other broken and propped and held together insecurely. It was never worth your while to investigate and find out which was good and which was bad; you just never sat on either.

It all made a hard and brittle and jiggly ensemble. It was of that period of decoration which included the cozy corner and the portieres of glass beads which tinkled as they were thrust aside. I am proud to say that my house never included either of the last named; I would remember if it had, as I was envious of other more ostentatious abodes which boasted them.

There must have been some candy eating, for Mother put two or three pieces of candy in a little china dish and placed it on one of the higher shelves of the mantel out of harm's, and my, way, and said it was for next time. Shortly thereafter I found the room unoccupied, and temptation was too great. I mounted one of the gilt chairs, the safe, sound one, I was sure, and greedily grasped the little china dish from off the shelf. The chair collapsed in splinters and a shower of little gilt balls, and down I crashed upon the hard, unyielding tiles. The little china dish was smashed to smithereens and one sharp sliver cut me badly between my eyebrow and the eye, just above the ball. I yelled and bled upon the cold and hideous tiles. I don't remember any punishment—I was too badly hurt—but the scar has been with me ever since. I came very close to collaborating with a black patch the rest of my life. This was my first lesson in the consequences of right and wrong, but did I profit by it? Did I learn the poor returns one gets from crime? No.

There was the time in Chapel Hill when I unlawfully entered the pantry and feloniously attempted to appropriate the powdered sugar. I was indirectly steered into the doing of this deed by Mother's cookies, and when I went after the cookies I had no thought of powdered sugar. (The name confectioners' sugar was unknown; we had no confectioners.) Gastronomy has always led to my undoing; my moral fibre, where my stomach is concerned, is weak; and Mother made the best cookies that were ever baked.

Mother was really not any great shakes as a cook—that is a regular cook of regular food—and I am not one to bring up the things that Mother Used to Make, other than her cookies. This lack of culinary skill was not to her discredit; always there was a slavey in the kitchen, that was an accepted fact of life and one you took for granted. Everybody had a cook. Even genteel poverty, if such was your lot, was not genteel unless you had a cook. Not that we were at all poverty-stricken; we did all right. But it was just that any Southern lady of the period, even though she be as poor as Job's turkey, had as soon be caught over a hot cook stove in the kitchen as

without her corset cover. What cooking she did was Art—
superfluous, of course, but tending toward the finer things—
cookies or fudge or some exotic, fancy, chafing dish creation,
or putting up preserves or pickles. And desserts. All ladies
were experts in desserts. They were theoretical authorities on
cooking, but they seldom did the work.

Mother had a wonderful cookbook called *Housekeeping
in Old Virginia,* published in Richmond some years after the
Civil War. It was a collection of recipes gathered and donated
by Virginia ladies in the lean days when the wolf was scratching at their doors, the object of which was to prove that even
in such hard times as those one could concoct palatable dishes
from poor and makeshift ingredients. There was a foreword
to that effect. However, a recipe might start out like this:
From the springhouse fetch one qt. sweet cream, into which
slowly stir one bottle best Madeira, or: Melt 2 lbs. fresh sweet
butter in saucepan for the basting of the pheasant . . . Stuff
like that! Mother seldom tried to use any of the recipes. We
have the book now, but my wife never uses it; we keep it only
as a quaint reminder of what slim rations our sturdy fore-
bears got along on.

Where Mother got her cookie recipe I do not know, but
the result would indicate it came straight from Heaven. She
made these cookies—tea cakes, she called them—fairly often,
and she made not just a pan or so, she made 'em wholesale!
Our pantry, where the cookies rested after their ordeal by fire,
was large as pantries go, but the cookies filled it. There was a
broad workbench or counter around three sides, with shelves
above, and on brown paper on this counter Mother spread her
cookies, thin and brown and hot, straight from the oven, to
crisp and cool. Afterward she filled crocks and tin boxes with
them, and the pantry door was locked. I don't like to think
that Mother distrusted me; the fact is the appetites of the
entire family, where tea cakes were concerned, were unrefined.

Mars' Phil and Mars' Pike could each have eaten a bushel at a sitting, if he could have got them, and of course there was no limit to my capacity. Mother liked them pretty well herself, and even Grandpa ate more of them than you'd think he would.

On the day of which I speak—the one involving the powdered sugar—a fresh batch of cookies had just been laid out in the pantry, and the pantry door carelessly left unlocked. This was very reprehensible of Mother, and eventually caused me, in my innocence, great distress. I entered the unlocked pantry only to snitch a few cookies; there were so many of them a dozen or so would not be missed. I was completely innocent so far as anything beyond this was concerned. In a way, you might say I was framed, for there on the counter beside the cookies was a large jar of powdered sugar.

I was helpless in the face of powdered sugar. My passion for it was blind, unreasoning. I knew it was a luxury, a rare and costly thing we seldom used except to sprinkle tea cakes, and never just to *eat,* and yet here was a whole large jar of it! Perhaps a little of that would go unmissed, also. Guiltily, I thought I heard a board creak, a step approach, and quickly I scooped up a big handful of the snowy dust and crammed it in my mouth. . . .

It was baking soda.

Apparently that lesson did me no good, either, for under almost identical circumstances occurred the episode of Grandpa's sacramental wine. This I knew he kept in a tightly corked jug under the counter in the pantry, and that small amounts of the mysterious dark red liquid were carefully poured out into a smaller container and taken to the church on Communion Sundays where people tasted it in the solemn rite of Holy Communion. I had a great and consuming curiosity concerning this sacramental wine. I asked Mother, one day when we were together in the pantry, if I could taste it and she gave me a very definite and horrified *No!* Not under any conditions, she said, until I was confirmed and became a Communicant. I decided to beat the gun, and when my chance came I slipped into the pantry, reached down in the dimness of the windowless room and grabbed and raised the jug and took a good long swig.

And this time it was vinegar.

Old, strong vinegar. I almost burned and choked to death.

You'd think I would have learned, wouldn't you? That is why my convictions are so strong that little boys, even little boys who Work Hard and May Become President of the United States Someday, have two strikes on them from the start, and just can't help these heinous things. It took another experiment to partly make clear to me that crime is not a remunerative employment; and this disgression from the straight and narrow path was really serious. I burgled the Cobbs' house.

I say "I" but it was really "we." I am not trying to shift the blame, understand—that is, not more than half of it—but I did have an accomplice, and, well, you know how easy and pleasant things are if done together. There was a boy named Loren Smith who lived, one summer, with his mother, at Mr. Pickard's University Inn. For some reason all my family were still in Chapel Hill while most of my friends were vacationing, and for company I began palling around with this Loren Smith. It was not at all that he was an Evil Companion, or that I was too easily swayed by his big city sophistication (he came from Charlotte), but he did seem to find my usual and favorite pastimes uninteresting and childish, he being a trifle older than I and having had far more experience in the really enjoyable pursuits of life. Anyway, the whole Cobb family was away, and their house shut up and empty, and we took it in our heads to investigate their pantry. There again someone else's carelessness was to blame; their pantry window was unlocked.

I knew that it was wrong—I was quite a big boy then—and I am covered with confusion, telling this, but we climbed through their pantry window from the Cobbs' back porch. It seemed fairly safe to do this, as we scouted around and were sure we could not be seen; there were no other houses within eyeshot, and only the tranquil vegetable garden was in our rear. When we got inside, the pantry did not contain the epicurean treasures we had hoped, however; and we had to settle for a can of salmon (this may have been intended for the Cobbs' cat) and a jar of cherry preserves. Nothing else seemed appetizing or readily movable. After carefully closing the window, just as we found it, we repaired to the woods and consumed our booty. I can't say that it was much of a feast, as—if you have ever tasted the combination, you will agree—canned salmon and cherry preserves without benefit of bread or anything leave something to be desired. But, like stolen apples, we enjoyed it. After a while, except for occasional slight twinges of conscience, I ceased to think about it, and when the Cobb boys came home listened with interest to the tales of their adventures. Collier, in particular, had a fine story of being caught on a great long trestle he was walking across by an onrushing train, and escaping a horrible death by climbing underneath the trestle and hanging by his hands from the cross ties while the train thundered over him. I was glad the Cobbs were home again, and my transgression was practically forgotten.

And then, one day, my grandfather called me in the study, and told me, very sadly, that Mr. Cobb had been to see him and that he knew all.

What Grandpa said was not all I suffered, either, though that hurt me very much. I really got what was coming to me, and afterwards I was made to go to Mr. Cobb all by myself

and apologize most humbly and promise him never, never to
do such a terrible thing again. What I could not figure out,
however, was how Mr. Cobb knew that Loren Smith and I
had done it. . . .

When I went fearfully to him to apologize, Mr. Cobb was
fine about it. He said that it was all right and that he hoped it
would be a lesson to me and that he knew boys would be boys.
This had not occurred to me before, and made me feel a little
better, but I told him I felt awful about it, which I did, and
that I would reform, completely. He was so nice about it, and
patted me on the back, that I screwed up courage to ask him
how he found out. He smiled at me and said a little bird told
him. I knew it wasn't a bird, and I have wondered many times
who it was.

At any rate, I was cured of Unlawful Entry. The in-
former remained anonymous, and I had the uncomfortable
feeling that should I ever do anything of the sort again, unseen eyes would see me, sure as anything. Grandpa told me
gravely that even though I thought no one knew, *God* knew,
always,—and that sooner or later one always reaped as he had
sown. But this did not entirely clear things up, as I felt certain
God had not told Mr. Cobb, personally. However, inocula-
tions take, sometimes. Demonstrations really demonstrate,
and there was one shameful instance of iniquity in which I
was shown the light, forcefully, effectively, and I learned my
lesson. It was the case of Edwin Black.

Edwin Black was Mrs. Black's little boy, and Mrs.
Black's name and reputation were such as to cause whispering
and eyebrow lifting. Even the house the Blacks lived in was
a sinful-looking thing, tall and dark and bare. It stood halfway
down Windy Hill, back from the road, and always I specu-
lated with a quickened pulse as to what went on behind the
broken shutters. The yard was always full of flapping sheets
and garments, for Mrs. Black took in washing. This was only

a blind, however, and Mrs. Black, a rawboned, knotty individual, spent long days over the washtubs only to make you think her an estimable and God-fearing woman. The truth was, Rumor said, she ran a *Blind Tiger* . . . and running a Blind Tiger, in those days, was the Ultimate Offense. She sold unlawful liquor to Our Boys, as the students were tenderly and sympathetically called, and ruined their bright young lives. I used to look at the baleful Black abode, protected by its wash lines, and wonder when the mob would form and burn it down and lynch the Blacks. Queer, quaint ideas . . . Since then, of course, many of the best friends of all of us have been Blind Tiger-running bootleggers, and the sin seems not so terrible. In the light of later years I am inclined to make allowances for Mrs. Black: it may be that the income from her washing did not close the gap between the ends, and that to support herself and family she may have occasionally disposed of, for some slight remuneration, an extra jug or so of scuppernong or elderberry wine. But then no such charitable point of view was ours. We boys, along with our elders, thought of the Blacks as well-named outcasts, a disgrace to the community, and their Blind Tiger as a sore and festering spot in our holy habitation. I don't ever remember hearing a specific discussion of their shortcomings in my home, for Grandpa was a very charitable man and no mudslinging went on within his hearing (Mother said Mrs. Black was a fine laundress, but we used Aunt Jinny Johnson, so I had no direct evidence of this point in her favor), but nevertheless the knowledge of the Blacks' perfidy was common.

Mrs. Black's family consisted of two sons. There was no Mr. Black. The two boys were Edwin and his much older brother—whose name I have forgotten. However, I remember other details of him very clearly.

Edwin was about my age, which at that time was nine, a shy, silent boy with enormous dark eyes and a patient,

frightened look. I believe now that he must have keenly felt
the cloud under which he lived, as he never tried to mix with
us; I don't see how he could have helped it, what with the jeers
and insults shouted at him, and the rocks thrown. Not that
I was any worse about this than the rest of us; we were
all little stinkers, unbelievably cruel as only boys can be. I
remember hearing Mother say that little Edwin had a face
like a choir boy, but I had never seen a choir boy and the
description meant nothing to me, and I thought only of his
wickedness and the Blind Tiger which his mother ran.

It happened one day when Edwin had been delivering
some wash. He emerged onto the quiet, deserted Back Street
from the heavy honeysuckle hedge by the Woolens' backdoor.
(They lived across from the Abernathys.) The devil
prompted me, and I spoke roughly to him. I could almost
smell his fear, the way they say dogs can. Self-righteously

I gave him a hard shove and he dropped his empty basket and fell in the dust of the street. I don't remember whether I hit him, but that was my intention, in my blind better-than-thouness. Perhaps I didn't have time to start beating him up, for something hit *me!* Something struck and sent me headlong in the road beside the fallen Edwin. . . . It was Edwin's brother. All the things I had intended doing to Edwin, Edwin's brother did to me! And he did them well. Nobody came, nobody pulled him off, and in his righteous rage he gave me almost all that I deserved.

When I got home I would not tell my mother where I got my mauling; I was too ashamed. I could not bear her sympathy and solicitude; she thought I was an innocent little martyr beaten up by bullies, and I could not bring myself to tell her that the only bully was I. I had to take my bitter punishment alone. Thinking of it now, my face gets red and hot.

The cut mouth and the blackened eye I took home with me that day I've always kept. They are very valuable. I learned not only never to pick on somebody when his big brother may be just behind the hedge, but I learned a little, too, about man's inhumanity. That was a lesson, to my body and to my soul, which did me good.

CHAPTER FOURTEEN

THE CHRISTMAS when my mother was so ill was a gray and dreary time around our house. On Christmas Eve I was packed off to sleep with Grandpa, a sobering experience in itself. It must have been tough on him, too, having the privacy of his big bed invaded by a jerky young wiggletail. But, as usual, he took it calmly.

My sleep was fitful as the night went slowly by and when I came wide awake it was still long before dawn. Grandpa, however, snored on, strongly and deliberately.

I had never really heard him snore before, that is at close range—point blank, you might say—and it impressed me. I wriggled further down toward the middle of the bed, but I was careful to keep one eye uncovered by the blankets, and I strained to see the picture we called "Lake Erie" in the cold blackness. Outside in the chicken house the young Brown Leghorn rooster crowed, and Grandpa snorted and turned over. I knew by the rooster's voice, high and thin, which one it was; as with us, it was the young rooster announcing the new day while the old roosters dozed on.

"Grandpa?" I whispered. There was no answer, but I thought by the way he breathed he was awake.

I lay rigid, and peered where "Lake Erie" ought to be.

The dark was heavy and thick. I tried again. "Grandpa . . . ? It's morning. The rooster . . ."

"Now go back to sleep," said Grandpa suddenly. "It's not morning yet. *That rooster!*" The way he said "that rooster" was the closest I ever heard Grandpa come to profanity, and it silenced me.

The clock ticked. Way off, somewhere, I heard a firecracker, then another. All of a sudden Grandpa cleared his throat and spoke again. "You can't get up," he said clearly, "until you can see Lake Erie."

"But *Grandpa* . . ." I was near to tears, and my eyes almost burst from their sockets in the effort to pierce the darkness. "I think—"

"Now listen," said Grandpa, and his voice held the quiet authority it carried from the pulpit. "You can't get up until you can see that picture. Your mother . . ."

The picture, in a tarnished gold frame, was a huge, faded oil, showing a wildly excited and imaginative body of water; towering curling white-capped waves of tremendous height, against a black and angry sky. The only relief was a great jagged fork of lightning which hung suspended in the heavens. Where the picture came from I do not know. I was told that it was Lake Erie in a storm. Bad storm, I thought. As far back as I can remember, it had hung in a dark corner over Grandpa's bed; if it had ever fallen it would have flattened the old gentleman into a bony little pancake. I often used to speculate on this possibility. When I saw the real Lake Erie, years later, I was disappointed. I do not believe the picture showed Lake Erie at all.

I would like to know whatever became of it. I have heard rumors, since, that my grandmother (whom I never knew) painted. Maybe she conjured up this conception of a storm at sea, inland. Maybe that's why it hung over Grandpa's bed.

I buried my head in the pillow and lay still and tried to

think of my mother, so very ill, and Dad probably huddled in a blanket before her fire. And I thought of last Christmas morning, and my stocking, and the orange. I must have dropped off to sleep again. Because when I came to, the big clock in Grandpa's study was striking six—I counted it—and the lamp was lit, and Grandpa, in his flannel nightshirt, with something over his shoulders, was hunched over the fireplace, trying to get a fire going. I gasped and sat up. His back was to me, and he was grumbling as he fed lightwood knots in under the logs.

He was unbelievably frail, and I used always to wait with great interest when a wind came up to see if what my mother said was true, and if he'd blow away. He had whiskers, a Van Dyke beard, they'd call it now, and when he was asleep his snore sometimes ended with a little whistle as the exhalation went through his mustache. His face, as I remember it, was very calm and beautiful; a big nose, and fine, deep eyes, and that white beard and mustache. He didn't talk much, that is idle chatter. He was, I know now, a Greek scholar; University of Virginia, and afterward the Episcopal Seminary—and then the War.

I was sleeping with Grandpa that Christmas Eve because we were in such a jam at the rectory. It was the Christmas when Mother was losing her fight with typhoid, and it was a strange and upset one. Early in the fall Mars' Pike had appeared (he lived down in the eastern part of the State then) and said, "Alice, I'm sick," and gone to bed with the fever. Mother had practically raised him and Mars' Phil, following my Grandmother's death when the boys were quite young, even though she was hardly more than a girl herself. And even though he had just been married, Mars' Pike turned to her, as usual, when he was in trouble. Everybody in the family, whenever anything went wrong, took it directly to Mother. She generally fixed it, too.

In this case she nursed Mars' Pike night and day, and about the time he was convalescing went down herself, all worn out. Mars' Phil had got a room uptown somewhere, and Mars' Pike had the big back room to himself. As Mother went from bad to worse, Dr. Manning got a nurse for her, and this helped, and when Dad took a leave of absence from his job and came in off the road things were better, but even so we were in a mess. That's when they sent for my Great-aunt Lucy, Grandpa being so helpless without Mother.

Aunt Lucy got to Chapel Hill on Christmas Eve. She was a tiny, dried up, porcelain figure in stiff black taffeta. She had my little room, up next to Mother's. In the daytime Dad slept in Grandpa's room, and at night I slept there, with Grandpa. Duke was inconvenienced more than anybody, as, deprived of my bed, he had to sleep on the floor. There we all were, jammed into that little cottage that Christmas when I was nine years old, a house of quiet and fear and prayer.

Dr. Manning came two or three times a day, and he would go into Mother's room and shut the door. People would come, bringing things, and ask if they could help. Dad went around looking tired and worried and white.

There was one little incident, though, that gave everybody a laugh, even Dad. Seems he was sitting quietly one night, dozing before the fire in Mother's room, when a mouse ran up his leg inside his trousers. He came to with this unexpected visitor climbing up him. Any ordinary man would have let out a yell and gone straight up in the air and turned his chair over and waked Mother, but Dad's reaction was heroic, and he simply grabbed his pants leg where the mouse was and throttled the beast to death. Then he shook him out, a bit shaken himself, all without a sound.

That's the way it was that Christmas Eve. Aunt Lucy had patted me and said silly things about Santa Claus (I knew better then, of course) and we had set up a cedar tree and trimmed it, in the front room. There wasn't much space in the front room, because Mother's big square piano took up almost half of it, and on the other side was the stove. The piano couldn't have been ebony—could it?—but it was black as ink. They'd put a lamp on one corner and my mother would sit down at the keyboard, and they'd sing, Mars' Phil and Mars' Pike. Songs like "Polly Wolly Doodle," and "Solomon Levi," and "Forgotten . . ." Sometimes Grandpa would come in from the study and sing, too. Always at Christmas we'd sing carols.

But there wasn't any singing that night. We trimmed the tree with tufts of cotton and strings of chinquapins and popcorn and chinaberries I had gathered for the occasion. Aunt Lucy bustled noisily around in her taffeta skirts and supervised. "Santa Claus is coming tonight," she said, "and we must be ready for him." She put out a little plate of cookies for Santa Claus (which she of course emptied later, before the mice could get to them). Dad came in and helped fix the tree. "Mother's better," he said. "Maybe you can see her in the morning. You're going to sleep with Grandpa, and everything's going to be all right in the morning."

In the morning, I thought—in the morning. Christmas would be the same, wouldn't it? The tree . . . ? My Aunt Lucy, so businesslike, Grandpa so worried and silent? It was different, and I didn't have the warm, happy feeling of Christmas Eve. Always before we had gone to the Church, and on Christmas Eve there had been a great litter of greens—laurel and ground pine and holly—and the ladies had made long ropes and festoons and the men had laughed over wreathes, and they had hung them around the walls and doors and chancel. But that night nobody from our house went, not even Grandpa.

"Grandpa," I asked, when I went to bed, "how soon can I get up?"

Grandpa looked at me, then he said, "Well, soon as it's light. You mustn't get up too soon."

"How soon?" I insisted.

"Well," he answered, "soon's you can see that picture over the bed. It'll be light then. Morning. Try to be quiet."

"Yessuh," I said.

And I went to sleep with the image of that impossible storm on Lake Erie in my mind's eye, determined to see it through the dark of Christmas dawn.

I've never forgotten Grandpa, squatting before that fire. It was pitch dark outside, as black as the inside of a tar barrel, but he'd gotten up and started the fire. As it took hold, he warmed himself, rubbing his hands, then he stood up stiffly and turned around. I can see him now, little and slight, with the checked blanket around his shoulders, and his white hair mussed, but with the dignity that never left him. He didn't know I was awake. I saw him look at the clock on his big mahogany dresser, in the firelight, then glance at me. "Son?" he said softly.

I jerked into attention. "Yessuh!"

"Guess you can get up, if you want to. It's early, but . . ." Then he busied himself with the fire again. "It's Christmas. Don't forget, our Lord—your mother—" he mumbled something then, and I couldn't make out the words. In one leap I was out of bed and into my long drawers.

"Grandpa, can I . . . ?" "Yes," he said, and on the word I was through the study and out into the front room where the Christmas tree was and where I had hung my stocking. Shadowy, mysterious. He followed me with the lamp. "Careful," he said. "Now wait . . ." There were the things I had asked for—a Spalding football in its box, a junior printing press, a jackknife and some Henty books— and other packages banked around the tree. I tore them open, shushed always by Grandpa, holding the lamp. There were some leather knee pads, a box of water colors. *With Clive in India, A Boy in Early Virginia* and an Alger book or two. And there was the big box of candy I knew would be there; only I would have to give it back to Dad and he would dole it out. And then, my stocking. Always you saved your stocking for the last. Always there had been the little packets of candy, a tiny gift or two, nuts, lots of nuts, and raisins—and finally down in the toe an orange. Just why oranges in North Carolina in the early 1900's, were so scarce, I don't know, but such was the fact. So much of everything we had then, but nothing exotic, like an orange. I never had one, for my own, except at Christmas. An orange was a great event. It was an institution, in the toe of a boy's Christmas stocking.

There wasn't any, that morning. I remember grabbing my stocking from the mantel. In the toe was a small, square package—a present from Cousin somebody or other—but no orange. I knew, then, that Christmas could be very different, and that my mother was sick. I remember emptying that stocking, not believing that an overlooked orange wouldn't tumble out. Aunt Lucy came in, fixing her skirts. "Happy Christmas!" she said. "Did Santa Claus bring you everything you asked him for?"

"Yessum," I said. He had.

Viola had come by that time, saying "Chris'mus Giff" to everybody, and we had pancakes for breakfast, Grandpa, Aunt Lucy and I. Dad came in, tired and pale, and gave me a hug. "Mother . . . ?" I asked him.

"Maybe later," he said.

We got all dressed up and went to church, then. It seemed to me the Christmas hymns didn't sound half so

good, with Mother absent from the organ. In the dark corner back of the organ I pumped away, however, while they
sang "Hark, the Herald Angels Sing" and "Little Town of
Bethlehem." When it was over I ducked out and hurried
homeward. Back to my presents and the glory of Christmas!
I wondered if the Cobb boys had oranges, and bet they had,
and made a mental note to go over to their house and have a
look at their take, just as soon as dinner was over. I remembered last Christmas, and that I'd kept my orange until
it began to shrivel and turn dark, and then I carefully cut
the skin four ways and peeled it, and ate it . . . At the same
time I thought of that brand new golden Spalding (stamped)
football, and that I must blow it up.

I walked along the quiet, sunny street, trying not to
skin my good shoes. It was almost warm, as it can be in
Chapel Hill at Christmas, and roses were still blooming in
some of the yards. Mrs. Kluttz came by (they were Presby-
terians, but everybody loved them very much) and said,
"Merry Christmas!" and asked me, "How is your dear
mother this morning?"

From force of habit I said, "Oh, she's much better this
morning, thank you, Miz Kluttz." Then I remembered that
she wasn't any better, or I could have seen her, as Dad said,
and I hurried miserably along.

Dad was in the front room when I came in, hadn't gone
to bed. He looked sort of played out. "Son," he said. "You
be mighty quiet. Your mother . . . You and Mars' Phil go
out in the chicken yard. He's got something for you."

Our chicken yard was quite a large one, and the ground
was beaten down hard and smooth. The rest of the back lot
was the corn field. Mars' Phil was there. I followed him out to
a long, level space, and he stepped off about sixty feet, and
shooed the chickens away. "O.K.," he said. "Go get your
mitt and your mask," and he grinned at me. Handsome as an

old-time Southerner in a daguerreotype, my Mars' Phil, six feet one of him, about a hundred and ninety pounds. He was a ball player, he'd played professional ball, and one of my earliest recollections is seeing him hit a triple and drive in the winning run in a game between Richmond and Norfolk. I was mighty young then, and all I remember of that game in Richmond is that I saw him, from a tremendous height, so our seats in the grandstand seemed to me, slide into third, in a dark blue uniform. Now, besides being express agent, he helped coach the University baseball team.

"Batter up!" Mars' Phil called. "Ready, pardner?"

"Shoot," I said. I had a catcher's mitt, and a mask; it had cost fifty cents at Mr. Neville's Sporting Goods, and there were pads on the sides and the mask itself consisted of some heavy bisecting wire. But it served.

"Put your cap down for a plate," Mars' Phil ordered. "Gimme a signal."

I threw my cap on the ground, and squatted behind it. Two fingers for an outcurve. He nodded, and drew himself up, with something in his hands. "Outside corner," he said. I crouched, and spread my arms.

"Strike one!" he said, as he threw.

It was. It was a mock orange that he threw, from the tree in the side yard, hard and green, about the size of a baseball. It whopped into my hands, and I threw it back and pounded my mitt. "Good work!" I yelled. "Knock him down!"

"Signal," he called. And I squatted, and signaled one finger for an incurve. He stood there, with the mock orange at his feet, something else in his hand, and shook his head. I showed him four fingers for a drop, and he nodded. He glanced right and left, watching imaginary base runners, then quickly threw. It thunked into my mitt, dipping across my cap, and "Strike two!" he called. It was a brand new Spald-

ing LEAGUE $1.25 ball! I'll never forget it. I stood there fingering it, looking at the snowy whiteness and the red stitching and the trademark, and then he called to me.

"Look out," he yelled. "This is the one he's going after! It's going to be high and fast!" And from his hip pocket he took another ball, I thought, all wrapped in tissue paper, and fondled it, the way pitchers do. His toe scraped an invisible slab, and he raised and flexed his arms high above his head. His fingers twiddled there, and then slowly he r'ared back and went into an intricate, double-eight windup, and his right arm swung through, with his back behind it.

"Watch it," he yelled, as he let it go. And then, *"Strike three!"* as it whizzed over my cap, high and hard. It was an orange.

Chapter Fifteen

"Sad'dy Evenin' Post, here.
Getcha *Sad'dy Evenin' Post!* D'yuh wannabuya subscription, Mister?" This was my Saturday afternoon song—my weekend wail—during a period in which I believed the advertisements and tried to make my fortune the easy way (the advertisement said).

The pack on my back was heavy, as the canvas bag slung over my shoulder contained a dozen or so copies of the periodical referred to, and the winter air had a nip which made my eyes and nose run. I was buttoned up and mittened, and the ear flaps on my cap were down, but I had to pull my mittens off every now and then to blow on my hands, or wipe my nose. Business was not so brisk as to help keep me warm, either. Duke sat shivering on the cold, damp dirt of the sidewalk beside me. The post office at my back cut off some of the north wind, and I moved closer to its protection, and looked up the street a little way at Collier, in front of Mr. Eubanks' Drug Store—who bore the same burden and chanted the same refrain. For we were Publisher's Representatives, and the long block on Franklin Street—on Saturday afternoons—was our beat, as most of the people in town passed up or down it during those hours. It was not strictly our beat, either; rather it was The beat, as several other boys, on

153

the same business bent, patrolled it. I stopped everybody who came along, black or white, large or small, in the hope of making a sale, as I knew you had to appeal to the masses and could not just pick your customers. It paid off, too, and I remember my astonishment, one day, when a colored boy named Gimpie, no bigger than myself, produced a greenish nickel and bought a *Post!* The cover picture got him, I think.

Dr. Bernard came out of the post office, and I blocked his way. "Wannabuya *Sad'dy Evenin' Post,* Dr. Bernard?" I inquired.

"Sure," he said, and fished in his pocket. I was relieved at the ease with which the sale was accomplished. "Got change for a dollar?" Dr. Bernard asked.

"Uh—no, sir," I answered, "but I'll get it." I took the big, floppy dollar bill in to Mr. Rob MacRae at the General Delivery window and he counted me out a handful of silver. "Business pretty good?" he asked.

"Yes, *Sir!*" I said.

"That's the stuff," he said. "Hit 'em hard!"

I was cheered, and warmed a little by Mr. MacRae's enthusiasm and my own false front of prosperity, and I took the money back to Dr. Bernard and carefully counted it out in his hand, all but the last nickel which I put into my purse. "Here comes Vernon Howell," he said, nodding over his shoulder, "you better get him before Collier Cobb does." But I knew what would happen. "Wannabuya *Sad'dy Evenin' Post,* Dr. Howell?" I asked, halfheartedly.

"Yes siree," he said, "I'll take six dozen."

"I haven't got that many," I mumbled, following the lines of the act.

"No?" he said, "Well, now, that's too bad. I want six dozen, but I don't want to shop around for 'em . . ."

"No, sir," I said, and turned away. He did this to me

every time I approached him on the matter of the *Saturday Evening Post*.

I moved on up the street, and Duke followed, to where Collier stood, whistling and shaking first one foot and then the other, and calling his wares. "Sellin' any?" I asked.

"Yep," he said. "Sold two—Dr. Gore and Mr. Jim Taylor. Mr. Jim MacRae's in the Drug Store now lookin' at one to see if he wants to buy it. [Mr. Jim MacRae was Mr. Rob's cousin.] If he does, that'll be three."

This was discouraging news to me, as a competitor, and I drifted on, hoping, perhaps, to head off some of the trade coming from that direction before it got to Collier. Beyond Mr. Eubanks' was Mr. Strowd's general store and meat market, with a watering trough in front. I remember there was a little ice in the trough that day. I paused beside the door to look at the game hung up on the clapboard front of the store.

I wonder if most of the memories of other oldsters have to do with summer? Things happened in winter, of course, but in my memory most things are brilliant in the summer sun. However, that is one of my clearest recollections of long ago winter, the strings of rabbits and quail hung up on the outside wall of Mr. Strowd's store (and occasionally a wild turkey). Only, then, we didn't call them quail; they were always "birds" or "partridges." They sold, dressed, for five cents. Rabbits were five cents, too. I don't know how much the wild turkeys were; we never bought one. But I remember so clearly standing on the cold sidewalk that day, my nose running and the heavy woolen muffler prickling my neck. And I remember taking off my mittens to touch the fur and the feathers, and I remember the beautiful designs on the feathers, and the tiny legs and feet of the dead birds.

Whatever hunting restrictions there were then were pretty sketchy and loosely enforced. People just went out and

shot. You could not trap "birds" however, and you could not
ship them to market outside the State. There was a bird dog
kept at the Greensboro Station to break up such attempts.
This dog, which I never saw, but which Dad would tell me
about, would be taken out to inspect a load of baggage or
express, and sure enough, likely as not, he'd stiffen up and
point a crate of eggs. They'd always find the inside stuffed
with birds, going to New York or Washington.

Mr. Strowd had three sons, Frank, Wallace, and Bruce.
(I don't know where the Scottish influence came from.) They
were all older than I, and therefore not among my intimates,
but I was allowed by Bruce, the youngest, to come along on
many occasions. Of Wallace I fought shy, as far as possible, as
he had a nasty habit of twisting my ears whenever he could get
his hands on me. Frank, the oldest of the brothers, was considered a grown man by us, so we didn't give him much
thought.

Next to Strowd's stood Mr. McCauley's Dry Goods,
and then the bank, and then Dr. Kluttz's. On the other side
of Dr. Kluttz was a tiny place operated by Mr. Willie B. Sorrell, who kept bees and sold knickknacks and eye glasses. In
a little back room he had a camera, a gingerbread wicker
chair, and one of those awful iron contraptions for keeping
your head where he put it, and made Photographic Portraits
of Ladies, Gentlemen, Infants and Family Groups Satisfaction Guaranteed. He developed my Brownie snapshots when
I first began taking pictures. I thought him a great photog-
rapher. Farther up was the hardware store. The Herndon
boys, sons of the proprietor, were friends of mine, though they
lived uptown. Then there was the blacksmith shop.

Across the street from Dr. Kluttz's was Tank Hunter's
big livery stable, one of the three the village boasted, back of
the neat brick building housing Webb's Store and Mr.
Neville's Sporting Goods and Ice Cream. I remember think-

ing that Poor Dave was probably inside the stable office, sitting by the stove and waiting for a call, and that I'd go over after a little while and see him, and get warm. But I forgot to do this when Dr. Pratt came along, just then, and I asked him, "Wannabuya *Sad'dy Evenin' Post,* Dr. Pratt? D'yuh wannabuya subscription?"—and to my joy and amazement he said, "Yes, maybe I do. Why don't you go down and see Mrs. Pratt? She said she thought she would subscribe—"

"Yes, *Sir! Thank* you, Sir!" I called back, already on my way.

This was only one of the ways employed to pick up an honest dollar around Chapel Hill—an honest dime, anyhow, now and then, here and there. As I grew older and my modest needs inevitably increased, my "allowance" became more and more inadequate (there were so many calls upon me) and I was forced to supplement my income by whatever means available.

I became a Village Nuisance, First Class, trying to secure subscriptions to the *Saturday Evening Post,* partly for the money involved, of course (if you ever sold any subscriptions, which was rarely), and because the *Post* of that time always carried in the back an enticing advertisement for agents, picturing in glowing terms the boundless wealth an industrious boy could accumulate by signing up subscribers. This wasn't all. Not by any means! In addition to getting rich, you stood a fine chance of *winning a pony* if you sold the most subscriptions in your town or district or continent —I don't know which it was, now—but there was a catch in it. There was always a picture of a smug, self-satisfied boy standing beside a beautiful, particolored Shetland pony of just the right size, beautifully turned out in a bucking saddle and all. "This Might be You," the advertisement said. But it never was. The boy pictured with the pony always lived in

Boston, or Dothan, Alabama. Nobody in Chapel Hill ever won one, but we were all trying. We were not readers of the *Post,* ourselves, but we highly recommended it.

The first letter I ever wrote to an editor was to that of the *Saturday Evening Post,* suggesting that it might be a good thing, and a fine investment, if they presented all their agents, regardless of competitive rating, with Shetland ponies, pointing out that an agent could get around better and cover so much more territory if he were mounted; but the *Post* never took the hint. This was also the first letter I ever wrote an editor which the editor did not answer.

My own magazine reading, I remember, was diversified. I myself was a subscriber to three periodicals, whose monthly or weekly arrival was eagerly looked forward to. The *Youth's Companion* was a weekly, and the backbone of my literature. The *American Boy* came every month, as did *St. Nicholas.* The *American Boy* was a great magazine for an outdoor sportsman, and after I had rabidly rushed through it from cover to cover there was a month's long, tedious wait until the next copy arrived. I was never very crazy about *St. Nicholas.* It was not exactly a woman's magazine, but it was definitely aimed at girls as well as boys—a mistaken policy, I believe, for any magazine to follow. Sort of takes the guts out. The *Youth's Companion* and the *American Boy* were as masculine as a pair of pants. I sold, or attempted to sell, subscriptions to all of these, too, but with indifferent success, as most of my boy friends were already subscribers or could borrow the magazine from other boys who were. I firmly refused to lend mine to anybody so long as there remained a chance of forcing him to become a subscriber.

An agent's duties and responsibilities did not end with getting the signature on the dotted line, either. The copies of the magazine came to him, and he had to deliver them to his subscribers! You earned your thin commission.

The prize of a pony for roping in the largest number of
subscribers was not a unique *Post* feature. The *American
Boy* carried the same alluring proposition, and strangely
enough it seemed to me that the pony the *American Boy*
pictured bore a striking resemblance to the *Saturday Evening Post* pony, one of which was awarded some hardwork-
ing and deserving boy (in Muskrat Falls, Minnesota!) each
month. Other publications baited prospective representatives
with ponies, too—or bicycles, at least. I had never heard of
psychologists who specialized in the workings of the juvenile
mind, then—and I doubt that they would have made a living because of public apathy toward the subject—and I am
sure that no such advisor could have been responsible for this
bait of a Shetland pony. No, it was just some smart, if under-
paid, circulation man who thought it up because he had a boy
exactly like Mr. Rob't. W. Prince's, who would have given
his right eye for a Shetland pony, and he, like Mr. Rob't. W.
Prince, was unable to buy him one. He knew how to secure
the desired result, from the magazine's standpoint, and everywhere you would see boys with white canvas bags over their
shoulders inscribed *Saturday Evening Post* or *Literary Di-
gest,* hawking the magazines and asking every passerby,
"Mister, d'yuh wannabuya subscription?"

In my later years I became a prolific contributor to the
pages of the *Saturday Evening Post,* and there is no doubt
(in my mind) that my pictures were at least partially responsible for the great growth and prosperity of the Curtis Publishing Company, but at the same time I believe that my early
efforts, with the canvas bag and a persuasive line of sales talk,
had even more to do with the great success of that organization.

Magazines don't seem to do much of that sort of thing
any more; the breed of man who undertakes to secure subscriptions is gradually dying out, like the Indian and the buf-

falo, and nowadays the offer of a private bombing plane or a custom built convertible with six whitewall tires and built in television would be the logical prize with which to entice the younger generation to get out and hustle. And this, of course, would greatly reduce the margin of profit.

I sold eggs, too—to the family—but as they were mostly Bantam eggs they brought only half price. Eggs were cheap, anyhow. I tried to work up a case for myself and Bantams, pointing out to Mother that it took me just as long to feed the Bantams, and to clean their house, and gather their eggs, and that it gave a Bantam hen just as much trouble to lay an egg, as if they were big chickens. But she laughed and said I ought to sell my Bantams and get some big chickens. "Yeah," Mars' Phil said, "invest in something that will pay you full size dividends." Ultimately I did this, but it was a wrench, as I was very fond of my tame and sociable Bantams, and I have never wanted to make a pet of a big chicken. But I kept one pen of Bantams, for old times' sake, and I got my pleasure from them and my increased revenue from my Domineckers.

I built up a small business on my Brownie Kodak, with snapshots of the University athletes. There were no press photographers hanging around then, and publicity was poor, so the athletes were glad to pose for a small boy with a Kodak. Afterward, if the pictures were even halfway decent, the subject was always good for a dozen or so, printed on postcards, or, if the picture made him look like a big-timer, maybe he bought even more. I got developing and printing paraphernalia from Mr. Willie B. Sorrell, the professional, and he threw in plenty of free advice along with my purchases of Hypo and developing powder and pans and Velox paper. I have an idea he didn't charge me full rates, as he would always do a lot of figuring with a pencil. I had no darkroom, but I developed my negatives, after dark, in my own room by the help of a red lamp. It was wonderful to watch the pictures come out, as you sloshed the film through the mixture, and I could hardly wait for them to get dry so that I could get to printing.

One spring, when we had a particularly good baseball team, I had a brilliant idea and really cashed in on it. After I had sold the individual members of the team all the pictures of themselves the traffic would bear, I carefully cut the heads off the bodies of the heroes, ruining my negatives of the full length figures, but of course they had already served their purpose. I had made an NC monogram—the standard design awarded the players for their sweaters—with the C superimposed over the N. My monogram, of black paper, was postcard size. In it I carefully cut round holes and pasted behind these holes the bits of negative of the heads of the players (there were only about a dozen on the team). When this was printed in the regular way the result was wonderful! On a black field I had a beautiful big white NC framing the portraits of The Team! And did they sell! Not only the players bought them, but lots of the students, too. The orders, and the money, rolled in. I was busy printing pictures all the time.

I wasn't so successful when I tried repeating the idea; after the first year the novelty wore off and sales resistance stiffened. Anyway it was good while it lasted, and that is how I got my bicycle.

One Christmas when I was still pretty small Dad and Mother gave me a bicycle—Santa Claus was the donor, I thought—and like me, the bicycle was pretty small. I had asked Santa Claus for it, and I remember the thrilling discovery of it in the lamplit wonder of Christmas morning! Dad had gotten home just the night before, and when he arrived I was made to stay in my room while a lot of bumping and laughing and happy Christmas noises went on. Dad said later that

Santa Claus had asked him to bring it, as he, Santa Claus, had no room for it in his sleigh. Can you imagine carrying a bicycle under your arm on a crowded Christmas train? That's what Dad did.

But that was as nothing compared with the time he brought the hook and ladder, also at Santa Claus's request, a real red and blue truck you could ride on, with a gong, and a ladder hanging on each side. . . . It was a wonderful vehicle, and I was the envy of every boy in Chapel Hill. A fireman's suit, complete with red shirt and helmet, was part of my Christmas haul. Little axes and red fire buckets came with the hook and ladder, too. How Dad ever managed it, through those Christmas crowds, I'll never know.

I had long outgrown my little bicycle, and I had been saving up for a long time to buy one. It wasn't easy saving up enough money to buy the blue "Coaster-Brake" dream I wanted, and for which I set my sights, even with the bonanza of the Kodak pictures. The bicycle, at Mr. Neville's Sporting Goods, cost sixteen dollars. It takes a lot of nickles to make sixteen dollars. Strangely enough, it was the novel game of golf which gave me a helping hand just when I needed it.

Golf made its first appearance in these parts just about this time, and Chapel Hill's first course—just east of the village and out beyond Battle's Park—was hacked from the wilderness. It also utilized a few convenient cow pastures. This was a godsend to me, and while I, as a caddy, had to learn the game just like the players, it brought in some money. Not an income you could bank on, however, as there were no fixed rates covering our services and we caddies were unorganized, and you might get stuck by some extra-stingy professor. Another thing that kept down my dividends from golf was the fact that Miss Nellie Roberson, my schoolteacher, had taken up the game, and as I adored Miss Nellie it seemed

indecent to take her money for the privilege of accompanying
her all afternoon o'er hill and dale and briar patch, and being given the proud if somewhat difficult responsibility of
keeping track of her ball. I caddied for Miss Nellie for love.

Dr. "Bully" Bernard was an indefatigable golfer. He
showed me something once, one day when I was caddying for
him, which made a lasting impression on me. He rolled up
his sleeve (there were no ladies around) and bent his arm and
pointed to the little hard knot of muscle on the outside of his
elbow. "See that?" he asked. I looked at it, hard. "That's the
golf muscle," he said. I have since learned that the muscle's
proper name is Extensor Carpi, radialas longus, but to me it
has always been the Golf Muscle.

My current expenses, along about this time, were pretty
heavy, also, and not conducive to much saving, what with
stamp collecting and the Approval Sheets all of us Philatelists
received through the mail. There was no ducking these approval sheets. Of course it was primarily your own fault that
you received them, as you had written the Scott Stamp Company, and other dealers, asking them to send you the sheets,
and giving your father as a reference; but you were practically
compelled to do this by all the news and suggestions on the
Stamps page of the *Youth's Companion* and *American Boy.*
The stamp dealers' advertisements, too, were deceptive. They
offered to send you these sheets of rare and valuable stamps,
marked at ridiculously low prices, which you could easily sell
to your friends, pocketing a fat and handsome commission for
yourself. It hardly ever worked out that way: sometimes you
did sell a stamp or two to a friend, if he happened to be flush,
but you yourself were usually the buyer. The stamps the
stamp companies sent us may not have been philatelic treasures, but they sure looked attractive, nay, irresistible, stuck
in their ruled spaces on little tissue hinges, with the price
modestly inscribed in the corner below. The letterhead on the

sheet was always most impressive, mentioning cable address and the names of foreign representatives. It made you feel that you were lucky to be doing business with such a firm! That's what I mean by being hard to duck; when you received one or two or a dozen of these sheets, you just had to break down and buy. They were so beautiful.

As my money disappeared I went, in desperation, into the approval sheet business myself. I got some blank sheets from the stamp people (they seemed to have anticipated this need) and with my hand printing press I set the rubber type and printed PRINCE STAMP CO., Chapel Hill, N.C., in the blank at the top. Then I filled the sheets with old duplicates I had, and peddled them around, but my luck was poor and my fellow collectors indifferent.

I was a sucker for pictorial stamps, the larger and gaudier the better. I had inherited a small collection from Mars' Phil and Mars' Pike, which had been given them when they were boys by some aunt or other, so there were a few really good things in my hodgepodge, but what we young collectors really went for was color and design and subject matter. It was sort of tragic not to have enough money to buy all the beautiful stamps that were thrust at you. I heard Grandpa say that stamp collecting was very educational, and I tried to work this angle and wheedle money out of him or Mother for educational purposes. I got a little now and then, but not enough to really count, or educate me very much.

There were large, bright Egyptian stamps, from the Sudan, each denomination a combination of different brilliant colors, which portrayed a running camel ridden by a turbaned Arab (we called them A-rabs) which I could not resist. There were the huge stamps, big as a cigarette picture, from Obock. You never heard of Obock? It is a French Colony on the Red Sea. There were the gorgeous and exciting stamps of the Central and South American Republics, showing strange birds and animals and ships and generals and flags and coats of arms and mighty waterfalls and smoking volcanoes. There were stamps of the Greek gods. The Oriental stamps had dragons, those of New South Wales emus and lyre birds and kangaroos. But the big Obock stamps were the most dazzling of all. They showed a group of hard-looking customers, long-haired tribesmen, squatting on the ground in council, their shields and spears much in evidence. Faraway Obock seemed a very dangerous place from which to send a letter, and a strange one to have such beautiful stamps. They were very different from the staid, prosaic stamps of Great Britian and Ireland (the words were spoken and written together, then) and France and Germany, which pictured mostly only dignified kings and queens. . . . The stamp companies used psychology, too, (just like the magazine people) in sending us more of the former than the latter.

Most of the garish South American and Eastern stamps were unused—bright and clean as though they had just been printed in New York—and this "brand new" feature gave them added value in our eyes; they seemed at a glance so much more desirable than old, postmarked, beat-up stamps from Italy or Canada. I think all these little heathen countries must have sold their gay stamps to the stamp companies cheap, whereas such a thing was beneath the dignity of old, established countries like England and France.

All the provinces and colonies of the different countries had their own stamps, even the various Canadian Provinces. Looking at my old album I note with surprise and pleasure that New Brunswick, where I have salmon-fished, had its own postage, back in the nineteenth century! In addition to our albums, one felt compelled to buy sets of flags and the arms and the rulers of each country, to be pasted at the top of its section in the album. These made a fine and colorful

effect. Some of those flags, as historical items, are very interesting now. I learned a lot about the world and it's geography
—that is the geography of that time. It doesn't do me much
good now. My dog-eared album is inscribed *The International: 1894 Edition: The Scott Stamp & Coin Company,
Limited.* I never did know what the Limited meant; certainly
their stamps weren't limited. The album contains such forgotten names as Hungary, Persia, Prussia, Servia. . . .

One or two of us had catalogues (which you also had
to buy; hardly anything was free in stamp-collecting) that
listed the values of the millions of stamps from all over the
world. It was a fine occupation to list your stamps and figure
up what you were worth. At one period I believed myself
worth about $10,000.00. But there was always the talk of
counterfeit, and you could never be quite sure. Dr. Venable,
the Venable boys' father, and the President of the University,
was our foremost Chapel Hill philatelist, and he could tell
about counterfeits, it was said, because he had a microscope.
I had no miscroscope, so I had to take my chances, and I just
bought what looked good to me. Like so many people and
Art, I didn't know a thing about stamps but I knew what I
liked.

A fine new issue of United States stamps came out in
1902 (I specialized in United States stamps, too; there were
so many of them around) and I invested and got as many of
them unused as I could afford. Benjamin Franklin was on
the 1¢, there were two different 2¢ with Washington on both,
Andrew Jackson was the 3¢, Grant the 4¢, Lincoln the 5¢,
Garfield the 6¢, Martha Washington the 8¢, Webster the 10¢,
Harrison the 13¢, Henry Clay the 15¢, and the 50¢ had
Thomas Jefferson's picture. I had them all *unused* up
through the 13¢. My 15¢ and 50¢ ones were postmarked,
and I felt pretty badly about it. There was a $1 one, and I do
not know whose picture was on that, for I never saw it. If I

could somehow have gotten a $1 one, I would have had a complete set.

I had two banks, one my own china one in which I tried to keep sufficient currency to meet any sudden and serious emergency, though this was very difficult and generally this bank was empty, and the other the Bank of Chapel Hill in which I had a savings account and in which I was sometimes able to deposit a dollar against the glorious Sixteen Dollar Day. When I got my bicycle, finally, it was in spite of the Scott Stamp Company, and for a while I forgot my stamps and the insidious approval sheets in the sheer joy of motion. It was beautiful and pristine and gleaming, that blue Coaster-Brake, and even though it represented the toil of my hands and the sweat of my brow and my hard-earned life's savings, it was worth it.

CHAPTER SIXTEEN

COLLIER and Billy Cobb
were my closest and most depended-upon friends, they and
Tad Lilly; but Tad Lilly was not always there when you
wanted him, as he was only a summer resident of Chapel Hill.
The Cobb boys—until Collier went off to school at Warrenton
—were my standbys.

Billy was a couple of years Collier's elder, and in point
of age and size I fitted right between. We made three steps,
as Collier was quite small and slight, and Billy (whom you
would never have taken for Collier's brother) a remarkably
tall and stringy boy who moved like an animal or an Indian,
and knew more about the woods than any boy I have ever
known. He grew up to be a distinguished naturalist.

The two boys were quite different in ways other than
their physical appearance. Billy loved, passionately, everything related to nature; Collier was only mildly interested.
Billy liked solitude, Collier was gregarious to an extreme.
Billy was quiet almost to taciturnity, and Collier a chatter-
box who could, and did, talk your ears off if given half a
chance. Billy never tried to convert you to anything; Collier
would have sold you the Woolworth Building if it had been
constructed then. Collier seemed on springs, Billy moved
slowly. Billy's carriage fell forward when it got up to his

sloping shoulders and long neck, and his arms dangled awkwardly, while Collier was a compact little fireball who stuck
out his chest and strutted like a Bantam rooster. I tried to
emulate the better accomplishments and characteristics of
each. By the way, there was a period in there where all of us
amused ourselves and each other by crowing. We got quite
expert at it, too, flapping our arms and copying the crows of
various breeds and individual roosters. Some of the crows
sounded quite authentic, and from a little distance you could
hardly tell the difference. I remember Collier occasionally
used to crow surreptitiously in school.

Billy could draw, and Collier couldn't. Billy could draw
better than I could; he did everything better than I. But this
was all right, he was older than I was, and his superiority
was to be expected. The Cobb boys' father was Geology
Professor. He had chunks of interesting rock—specimens, he
called them—sitting around the house, and he had a fine
library which went far beyond ours (which consisted mostly
of Grandpa's theological books) including a wonderful natural history, and we spent many hours copying the animals
from these books. Mr. Cobb had spent his undergraduate days
at Harvard, way back in the olden times, and his library also
contained a lot of bound copies of the *Harvard Lampoon*.
These were very stimulating and there was a time when we,
Billy and I, thought it possible that with the inspiration afforded by the *Lampoon* we might become cartoonists instead
of natural history artists.

Both boys were athletic to a marked degree, as were
most of us, I guess. Billy was a pitcher on our Little Downtown baseball team, on which I caught, and Collier was a
remarkable runner even as a boy, his short legs pumping tire-
lessly. We used always to send him when long-distance mes-
senger service was necessary. His slight stature was an asset
in many ways, too. Once he wriggled all the way through a

ten inch culvert under Franklin Street. There was no special
reason for it and nobody suggested it; it was his own idea. It
seemed very important at the time, however, when he in-
formed us of his intention. If he *had* gotten stuck under the
street somewhere we had no plans to rescue him, but it would
certainly have been an exciting and enjoyable occasion. Later,
in his student days at the University, he stayed above ground
and became a famous miler, and even though he still looked
like a small boy he ran rings around the best distance runners
in the South and set several records besides winning a boxful
of medals. He says that when he went with the track team
to meets at other colleges where nobody knew him they
thought he was a joke and laughed at the idea of his running a hundred yards with grown men, let alone a mile. Then
his Chapel Hill-hardened legs would bring him home far
ahead of the pack, the puffing big guys wallowing laboriously
behind. He is now a political power in the State, and as a
dignified and successful businessman and civic leader the pride
of Chapel Hill.

Tad Lilly, whose real name was Edmund, came in the
summers from his home in Fayetteville to visit his grandfather,
Judge MacRae, and his uncle Duncan, the Judge's son, who
was only some two or three years older than himself. He was
very blond, almost a towhead, with an impish, laughing face
mostly mouth. My father said that Tad's mouth looked as
though it had been put on hot and allowed to run all over his
face. I gleefully reported this to Tad, but he didn't seem to
think it particularly funny. By background and connections
he was a very "nice" boy, but at the same time he had a rough,
tough swagger which made him resemble a thoroughbred-
Wire-Haired Fox Terrier. He could cuss beautifully and
was handy with his fists. He was considerably toughened up,
I have no doubt, by his uncle Duncan.

One summer Mother took both of us (Mother was a

courageous woman, for all her softness) with her on a trip to
Wilmington to visit the Cranmers, and enjoy the beach. Dr.
and Mrs. Cranmer had lived in Chapel Hill, and their son,
Jack—while he was a little younger than we—was considered
a fully privileged member of the Little Downtown set. We
would go down to the dock and get on the little steamer to go
down the sound to Wrightsville Beach. We'd sit on the bench
which ran around the rail of the top deck and watch the flat
marshlands go by and look at the ruin of Fort Fisher, the old

Civil War fortification guarding the entrance to the harbor.
We were stirred by the romantic clang of the ship's bell and
the throb of her engines, and imagined ourselves fearless sea-
men on the bounding main as we chugged down the placid
waters of the sound. The steamer seemed a great liner to us;
later on the *Majestic* and the *Leviathan* impressed me not half
so much. It was the first time either Tad or I had ever seen
the ocean, and we agreed with the old conclusion that it was
a mighty fine body of water. I saw Mother's legs at Wrightsville Beach. She and Mrs. Cranmer put on bathing suits which

reminded you of cut-off "wrappers," with bloomers and black
stockings, and all of us had great sport playing around the
edge of the surf and screaming when a wave upset us. I have
a Brownie snapshot of Tad Lilly taken at Wrightsville Beach,
that summer. Jack Cranmer appears beside him, half buried
in the sand which Tad was heaping on him, and Tad, on his
knees, is leering and thumbing his nose in a most ungentle-
manly fashion at me and the camera. The picture is very indic-
ative of his general attitude toward things. He never backed
down from anything he started, and always took a dare. I remember, once, on Judge MacRae's side porch, a couple of
diabolically inclined students who lived in the back room
offered us some licorice (they said). It was the strangest
licorice I ever tasted, but they told us to keep chewing and the
good licorice taste would develop. After a while I felt awful
and I couldn't keep on and had to spit mine out, but Tad continued chewing nonchalantly, even after he began to turn
green. We finally strolled away, Tad still chewing, until we
were hidden by the hedge, and there Tad let go and was sick.
This was my first experience with chewing tobacco, and I am
just as unenthusiastic now as I was then. Tad was an able
infielder and a great bulwark to the Little Downtown baseball
team, although he was what you might call an umpire-baiter.
We wrote to each other a few times after I left Chapel Hill,
but the correspondence died aborning.

I didn't see Tad Lilly for almost forty years. Early in
1941, and after I had returned to Chapel Hill after so long
away, I had a letter from him. He had stayed in the Army
following 1918, and become an Infantry Colonel. He was coming home to North Carolina on leave before going out on a
long hitch in the Philippines, and wrote that he wanted to see
me if and when he got up to Chapel Hill before his departure,
but he never came. His name was announced as one of the
officers captured on Corregidor—and then silence. Later I

learned that he had survived the Bataan Death March; that
for more than two years, firm in the faith that he was alive,
his wife had written to him daily, though he never received
any of her letters, while she never heard from or of him. And
then finally she heard his name in a list of men in a Japanese
prison camp in Manchuria. My own thrill came when just a
little while back I was called in from my studio one day because "an Army Officer" wanted to see me. In the hall stood
a Colonel who could make his fortune on the stage or in the
movies, a hard, wiry military figure, gray-haired, and with a
back like a board and a face cut from solid rock. I had never
seen him before, I was sure. I said, "How do you do, Sir?" He
said, "Tad Lilly" . . . and we threw our arms around each
other. I am confident that he thumbed his nose at the Japs just
as he did at everybody else.

How many years ago, all those boys and dogs and days
and places—so many details lost in a golden haze—and yet, as
I write, how close they seem!

We devoured the Ernest Seton Thompson books, *Wild
Animals I Have Known, Tito,* and *The Biography of a
Grizzly,* and *Lives of the Hunted.* (The Cobb boys named
their dog, which was a sort of Chow, Tito for Ernest Seton
Thompson's wolf.) When *Two Little Savages* was published,
our cup was full. Here was a practical plan of life as it should
be lived, complete with illustrations, charts and diagrams. By
the way, the author's name, then, was Ernest Thompson
Seton; just why he switched things around like that, I don't
know, but under both names he wrote great stuff.

We studied animal tracks and habits. It was very easy to
imagine the cloven hoofprint of a cow as a buffalo's, and that
of a pig as a deer. Big dog tracks might have been made by
small bears. But we did learn the tracks of rabbits and squirrels and 'coons and 'possums and weasels. Lizard tracks were
always interesting, with the long mark between the footprints

where the tail drags. We learned how to construct the most elaborate traps and snares for bird and beast and fish (but at Mr. Seton's direction we practised conservation, too, such as taking only one egg from a nest and putting back the fish we didn't want). Billy Cobb and I tried hard to shoot the few suckers or catfish we occasionally saw in the creek with bows and arrows, the only result of such attempts being that we had to grapple in the muddy water for our arrows. We learned to skin rabbits and chipmunks and squirrels, and to stretch and cure the pelts which we sometimes actually sold for a few cents. When this occurred we imagined ourselves real backwoodsmen and called each other Podner. We tried with mediocre success to stuff birds, and built armatures and ordered beautiful glass eyes of various sizes and color from a taxidermy outfit whose advertisement appeared in the *American Boy*. They sent you full directions, but some of them must have been too technical, or something, because we had to take short cuts and improvise, and some of our stuffed birds turned out to be creatures never seen previously on land or sea, and did not keep very well. The stuffing of owls gratified us more than anything else, because the glass owl eyes we got from the taxidermists were so impressive. I remember once finding a little too-long-dead screech owl and stuffing him perhaps unexpertly. The only eyes I had on hand were a trifle large for the screech owl and gave him an odd and commanding appearance. I didn't like him much, when the job was done, and anyway I was forced to bury him.

But as Indians we excelled. We learned to tread softly in the woods, leaving no trail behind us, and to be careful with fire. We never left a burning fire. We blazed trails, where necessary, in what we were sure was virgin forest. Our pockets usually contained lizards or small snakes, grass or garter or black, which we carried as charms or talismans. During one period we even tried to live off the land, that is for lunch, and subsisted on raw turnips and sweet potatoes, which we would steal—wriggling stealthily on our bellies—from quiet garden plots, and crawfish from the branches, which we boiled in tin cans. The fish we caught we'd roast on sticks. Usually these meals were backlogged by jam or jelly sandwiches brought along just in case the chase proved unsuccessful.

The building of our tepee was a major operation. We constructed it, slowly and laboriously, out of burlap bags (croker sacks) sewed together. *Two Little Savages* gave detailed directions covering pattern, poles, smoke flaps, etc. Space was needed for laying out the materials and doing the work, so we took advantage of the open floor of the Bruners' barn. Mr. Seton's pattern called for a rectangle of twenty by ten feet from which the half-circle of the tepee cover, and the smoke flaps, were to be cut. Making the cover out of skins (which we should have done) was impossible; there were no deer available and there weren't that many rabbits in North Carolina! and even enough croker sacks to cover that large an area presented difficulties. But we assembled 'em. We exhausted our families' supplies and then turned to our livery stable friends who were reluctantly accommodating and gave us grain sacks. Some of the sacks had seen better days, but we figured some holes were allowable, not only for extra ventilation but also because real Indian tepees probably had holes where arrows and thrown knives and tomahawks had pierced them, so we were not too particular. We sewed the edges of the sacks together with heavy string, using sharp sticks, easily pushed throught the burlap, as needles to which our string was tied, and while our stitches may have been a trifle long, they held the sacks together, and our ten by twenty began to grow. But that's a big area, and covering it seemed endless. For hours on end we'd sit or squat or kneel in the gloom of the Bruner barn, stitching those sacks—mostly only Billy and I— buoyed up and on by the shining vision of our finished tepee.

It was a great day when the last sack completed the big rectangle, and we carefully spread it out and pegged it to the dirt floor. Billy drove a stake in the middle of one of the long sides, and using a string and a piece of chalk as a compass, marked off the half-circle we had to cut. I remember rushing home breathlessly to borrow Grandpa's scissors with the serpents on them, and I remember the slight delay and my fussing and fuming because Grandpa wasn't there, and I knew better than to take the scissors from his desk without asking him. But Mother said she would tell him and she'd "stand for it," so I dashed out, clutching the scissors. ("Careful, now! Don't run. Be sure you don't forget them when you come home.")

We cut the cover out, then marked and cut the smoke flaps from the remnants on either side, and we could *see* our tepee rising majestically. But there was still a long way to go, and we started the tedious task of turning up and binding the long outer edges, and those of the smoke flaps. More days of work. Holes had to be punched and bound, and rope loops set in, at intervals around the bottom for the pegs which would hold the tepee to the ground, and then the smoke flaps sewn to the center of the long straight edge. But always we saw our tepee in the woods, and though our knees and hands got raw, and our backs were fit to break, we sewed and sewed . . . knowing that the great thrill of decoration lay ahead!

There were two beautiful charts in *Two Little Savages*, one showing the pictorial adornment of Black Bull's tepee, and the other of Thunder Bull's. We not only swiped these decorative designs, we improved on them, and we also appropriated the two names as ideally suited to our personalities and purposes, and I became Chief Black Bull Prince and Billy, Chief Thunder Bull Cobb. All the members of the tribe were allowed to choose their own names, and I believe Collier designated himself Howling Wolf, or was that Willis Bruner?

No, Willis Bruner was Great Yellow Rabbit. We secured unto ourselves all the odds and ends of paint from our families' tool sheds, and went to work. Naturally most of the braves and hangers-on just stood around and watched, or held impromptu war dances in the corner, while Billy and I, accepted Chiefs and head artists, laid out and painted the Sioux symbols and characters on the burlap. There was a striking looking bull on either side of the entrance flap—a sort of buffalo bull rampant, not just an ordinary cow bull—one, a black one, for me, and on the other side a red one for Billy. We were all vague as to proper Thunder color, so we held a council and decided red was best. Those two bulls were really impressive. Around the tepee we painted a frieze of mounted warriors dashing at each other, spears in hand, and from decorative medallions we hung scalp locks made of raveled rope dyed black. When at last our labor was done we climbed up on the haymow and the rafters so that we could gaze down on all the glories of our making spread below us. We looked and looked, and knew the unspeakable joy of accomplishment and creation. "You think we all done, Chief Thunder Bull?" I asked, after a while.

"Ugh. How," said Billy.

Of course, after we had allowed the painted embellishment to dry sufficiently to allow handling, and then tenderly lifted our cover from the ground, it was partially stuck where the paint had gone through, and the floor beneath it was a mess of half-dry and sticky paint puddles. We got this on our feet and hands, and subsequently on our clothes and faces, but it all added to the color and brilliancy of the occasion.

The whole tribe was put to work cutting fifteen foot poles, or thereabouts—eight or ten of them, we needed—and then came the portage to the woods. That was an impressive procession, accompanied by much grunting and brow-mopping

and gosh-amightys, as we struggled along. I wanted to tie the
poles on either side of Dan, the Cobb's pony, and have him
drag them, in the manner of the migratory Indians I had seen
in a picture, and we tried this—but Dan objected and would
have none of it. So we untied the poles and went about the job
by hand and back. A level space down back of the Hertys'
house was the site selected, a spot at the edge of the woods
below Dr. Battle's pond (Always choose a campsite close to
running water, Mr. Seton's book said) where the tepee would
show to the best advantage across the broomsedge field. One
important item we lacked in the personnel of our tribe, and
that was squaws to do the hauling and the heavy work, but we
partly overcame this deficiency by enlisting Wump Whitted
in the enterprise. Of course Wump had been an interested
spectator and helper in all our preliminary activities, but
necessarily he was on the outer fringe of things until called
upon to do something, and he had no official status. Billy and
I went into conference, or private council, and decided that it
might be a very good thing to give Wump a real and responsible part in our project, a role of which he could be proud,
and duties best suited to his own particular talents. So we
made him Medicine Man, and gave him the name of Doctor
Whitted.

Wump's exalted position may have caused a little jeal-
ousy among the lesser braves such as Frank Herty and little
Arthur Bruner and John Abernathy, but when they saw how
much work he saved them they accepted the arrangement
gracefully. With a minimum of training and practice Wump
later became one of the best Medicine Men I ever saw, making
up his own jargon and working out his own dances. With
paint on his face and feathers tied around his kinky hair
(sometimes for a headdress he wore an old dog skull he had
picked up) and his blue overalls rolled up to the thigh, and
bunches of bright feathers and flannel streaming from his legs

and arms, strings of beads and berries and other impedimenta flying from his neck, he filled the part even better than we could have hoped, as he leaped and twisted and writhed around, shouting his incantations and making mysterious and significant passes with his decorated forked sticks. So when we moved the poles, Doctor Whitted was the foremost burden bearer.

We laid out our poles in a ten foot circle, and then lashed three of them together, ten feet up, in a tripod, accomplished by means of the Medicine Man and the Hertys' stepladder. This took a bit of doing, but the other poles, laid into this tripod, were easy, and finally came the long awaited climax of stretching on our cover! Miraculously, it fit! We laced it tight together down the front, and threw open the flaps for the entrance, and raised and set our smoke flap poles. Everything dovetailed, everything was *right;* Mr. Seton knew his stuff! That completed tepee, shining and colorful against the forest backdrop, was a magnificent sight, a sight to cheer the heart of any tired, homesick Indian. It became a shrine, a temple— the home of the Battle's Park Blackfeet—and for days and weeks it was rarely without its occupants.

In our war bonnets, we sat cross-legged inside before a fire, choking on rabbit tobacco smoke from our peace pipes (I had found some old, blackened, smoked out clay pipes of Grandpa's, and we cut and decorated extra long stems) or the acrid fumes of burning bacon or sowbelly we had brought from home. Somehow we always had difficulty with our ventilation, even though we carefully wet our fingers and held them up to determine the exact direction of the wind and adjusted our smoke flaps accordingly, just as the book said, quartering them into the wind so as to create a draft. I believe Indians must have had trouble with theirs, too, for ours were never very successful. We would emerge red-eyed and gasping, but anyway we had been living in our tepee. We held many councils and war dances, of course, and ceremonial rites of all kinds.

We were told exactly how to make our war bonnets, and we pored over directions and specifications as we worked. We even got, by fair means or foul, white turkey tail feathers and dipped the ends in black paint, and bound the quills in flannel and downy underfeathers, and sewed them to an old cap base on which a frame of sticks and wire held the feathers as they should be, a long feathered tail flowing down the back. With these bonnets on you assumed character and had to speak pidgin Indian. Billy was undisputed Chief and leader of our tribe (even though, nominally, I held equal rank) and, with the exception of Wump, its hardest worker, but he wore his honors modestly and never tried to boss anybody. We weren't *Playing Indian;* that term infuriated us. It seemed to denote "little boys," dressed up in cheap store Indian suits, who hid behind bushes and jumped out at people and shouted Bang, Bang. No, sir. We were past that stage, in years and in experience, and this was the solid, serious business of woodcraft. Of course we could add a few trimmings to make it more fun.

Billy, as First Chief, awarded the *coups,* prizes for such feats as killing an enemy or a buffalo, best at cooking, knife-throwing, scalping, crawfish-finding, etc., and he didn't hand them out indiscriminately, either; you had to earn them, as Chief Thunder Bull's standards were high. *Coups* (which we pronounced "coops") was the name given, according to Ernest Thompson Seton, the fancy feathers awarded for the various feats, and were decorated with a bit of rolled red flannel at the feather's tip, from which waved some red strands of darning cotton. These highly prized feathers were worn in the front of the war bonnet. Where practicable they might bear a small design symbolic of the mighty accomplishment which had won the coup. At a glance you could determine a man's stature by the coups in his war bonnet.

Dan, the Cobb pony, was full of color and romance because he was wild. He was a Banks pony, one of those free-ranging creatures which live unfettered on the eastern shore of North Carolina, the descendants, it is said, of horses brought over by the early colonists or even the Spaniards. He had been given the name of Dan, and a tamer, more lethargic beast I never saw. He was quite fat, and seldom moved faster than a walk. The Cobb boys were very proud of his having been wild, and bragged about it, but civilization and easy living had killed his spirit and practically all he did was eat and sleep. He was stubborn, though, with a will of his own, and if he didn't choose to go somewhere when you wanted him to, that settled it. Anyway, when Billy, in full regalia, mounted him and became a Sioux scout, it was a fine sight. Billy's legs were long enough so that he could hook them around Dan's withers and shoot an arrow from the off side under Dan's neck, Dan standing quietly the while with half-closed eyes.

We made really good bows and arrows, the bows of tough hickory or ash, and the arrows, some of them nail-headed for serious work, beautifully feathered three ways (you carefully split the quill and lashed on a half-piece of feather at a time after you had glued the flat side of the split quill to the arrow). We made canvas quivers, and cut and sewed and painted canvas moccasins, deerskin being somewhat awkward to secure. We made a fine dummy deer out of a saw horse and sticks and wire and burlap stuffed with leaves. Our deer hunts were paper chases, with a brave being given time to lay a trail and hide the deer. It was a good deer and gave you a fine illusion when you saw it at the edge of the woods and then crawled up on it through the weeds. Wonderful, when you rose to one knee and raised your good ole bow and swiftly let fly an arrow straight and true to the deer's heart—or rump. A certain amount of time was spent, of course, in looking for arrows which had fallen to earth we

knew not where. We were pretty good with slings, too; not
the familiar "sling shots," constructed with rubber bands and
a forked stick, 'though of course we knew and used them, too,
in their place. No, our slings were the real article, a leather
thong wide enough in the middle to support a rock, the sort of
rig David used. They were erratic weapons, however, and
like as not you might conk one of your own men instead of an
enemy or a charging bison.

We generally had a pot boiling over the regular—or
camp—fire outside the tepee. The fire inside was the sacred or
ceremonial fire, and even though we used it for cooking because it was out of the wind, we treated it as a superior fire and
one due our ritualistic worship.

In this boiling pot we brewed some weird concoctions,
recipes given us by Aunt Jinny Johnson, whom we thought
of as something of a witch doctor because she knew a lot of
homely remedies and superstitious preventives. Aunt Jinny
was the old colored woman who did our washing. She was almost a member of the family, and Mother called on her for any
and everything. We depended on Aunt Jinny as far back as I
can remember. When I was very little she was the nearest
approach to the Old Negro Mammy, beloved of song and
story, that I ever had. Every Southerner of any consequence
is supposed to have an Old Negro Mammy who held him on
her lap and sang spirituals to him and called him Honey Chile,
while the Darkies, down under the Plantation's great, moss-
hung trees, played banjos, and the people up in The Big House
danced and gambled and drank. We didn't have any of that—
and I am overreaching myself when I claim Aunt Jinny as my
Mammy, but I do remember well what a broad and comfortable lap she had, and how kind she was. This was naturally
before my Indian days.

She was a huge old woman, with a rugged, almost masculine face, which was covered by an eternal smile. She moved

like a runaway truck, running over and scattering pickaninnies before her. Her arms were like a stevedore's and her bosom like a feather bed. She lived in a little house on the outskirts of the village, in the opposite direction from Sunset, where most of the colored folk lived, on the brow of the long, winding hill as you start down the road to Durham. There was a huge boulder and a huge oak tree before her front door. I always think of everything connected with Aunt Jinny as huge, beginning with her heart. The house stood where you passed close by it on your way to the farm where the Strowd boys lived. There was the boulder, and the tree, timeless and beloved landmarks to me, when I came back to Chapel Hill, but the little cabin is displaced by fine residences now, and even Mr. Strowd's farm is occupied by a development known as Strowd's Hill.

Aunt Jinny was an authority on herbs and their uses, and to her we went for suggestions as to potent and magic mixtures, not only to appease the gods, but also to make us better Indians. I remember the tongue-tied group of us standing before Aunt Jinny sitting in the door of her little home, scraggly chickens pecking around the doorstep. It was difficult to put our needs into words which Aunt Jinny would understand, we thought. We began by asking what was good for a bad cold. Aunt Jinny smoked a corncob pipe, and she waved this expansively. "Slippery ellum," she boomed. "Ain't nothin' better'n slippery ellum tea, 'cept maybe catnip, but 'at's hard t'find. You jest drink all y'kin hold and go t'bed and cover up and sweat hit out." That didn't appeal to us in the least.

"What's good for toothache?" I asked her.

"Ain't nothin' s'good as a li'l whiskey," she chuckled, "pou'd on d'tooth. Ef hit don' stop achin' jest swallow d'whiskey. Den hit stop achin'." This presented difficulties, too. (I thought of Grandpa's sacramental wine, and shuddered.) I

tried again. "I don't like whiskey very much," I said. "Isn't there something tastes better?"

"Dandelion roots is good," Aunt Jinny laughed. " 'At's a fine drink; some folks uses hit f'coffee."

"Thank you," I said. "That sounds better."

"Y'all boys playin' Injin?" Aunt Jinny asked, noting our feathers.

"Well, sort of," I said, embarrassedly.

"You be keerful now," she said. "Don' you go git snake-bit, playin' 'round in dem woods! Ef you do, jest split a fresh-kill' chicken n'put on d'place, a fresh'un ever' hour. Make yo'sef a witch hazel tea and taub on d'place; you be a'right." Once she got started, her incredible fund of knowledge flowed from her like a stream, and we listened wide-eyed as it poured over us. She had boxes and jars and cans of dried herbs and grasses and leaves, and bundles of roots all looking alike to us, but unhesitatingly she picked out the various remedies and told us of them.

"Dis hyah," she said, "hit's gol'n seal, an' hit's d'best thing f'proud flesh. Hit humble hit right away!" She let out a horse laugh. "And dis hyah—ef you has spasms, you use blue cohosh. Ef you has his-sterricks you uses dis 'sterrick weed, an' ef you has d' *high* his-sterricks you uses dis hyah Injin moccasin." She went on and on, pawing over her stores.

She told us that may apples are good for the bowels of man and beast, and if we wanted to throw up, all we had to do was chew up and swallow some rabbit tobacco. "Hit's good t'mix in wid the store-bought for y' smokin', too," she said. "Make hit go further." She told us of the therapeutic properties of lobelia, and that claver leaves, made into a strong tea, are fine for sickness of the kidneys, and that when you had cankermouth all that was necessary would be a good shot of goldthread. Just in case you took too much of any of these, wintergreen leaves was a fine antidote and would save you.

She told us much, much more, which of course I can't remember.

We all felt we had a lot of valuable information.

"Thank you, Aunt Jinny," everybody said, as we departed.

"Don' eat no green persimmons!" Aunt Jinny shouted after us, laughing. This was a sort of Chapel Hill version of "Don't take any wooden nickels!"

We learned to identify trees by their leaves and bark. We learned to differentiate between the many oaks—chestnut, black jack, swamp and white and red and pin oaks, and water oaks and live oaks. We learned the differences of silver beech and blue beech, and leatherwood and ironwood.

We learned, with Mr. Seton's help, the invaluable code of Indian signs, and many a stroller in Battle's Park must have been puzzled by coming on a strangely arranged little pile of stones beside the path, or grass tops tied in odd shapes and directions, or broken twigs and blazed trees.

Sometimes, if some sort of home work or other prevented our getting together, we would signal each other by means of smudge fires in our yards, until our mothers, holding their noses, put an end to it. In short, we *were* savages, noble red men, under a spell, and we went around in a glassy-eyed trance.

We heard some talk from jealous Little Uptown boys about starting a rival tribe, but nothing ever came of it; they didn't have any inspirational leader like Billy. If it had, we were ready for them, with delightful tortures devised and a place picked out where we would burn hostile spies at the stake. We were prepared for war, but we followed the paths of peace, and we learned a lot.

As Mrs. Spencer, the lady who pulled the bell rope with Dr. Battle, wrote in an earlier day and of an earlier Chapel Hill,

"All educational work was slow and done without any
thought of training for mind and body as training is
understood in this day. There was a good deal of simple
happiness, and much converse with the woods and hills
and streams, the wild flowers and fruits of the country,
mixed with the books. The children grew up strong and
healthy, ready for any work that might offer."

Wonderful days, those, of tramping the hills and fields,
of finding real Indian arrowheads, chiseled from bluestone or
flint or quartz; of hunger satisfied beside a campfire, of thirst
quenched in a tumbling stream or a shadowed spring. And
when the day was over, and you called your dog, and plodded
tiredly across the fields, the yellow lights in the windows of
the houses, shining out through the autumn twilight, caused
you to forget about being a woodsman or an Indian until tomorrow, and you felt the warmth and security of home before
you reached it.

Years later, I saw in a New York exhibition a tiny landscape by Bruce Crain—hardly more than a thumb-box sketch
—which was the only landscape I have ever wanted to buy,
and I couldn't, then, because I was only an art student living
on a shoestring. But I was alone in New York, and young, and
homesick, and the simple little scene was of an open field at
early dark, the dim woods beyond, and it was *my* field, *my*
woods—with the tepee in the background. Mr. Crain didn't
know it, but the tepee was there.

We hadn't heard of the Boy Scouts then, but we could
have taught them things. Before I forget, I'd like to tell you
about a little incident I witnessed recently, not more than a
year or so ago. My home is in the woods, a couple of miles
from town and not far from the local Boy Scout cabin and
camping ground, down in the valley behind us, reached by a
trail through the woods from the highway. As I drove home
one day a yellow taxicab ahead of me drew up and turned

around at the head of this trail, and from it descended, so help me, two little Boy Scouts. They were covered with scarfs and badges and whistles and hunting knives, and neither could have been more than ten or eleven years old. The smaller of the two glanced at the meter and paid the fare, and off they trudged into the woods!

This is intended as no disparagement of the Boy Scouts. Theirs is a great and wonderful organization, and I only wish it had been in existence when I was eligible. It is only that things were different then, and perhaps our legs were stronger.

Chapter Seventeen

Among the colored folk of
the South and of that day there was a small minority born to
rest. From the beginning, and all through their lives, they
rested. Labor of any kind, for them, was akin to sin; they were
touched by The Finger, and they were foreordained to rest.
Even light or pleasurable endeavor, if calling for the expendi-
ture of any energy, was denied them. They were the chosen,
upon whom the yoke of work was never laid. Their friends
and relatives recognized their unique status, and provided for
them bountifully. Collard greens and pork chops flowed their
way, and shelter and shoes and raiment—all was offered,
nothing asked—while they lounged in the shade and plucked
a guitar, maybe, or just lounged, for they were born to rest,
as everybody knew. Even to this day, some rare souls receive
this gift, though it is becoming increasingly uncommon.

I used to envy the few of these Untouchables I knew.
There was old Uncle Dan'l Pendergrass, who lived down near
the mill and could hardly ever bring himself to climb up
Windy Hill; and there was a colored boy named Rufus Gooch
who didn't even have to go to school because his mother said
he was born to rest. And there was Asia Jones, whose daughters did all the washing and the ironing while she sat on her
front porch and rocked. God's favorites, I thought—the ex-

ceptions which proved the rule drilled into me that every mother's son of us must work. Never from the start of things was I given opportunity to don the mantle, to claim that I was born to rest. Always from the beginning there were things that must be done.

When I was old enough—that is, when my physique allowed it—I was given a solemn responsibility, a post, I was told, few boys attain; I was to assist, in a way, in the church services. I was to be allowed to pump the organ. My mother played the organ in our church, and to me was given the honor of collaboration.

I was properly elated at first, and it gave me a proud and exalted feeling to hear the music swell out because of my efforts; it gave me a sense of boundless power, and I toiled with enthusiasm and abandon. But after a while the glamour faded and the labor began to seem more and more just ordinary hard work, and finally I became disillusioned and convinced that it was exactly that, and I felt that anybody who wanted the job could have it. But nobody did, and I became resigned. The heart, the verve, went out of my pumping, and it became mechanical, like pumping the air into my own lungs. It came to seem just as much a part of me, too. I got my fill of it, and I want no part of it, any more. My mother may have played uplifting and inspiring music on that organ, for she played it well, but I furnished the boy-power which enabled her to do it. For years and years.

Every member of the family, with the exception of Dad, of course, who was absent so much of the time, participated in the church services. I doubt that Dad would have taken any active part even if he had been there, as he couldn't sing a note, and I don't believe that a post could have been created for him, even with all his good qualities. Unless it might have been passing the collection plate, maybe. But everybody else took part plenty, from Grandpa in the pulpit down through Mother on the organ bench and my two uncles in the choir, to my own long-suffering self packed into the tiny space behind the organ where there was only room for the pump handle and me. It was hot in there and dim, and sometimes between hymns, as I sat on my stool, I would doze off listening to the soothing sound of Grandpa's voice,—even though the discomfort of my Sunday clothes usually kept me awake. But always when I began to nod I would be brought back to reality by Mars' Phil, who kept a watchful eye on me, I suppose, just in case I did go to sleep at the switch, and he would reach a long arm in and shake me gently. Usually this was in time so that I got Mother off to a good start, but sometimes the music began with a most uncertain wheeze, or didn't begin when it should, at all. Once started, however, I pumped patiently and con-scientiously, so as not to make Mother look bad.

Church music has undergone a change of recent years; the good old days when everybody sang are gone. Choirs now-adays seem to like to sing, for the most part, hymns nobody else knows. But our choir, then—with Mrs. MacRae and Miss Dora and Mrs. Mangum and Mrs. Herty and Miss Nellie Barbee and my uncles and Mr. Woolen—was wonderful. When Mother played and they sang "Rock of Ages," or "There is a Green Hill Far Away," it was something to hear and remember. Their hearts were in it even though their voices may not have been trained, but they stayed together pretty well and it sounded wonderful, especially Mars' Pike's tenor. From where I was I could see Mars' Phil tapping his foot a little to keep time, and every now and then he would lean over to the organ and turn the music sheet for Mother.

The choir was a handsome sight, too, though I never saw much of it, back where I was; Mars' Phil and Mars' Pike and Mr. Woolen in their Sunday suits and stiff, standing collars with stickpins in their cravats and their hair slicked down, and the ladies in their best dresses and big hats (Miss

Nellie Barbee, in the front row with the sopranos, had a wonderful hat with ostrich plumes) and some of the ladies had
feather boas around their shoulders. When I first heard the
term "boa" (Mother didn't have one, but I was interested in
Mrs. Herty's) I thought instantly of a boa constrictor, and
imagined a great snake draped around Mrs. Herty's neck
choking the life out of her, but what she wore was of course
very light and soft. And how our choir *gave out:* when they
really got going on something like "Jerusalem the Golden"
the church seemed to rock. It gave me a strange, shiver-down-
the-spine feeling, and I pumped away with a will. They really
went about their business with a spirit hard to beat.

I know a lot of jokes are made about village choirs, but
you can take your vested outfits with opera-singer soloists
and parades and pomp and ceremony, and leave me ours!

At the Sunday evening service we didn't have any choir,
they got the night off, but not Mother and I. It was a strangely
moving little service, though, with not so many people as in
the morning, and only the small congregation to sing the
hymns. As a choral symphony it may have left something to
be desired, even though without the choir you could hear the
organ better. But it sort of got under your skin when the thin,
quavery voices sang—and Mother played softly—*"Abide
with Me, fast falls the eventide"* . . . while it was getting
twilight outside, and you knew that in a few minutes Grandpa
would speak the Benediction and everybody would go home
through the dark.

When we first went to Chapel Hill, there was only the
small reed organ, or a melodeon, inflated by foot pedals, in
the church, and Mother's feet did the work. I was too small
for pumping, anyhow. I was as excited as everybody else, however, when the new pipe organ was discussed (which it was
for a long time at my house) and finally financed and ordered,
and I awaited its arrival and installation with much enthu-

siasm. Mother was very proud of it, and when she got hold of
the new organ—if I do say it—she pulled a mean stop.

The organ, with the choir—which consisted of three
short benches at right angles to and in front of the organ—
was in one corner flanking the chancel. Mars' Phil sang bass
and Mars' Pike sang tenor. When Grandpa stood at the lec-
tern, fashioned of a wonderfully carved eagle with spread
wings holding up the big Bible, and which was on that side of
the chancel, they could all have reached out and touched each
other if they had wanted to. Nobody could touch me, though,
back behind the organ.

Even Duke attended services, when he could. Dogs, even
to this day, wander in and out at public functions in Chapel
Hill, such as church, formal receptions and football games—
they are accepted as part of the routine life of the village—
and Duke, even though on Sundays we shut him up at home
to guard against it, would sometimes get out and follow us.
If it was in the winter he would wait outside in the cold,
scratching at the door occasionally, but if it was in warm
weather and the doors were open he usually made a beeline
for the chancel, where he would join Grandpa, and with
tongue lolling out and tail wagging, gaze up at him lovingly.
Grandpa, naturally, never paid him any heed (except once
when Grandpa absent-mindedly reached down and patted his
head) and he would finally lie down and go to sleep against
the eagle. It would have been frightful if the trick I told you
about had ever occurred to him in church and he had started
weaving in and out between Grandpa's feet, but a certain sense
of propriety, I guess, held him back. Also Grandpa's long
surplice and cassock may have given him pause.

When sermon time came, I could come out of my cubbyhole and scrouge in by Mars' Phil in the corner of the last
pew. This afforded a certain advantage and was the only thing
I really liked about my work; whereas in church you generally

saw only the backs of other people's heads, up front in the
choir you saw their faces and kept tab on everything that went
on, whether it was a fly on Judge MacRae's bald head or Dr.
Battle taking a little nap, or Mrs. Venable doing an interesting pantomime as she silently reproved the Venable twins for
something. Also, being up front, and helping to run the show,
as it were, gave you a certain feeling of importance and responsibility.

Grandpa's preaching, like everything about him, was
quiet and gentle. I believe he must have made allowances for
sin, because his sermons had to do mostly with love and goodness. He seemed to think that most people are good, or try to
be, and that if you do somehow get involved in a little sin,
maybe a combination of circumstances beyond your control
was partly responsible, and the temptation was too great; that
you yourself were perhaps not so all-fired wicked, and you
mustn't feel discouraged. All you had to do was rise up in your
strength and slap sin down and throw it out the door. Sin was
not your natural habiliment, and if you got messed up with it,
it was very easy to shed. He gave you the impression that the
devil didn't stand a chance, really. He made you feel that the
devil was only an offensive stranger, who came up and tried to
butt into your business, and that you didn't have to have anything to do with him, unless you wanted to. Anyway, he didn't
shout and wave his arms and threaten you with damnation
and the fires of hell. You never felt frightened when you listened to him, but warm and better, and sure that everything
was going to be all right. His parishioners must have thought
a lot of him, because there is a beautiful stone cloister now, in
his memory, connecting the little old chapel with the fine new
church erected later.

Two services on Sunday, one on Wednesday night, and
choir practice on Thursday (what a session that was!) made
for a full week for me and all of us. Seemed as though I hardly

got through one spot of pumping before I had to start another! In addition to these fixed dates we played many extra
performances such as weddings, christenings, etc. Lent was a
time of horror for me, not only because of the sweets and
pleasures given up, and the endless pumping, but also because
practically every cent of my small allowance, and much of
what I got in various ways outside, must go into my pyramid-
shaped mite box to help the Heathen Chinee, and all. I used
to look at that mite box, and pick it up and shake it, and wonder what the Chinaman who would get it would spend the
money for. I used to see him tearing it open, my money spill-
ing out into his hand. . . . It was quite a good feeling, however, to have it so heavy with nickels and dimes and pennies
when Easter finally came and found me broke and arm-weary
and wishing the organ at the bottom of the sea. But somehow
I held on and stayed in there and pitched, or rather pumped. I
held my position for a long time, mind you, so long that I
have no wish to pump an organ ever again, or to be identified
with an organ to the extent of joining the Ex-Organ Pumpers
Association, or whatever they call the society which keeps the
sport alive. Comparative amateurs, I bet you, the most of them.

In the beginning, when I was very young and before my
organ-pumping days began, I got off to a bad start insofar as
the forms of the church were concerned. I had just accepted
the big words and the ceremonious and stilted phraseology of
the prayers and psalms and supplications as so much unintel-
ligible gibberish, which had a meaning, I supposed, but which
could be mumbled phonetically and got away with. And then
one day a sequence of words which Grandpa used formed and
impressed themselves upon my mind in horrifying clarity. In
the Lord's Prayer Grandpa, using the old-fashioned pronun-
ciation of the past tense as a separate syllable, would say
"Hallow-ed be Thy Name." To my untutored ear this came
as "Hello, Ed be Thy Name," and I felt quite confused and

shocked. It seemed to me that Grandpa must be addressing God by his first name, which was Ed, and even though I was very small I had sense enough to feel that this familiarity was not at all the proper approach. I hadn't even known that God had a first name, let alone that anybody could call him by it. On the other hand, if Grandpa did it, it was all right. After all, he had known God for a long time. But I couldn't help worrying about it a little, 'though I never said anything about it, and I was greatly relieved later on when the truth finally dawned on me.

Sunday School was all I could manage, too. My class was taught by a sweet and enthusiastic lady named Mrs. Webb (she was Jack Cranmer's grandmother), who, for all her sweetness and charity, was a stern taskmistress and one to put up with no foolishness. I was thrown in with the two (older) MacRae cousins, Duncan and Don (big and superior; smart, too), to learn and recite not only the Creed and the Catechism, which were long and difficult, but every Sunday's Collect, to boot. The learning of these I naturally forgot or postponed as long as possible, and Saturday night came to be a dreaded time. Sometimes I would have to get up early Sunday morning and study until I felt myself letter-perfect and equipped to face Mrs. Webb. I found that I could not recite if I happened to meet the coldly calculating gaze of either Duncan or Don MacRae, and so I would spout out the words with my eyes tightly closed. With all that training, how I could ever have turned out the way I did is something hard to understand.

My religious life at home was just as rugged. The day began, right after breakfast, with family prayers in Grandpa's study. (Duke was always welcome at this ceremony, and no questions asked.) During the school year we had breakfast extra early so I wouldn't have to miss prayers. The day ended the same way at bedtime. I can still see very clearly the design in the faded green rug in Grandpa's study where my eyes rested twice a day when we were on our knees praying. Grandpa would read a psalm and then we all knelt down while he prayed, and then said Amen when he finished and we could get up. You weren't quite through then, either, as the final act before blowing out the light was to say your own private Now I Lay Me. But you always went to sleep with the feeling that you were being safely held in the hollow of God's hand, and that God was wide awake and well able to take care of anything that might come up during the night.

Much of Grandpa's work, necessarily, was with the students, those theologically minded and others who might have gone to the dogs without him. Episcopal students, that is. The Methodist and Baptist preachers, and the others, were supposed to look after their own black sheep, and entertain their own white ones. But denomination didn't seem to make any difference to Grandpa, and if he liked anybody, right away he wanted to give him food, for the stomach or the soul. He was just as apt to bring a Unitarian home to supper as not.

Suppers and Sunday dinners were always a gamble for me. At the very last minute Grandpa might show up with some big ox of a football player, or an undernourished Bible student, to share our meal. This always meant slim pickings for me. Sunday night suppers were the worst. These Sunday night suppers Mother fixed herself, Viola having got off right after dinner, and they were usually pretty light affairs, even at best. We had our Sunday night suppers at six o'clock. This early hour not only resulted in the meal's being a very light one, as it followed so closely on the heels of the heavy midday dinner, but it also enabled us to get to the church for the evening service without getting in a swivet, as Mother said. And six o'clock meant six o'clock. As the hour approached Mother became more and more efficient, banging things around in the kitchen and adding last minute touches to the supper table.

"Draw me a bucket of water from the well, please, Sonny—
and hurry," she would say, and I'd dash outside and turn the
heavy windlass until the dripping oak bucket bumped against
the well cover, or "Sonny, run to the front door and see if
you can see Grandpa coming," as she took the muffins from
the oven. And there would be Grandpa coming down the walk,
for he was ever one for punctuality. And almost always, it
seemed to me, there would be a student with him. Maybe not
almost always, but far too often, anyway. The two of them
would come in and stand in the door, the student grinning
foolishly (darn his hide! I · would think viciously) and
Grandpa would say, "Alice, this is Mr.—uh,—Mr.—uh," and
the student would say, "Entwhistle," or something. "Oh, yes,
Mr. Entwhistle," Grandpa would finish up, "He's come to
have a bite of supper with us." And Mother would beam, and
say so cordially, "Why, of *course;* how *nice!* Come right in,
Mr. Entwhistle, supper's all ready." Oh, hell, I would have
thought had I dared.

The highlight of our Sunday evening repast generally
consisted of these hot corn muffins, two for Mother, one for
Grandpa, and three for me, as our muffin tins held only six. A
second tin was divided between my uncles, if they were there
(if their names were in the pot, as Mother said). This was
ample, for the family, but with one of Grandpa's unexpected
guests added Mother and I were left holding the bag, Grandpa
oblivious to what was going on. But well Mother and I knew
what self-denial hospitality demanded of us. Both Mother's
muffins disappeared down the guest's gullet, as did also all but
one of mine. "Have another muffin, Mr. Entwhistle," Mother
would say graciously, and to me, as she gave me a little kick
under the table, "Sonny, wouldn't you like some nice light
bread [or some nice cold pone, as the case might be] with
some nice watermelon rind preserves?" (Our pantry was

stacked up with watermelon rind preserves, a delicacy highly esteemed by some people who were not practically weaned and brought up on them.)

In this connection, I would like to point out that excessive organ pumping is not the only thing in which I hold some sort of record; I have probably eaten, in my time, more watermelon rind preserves than any man living. If there was one thing that was plentiful, one thing of which there was a surplus, one thing with which the market was glutted, it was watermelon rind. Except for the sugar, which was cheap, the preserves cost nothing and they were easy to make, and our pantry shelves groaned with them. I don't believe Mother could have borne seeing a piece of watermelon rind wasted or thrown away. A fanatical light would come in her eye, and you knew while you were eating the watermelon that Mother was already inwardly gloating over the fine new batch of preserves she could put up. I ate the sickly sweetish things until they were running out of my ears and I halfway expected to grow a watermelon, à la the rabbit tail. I think, now, with a sort of affection, of the big, bubbling pot on the kitchen range, and the rows of sealed and shining jars on the pantry shelves. But I have an intense antipathy, long developed, toward the idea of ever eating any more watermelon rind preserves. Like organ pumping, I had my fill long ago.

Oh, well, it was all in a good cause, even if sometimes on Sunday night I rebelled and couldn't take it, and did my pumping on an empty stomach.

When I entered the door of that little church, after thirty years, I could hardly believe my eyes; it was just the same as I remembered. The eagle, the organ, the plain little dark wood altar, the shabby carpet and the same narrow pews with their thin, worn cushions. Only the church itself seemed so tiny, not the huge, humbling place it had been. The little font was

there, and the rickety steps to the belfry, and the bell rope.
And there *they* all were, up front in the chancel and the choir,
those dear ghosts.

I had a lump in my throat the size of a baseball. It was
only when I climbed in back of the little organ, its once rosy
painted pipes faded and listing a little, that I realized how long
ago it all was . . . the pump handle wasn't there, and the
organ had been electrified.

CHAPTER EIGHTEEN

Love smote me unexpectedly when I was ten years old. It happened on a summer night, soft and warm and moonless, beside Mrs. MacRae's joggleboard.

Up to that time I had moved happily in a strictly masculine society, experiencing little contact with the opposite sex, except of course my mother and my great-aunts and a couple of female cousins in Charlottesville, who, strictly speaking, didn't count. There were a few girls, too, among my acquaintances in Chapel Hill, whom it was difficult to avoid at times, but they seemed almost nonexistent, they appeared to be of little consequence, with no real place in the world, and we boys paid them little heed. Practically everybody had only men-children, in most cases two or three or them. Just why this was I have never even wondered until this minute. Perhaps it was nature's way of preparing for 1917. As exceptions which proved the rule, there were two little Wilson girls, and no Wilson boys; the Venables had two daughters, also—and then much later, still a third, a great and stirring event in the community and the Venables' house—but they more than atoned for this by their strenuous boy twins. On the long block which constituted most of Downtown, and on which lived the bulk of my intimates, there were two Cobb boys, two Bruners,

two Hertys, two Venables, two Holmeses and one Abernathy.
In only one or two instances were these supplemented by baby
sisters. A trifle farther away were two Tenny and three Strowd
boys, sisterless. I had had a brother, too, and there was my little sister, Patty, but they had both died when I was very small,
and I labored under that only child handicap. People seem to
think that an only child gets spoiled through a lot of petting
and stuff, but I think an only child gets the dirty end of the
stick because he has to bear the brunt of everything and there
is no one to help him with the chores.

Even the student body at the University was almost
entirely male, and had been from the beginning. Only a few
years before, the University—upsetting its long-time masculine tradition—had opened its doors to women. The women
were very slow to respond, possibly preferring their secure
and established place in the home. (This was very popular,
then.) The girls seemed loath to take advantage of the opportunity afforded to explore the mysteries of higher education,
and snuggled down the deeper in their feminine retirement,
perfecting their domestic accomplishments and modestly
counting up their beaux and their dance programs. Girls were
sought after in those days, if you needed them; you weren't
tripping over them every time you turned around. Why, I
even remember when it wasn't considered very good taste for
a lady to have her name appear in print . . .

Only now and then did a girl student muscle in to disturb
the male serenity of the University. The professors would
never call their names in class rolls, because they knew that
the girls, or rather the girl, might not wish her name spoken
out that way in a room full of boys; and the boys always allowed her a bench all to herself, shunning her as though she
were a leper. It took a brave boy to sit by a coed. Today, of
course, all that is changed, and many hundreds of pretty girls
adorn the Campus, and brighten up a lot of corners. Other

hundreds, not so pretty, are there for more practical purposes. But I grew up in a forest of trouser legs.

I had no aversion to girls as such. It was simply that my life was so full of so many satisfactory things that there was no room for or need of girls. I hardly knew, in fact, that there were girls. That is, until Virginia Taylor came, that summer, and for a brief period changed and glorified and ruined my life.

Love struck me suddenly, viciously, without warning, and in one lightning flash I was bound and helpless. This has happened before to men too happy in their bachelorhood. She came, with her mother, from Away, and as has also happened many times before, the local boys cast their sheeps' eyes at her and left the local girls swinging alone on their own front gates.

I had gone with my mother one evening to Mrs. Mac-Rae's. Mrs. MacRae ran one of the village's most popular boardinghouses (I believe they called it "taking guests," however) and in the summers, when her student roomers were away, her big, rambling house was likely to be filled with people from all over, because Chapel Hill was not quite so hot as some other places in North Carolina. In fact, the people who lived in the torrid heat of the flat "Eastern Part of the State" considered Chapel Hill a summer resort. Mrs. MacRae and my mother were very close friends and co-workers, of course, in the choir and the Women's Auxiliary, and visited back and forth. Mother sometimes took me along, particularly if it was after dark, partly I think as escort and partly that she might have no doubt of my whereabouts and doings.

I remember that evening in the MacRaes' big yard, shadowy and mysterious under the trees. I remember the laughter and chatter and waving fans and the dim white dresses of the ladies in the hickory chairs, and then Mrs. MacRae's voice, ". . . and this is Virginia, Mrs. Taylor's little girl. Why don't you two run and play?" and the agony

of awkwardness that overcame me. I think that I said not
one word during all the time I sat on the joggle-board beside her. I was extremely uncomfortable. I don't remember
that she said anything, either. She was a presence, that was
all. I am sure I did not look at her face, and anyway it was
dark. I was only aware, dumbly, that she had long, pale-
gold curls, and long, slim, black-stockinged legs, and a frilly,
starchy white dress, and that she smelled terribly, terribly
sweet. Totally unlike my boy friends. I think I must have
feigned indifference to her, and interest in the joggle-board's
bouncing, for after a while she rose and moved away in the
dark. Afterward, on the way home, Mother asked me if I
was nice to Virginia ("She's a real pretty little girl") and
I said yessum. But I was tormented by the fear that Virginia
thought me a lout, which she probably did, and in a way I
hated her. I couldn't put her out of my mind.

In the days that followed I suffered. I recall going by
Mrs. MacRae's on any and every possible pretext, usually
on the far side of the street, however, where my faint heart
drove me. Two or three evenings we boys just happened to
drift around and play Wolf, or Run, Sheep, Run in Mrs. Mac-
Rae's yard, for I was not the only one smitten. Virginia
joined in the games, of course, but boylike we ignored her
or pretended to. At times I saw her at long range uptown, but
panic came and I went no nearer. Once I slammed head-on
into her and her mother, coming out of the drugstore, and
in my confusion mumbled something and brushed by. My
emotions choked me and I bled inside. I can still hear Mrs.
Taylor's cheerful greeting.

I resorted to love songs, the few I knew, and when sure
I was alone hummed passionately "When the Robin Nests
Again" and "When You Were Sweet Sixteen" and "You
are the Ideal of my Dreams"; anything that had sweetheart
or I love you in it. I sat out back of the woodhouse or in the

chicken yard and mooned about her and in my fancy wrote her the most flowery love letters.

This period of torture could have lasted no longer than a week, but my condition was becoming critical when on a Friday afternoon I happened to overhear my mother casually remark that she was sorry Mrs. Taylor was going home. *Going Home* . . . somehow I had not faced that dreadful eventuality, and now here it was. The reason I know that it was Friday is that I was quite penniless, my bank empty except for my lucky piece, a big copper penny, and having just bought my bicycle, my savings account was gone, too. My weekly "allowance" of twenty-five cents was not due until the next day, and my love was leaving town. I could not ask my mother to advance the twenty-five cents without an explanation, and I felt I'd rather die than admit what was in my mind. But I was desperate. Faster than ever I went on an errand before, I raced uptown to the express office and Mars' Phil. And Mars' Phil lent me the money. He was a man, Mars' Phil was, and man to man that transaction was made. I merely asked him, my heart in my miserable eyes and my voice, I guess, could he lend me a quarter 'til tomorrow, and with never a question he said he reckoned he could. What a great man, what a kind man, what a bulwark in a stressful time! In my overwhelming relief I never thought to thank him.

With the quarter in my fist and music in my ears I sped to Mr. Eubanks' Drug Store and possessed myself of a long, slim box of chocolate mints, just the thing, I knew, to win a lady's heart, even at the last moment. I could hardly wait while Mr. Eubanks tied up the little package, and I ignored his remark that I was spending my money like a drunken sailor. My feet scarce touched the ground on the way to Mrs. MacRae's—and suddenly I stood before the door behind which was She.

My knees began to buckle then, but I knocked. The porch was empty and the house was still, deadly quiet, it seemed to me. It was ladies' nap time, and a sacred hour, but I hadn't stopped to consider that. Finally Mrs. MacRae's black Mary answered, wiping her hands on her apron, and regarded me with disfavor and suspicion, chewing her snuff stick the while.

With my last puff of breath and my last atom of courage I blurted, "Miss Virginia Taylor . . . is she home?"

" 'At li'l Virginia?" Mary inquired. "Naw, she ain't hyah. She'n her mother dey gone back to Po'tsmouth—lef' dis mawnin'."

That was the end, for me, of Virginia Taylor in the flesh, and I think I have never heard her name spoken since except in my own whisper. But in spirit she never went home, and after that first shocked minute when I felt so sick in my stomach and my heart, I hugged her to my bosom. She has been there ever since. For more than forty years, off and on, man and boy, I have thought of her—although I never saw her. When I stood before her, so long ago, I could not raise my eyes. All I know for sure is that her long black legs were beautiful and her dress was white and crisp; where her face should be there is a blank space in my memory, framed by the long gold curls which smelled so sweet and clean.

I hid the box of candy in the bottom of a drawer, and for a long time I would take it out every now and then and turn it over in my hands and look at it, and then one day I opened it and ate the mints.

CHAPTER NINETEEN

C HARLOTTESVILLE, Vir-
ginia, is one of the two hottest places (on earth). The other
is New Guinea. Also, being in the mountains, it can be
brutally cold in winter. It is situated in gorgeous country
kindest to apples and foxes, and except for its beauty not a
fit habitation for man. Old Tom Jefferson, its patron saint,
must have been a tough and hardy soul to build his famous
University there, and Monticello, his stately and beautiful
home. I have frozen and fried in Charlottesville. I have encountered frostbite and second degree sunburn. I have heard
tell that the man who invented the pressure cooker was a
native, and that the gent who thought up the deep freeze had
lived there for a while.

If we ever went anywhere in the summer, Mother and
I, it was to Charlottesville. Charlottesville, anyway, would
be included in the itinerary, the other ports of call being
Richmond and "Summer Rest" at Greenwood, up in Albemarle County, which I shall tell you about when I can get to
it. There were many practical reasons for these trips to Charlottesville, most of them of a family or intimate nature.

To begin with, when it was decided to go someplace, and
the date tentatively fixed, Dad would apply to the Southern
Railway for passes. When the passes arrived, some weeks

later, it was most stimulating, and we knew, then, that we were going. Dad said that it took so long to get the passes because of the red tape, and I never got over the expectancy of seeing the passes arrive all bound up with long strings of it. These railroad passes were impressive and beautiful documents, of varied design and size, but always signed with a stamped and illegible signature over "Assistant General Traffic Superintendent," or some such resounding title, and gave the right of way to and from a specified destination, for ninety days, to Mrs. Rob't. W. Prince and son. Seeing the "and son" in print, and knowing it meant me and nobody else, made me feel important, as though I were an honored guest of the railroad whom they were happy to accommodate.

Charlottesville could be reached from Chapel Hill by a tortuous route, involving some stirring connection-making and train-changing, via the Southern itself. It was fortunate that this was so, as it was of course much easier to secure passes on one's own railroad than on any other, Dad said. Of course the other railroads would extend, or rather exchange this courtesy, if sufficiently pressed, though sometimes they seemed to be a trifle reluctant and dilatory about coming through. Dad said he guessed your Request for Transportation (that's what he called it) had to reach the desk of the Assistant General Traffic Superintendent of the other railroad some morning when he was feeling good and his wife had given him a fine breakfast, otherwise he might throw your application in his big scrap basket. "But how can you tell?" I asked him.

"Can't," said Dad, "you just have to take a chance."

The Assistant General Traffic Superintendents must have been uniformly good-natured and well-fed men, however, for sooner or later these other railroad passes always came, and we rode on new and exotic lines like the C. & O., or the Richmond, Fredericksburg & Potomac, or the Nor-

folk & Western the time we went to the Jamestown Expo-
sition in 1907 (that was when I heard Teddy Roosevelt make
a speech; he was 'way across the parade ground, but I could
see his teeth and hear a lot of shouting. I remember much
more clearly Buffalo Bill, whom we saw at the same time,
and his Wild West Show; I saw Annie Oakley, too. I guess
I saw her even before Ethel Merman did. The Attack on the
Wagon Train was very exciting, and the Custer picture come
to life!).

I remember that I was particularly anxious, at one
period, to ride on the Union Pacific, having read about the
driving of the Golden Spike and seen a picture of the ceremony which showed soldiers and gentlemen in silk hats and
feathered Indians standing around in harmony and brother-
hood. Two of the silk-hatted gentlemen had sledge hammers in their hands, and this presented an interesting anomaly
to me, as I had never seen track laborers thus arrayed. I always pictured the necessary work (maintenance of the right
of way, Dad said was the correct term) on the Union Pacific
as done that way. But Dad said getting passes from them
would be difficult, and even if we did they were too far
away for us to get to, and that the picture represented things
as they were a long time ago, and that it wasn't that way now,
at all. There was really very little to see on the Union Pacific
nowadays, he said. So I had to give the idea up. But anyway, way back there, there was no railroad anywhere could
compare with the Southern. There was something about it
. . . and it was our own.

The C. & O. went to Charlottesville, too, and its sta-
tions in those days were painted a violent yellow, a sort of
rancid butter shade, with the trains to match. You couldn't
miss seeing either of them; there was nothing drab about the
C. & O.

Piedmont, the family place we visited in Charlottesville,

was only a long block up the hill from the C. & O. station, and it was fine to hang on the fence there, in your own back yard, as it were, and watch the yellow trains come in. The first real sidewalk I ever remember, made of bumpy black asphalt, burning hot to my bare feet, led down to the station.

Piedmont was built early in the nineteenth century, a big and gracious Georgian house of rosy brick, with a hip roof and four chimneys, and a great center hall. Even when I knew it the old house was a little shabby, but mellow and easy in its down-at-heelness, brooding drowsily upon its better days. After the rickety rectory with its low ceilings and small rooms, and its atmosphere of piety and frugality, Piedmont always seemed a vast and dim palace to me, filled with heavy mahogany and silver and antimacassars and dark portraits and candlesticks and whatnots. Across the front hall from the casual and lived-in sitting room (behind which was Aunt Lucy's bedroom and domain) was the large and sacred parlor. It was seldom entered, by me, anyhow, and to this day remains in my memory dark and unexplored, a sombre place where I tripped over rugs and stumped my toes on the projecting feet of big, horsehair-covered mahogany sofas, which were slippery and difficult to stay put upon, while shadowy and mysterious late Meade ancestors and connections glowered down at me from the walls. There was a round center table (it was cherry, and Aunt Lucy's pride) covered with a looped and fringed red thing upon which rested a tall and ornate lamp, a big black Bible, and various intriguing articles (including a glass slipper like Cinderella's) which I was told were "curios now don't touch them." The shutters were kept closed in the parlor until the minister came to call, or other company who rated being entertained there, when one or two of the blinds would be prudently opened, to be immediately closed upon the guest's departure, and I remember the darkness and the musty smell of the big room when I was occasionally allowed to enter it with Fanny, my cousin, for her piano practice. She would open a window by the upright piano and adjust the stool. She would always have to adjust the stool because I would always beat her to it, while she was fixing the window, and jump on it and propel myself around. Then when she had it back to its correct height, she would carefully and sedately sit upon it, arranging her skirts just so. She would open the keyboard and begin to play, while I would sit there and watch the street as she ran scales and thumped out *Hearts and Flowers* and Mozart's *Minuet*. Sometimes Aunt Minnie, who was her music teacher, would come in and stand beside her and beat time. When the hour was up she would say "There!" and carefully close the piano again, and then the window and the shutters, and we would go back into the house, closing the parlor door behind us.

Upstairs, reached by a narrow stairway, steep and dark, in the rear of the house, the bedrooms were huge and high, with fat pincushions and flowered washstand sets, and ruffled curtains at the windows, and framed mottoes on the walls, and huge and high four-poster beds which one attained by means of wooden steps from the matting-covered floor. These steps were pushed back under the bed when not in use, alongside the trundle. (Children, when jokingly censured, were called little Trundle Bed Trash.) The rooms, upstairs and down, in addition to all their interesting clutter, seemed always filled, too, with chattering old ladies in rustling black taffeta—my maiden Great-aunts Lucy and Mary and Margaret and Harriet. Never have I known of such perversion of such beautiful names as theirs, the last three being called respectively Mamie, Minnie and Hallie. I always associated Aunt Hallie with the mocking bird song, and felt sure that if she died there would be a mocking bird singing o'er her grave. I wouldn't be surprised if this turned out to be a fact.

She was plump and jolly, the youngest of these four sisters
of my grandfather's. Only slightly older was Aunt Margaret ("Minnie"), small and gay and birdlike. These two were
inseparable, and were known as The Girls, or Minnie 'n'
Hallie. Every now and then they would kick over the traces
and appear in soft and cool white organdy dresses, Summer
Things, they called them, instead of the eternal black taffeta.
I used to like to see them like that; it seemed to take them out
of the Old Lady class. My Aunt Mary was tall and thin, and
sharp of eye and feature, but her grim face could break into
a heavenly smile. At such times she was almost pretty. Mamie
was all right . . . The eldest, and the boss, was tiny,
dried-up Aunt Lucy. I remember her, in the mornings, her
sparse gray hair in curl papers sticking out around her
wrinkled little face, bustling about and tailed by a colored girl,
with a great bunch of keys which she wore at her belt or
carried in a wicker basket, unlocking pantries and closets and
drawers, getting out the day's provisions or the silver which
she carefully counted and locked up every night. She always
talked to herself, low and soft, while she did this. I remember her, too, at the head of the dining room table, almost hidden behind a lot of silver things over which she presided.

The four sisters had lived their lives in Piedmont. My
great-grandfather, from whom they had inherited the place,
was an Old Buzzard. I know this to be a fact because I once
overheard Mars' Phil say so to my mother, and of course I was
enormously interested, craving details. Seems the Old Buzzard had tied them down to the place through some pro-
vision in his will whereby if even one of them got married
they'd lose the house. Young men who had come a-courting
were gently discouraged by the sisters, and there they had
waxed and waned into resigned spinsterhood keeping a roof
over each others' heads. They were a happy family, though.
My Cousin Fanny, their niece—a few years older than I—

lived with them and they worshiped her; they had taken her
as their own at the time her mother died, when she was tiny.
Fanny was a quiet, gentle girl, but pretty as could be, with
lots of blond hair and very pink cheeks. I liked her very much.
("When she gets away from Piedmont," I heard my father
say, "she's going to break some hearts!" I looked at Fanny
with added respect and interest after I heard this.)

Uncle Bob, the man of the house—small, gray, ruddy,
and always laughing—was seldom around, and he was mysterious to me because I saw so little of him. He was up and
gone to work in the mornings when the rest of us sat down
to breakfast, and often did not come in until late at night.
When he didn't show up for supper Aunt Lucy would always
say, "Robert must be detained at The Mill." This was an old
stone, and vine-covered, woolen mill, down the river, which
for generations had manufactured heavy cadet-gray woolen
cloth. I was told that the stuff for the V.M.I. and West Point
uniforms came from there, as it had long ago for the Confederate Armies. Uncle Bob was a bookkeeper, and had spent
his life, a bachelor, on a high stool at The Mill. It meant as
much to him as the Southern Railroad did to my father. He
had glittering blue eyes and long and gray walrus mustaches.
His face was very alive and attractive. I am pretty sure he
could not always have been detained at The Mill, and from
somewhere I recall a vague something about poker games.
(I used to pick up a lot of stuff, here and there.) He must
have spent a somewhat lonely and monastic existence as the
protector and representative of his four old-maid sisters, and
when he died, a martyr, in the carved four-poster bed in the
front bedroom, they found many empty Bourbon bottles in
his secret hiding places. People in Charlottesville felt mighty
badly, they say, when Uncle Bob passed on.

The old ladies seldom, if ever, got away from Charlottesville, although Aunt Lucy, when she was a girl, had

been to Louisville. Just why this trip was necessary I do not know, but it was the great adventure of her life, and she recounted it whenever possible. Always when the talk was of travel, or even when the conversation lagged, Aunt Lucy would chip in with "When I went to Louisville . . ." A little later when I read about Daniel Boone I thought of Aunt Lucy. It seemed to me they must have had a lot in common, hacking their way through the wilderness to Kentucky, 'way back yonder. It occurred to me that she might well have gone with him, or at least have known him, and once I asked her about it, just on the chance, but she laughed and said No, she had never met the gentleman, and that she had gone to Louisville on the steam cyars. Nowadays, of courses, trips to far places are nothing out of the ordinary, and—particularly in recent years—millions of young Americans have gone easily and quickly to the ends of the earth, but in Aunt Lucy's day a trip to Louisville must have been quite an expedition, and it stayed forever fresh in her mind.

The Misses Meades' Female Institute, which the sisters had conducted for the most of their lives, was justly famous and respected, and many young ladies of Albemarle and Orange learned a little Latin and Greek and mathematics and music, and much of manners and the Scriptures, within those walls. My mother was an alumna of the Institute, as were many of the ladies in Charlottesville whom we knew. The school was highly recommended by the church, and many of the clergy sent their decorous daughters there for a little polishing.

The house stood close to the street on a corner, with a big, shady lawn behind it. There was a stout board fence all around this lawn, so that the young ladies might frolic, at recess time, in perfect safety and seclusion. There was a side entrance for the students of the Institute, and the fact that the house had two entrances of almost equal importance

gave it added grandeur in my eyes. I used to like to go out
one door and slip around the corner to come in the other.
Across the rear of the house was a large schoolroom (always
shuttered and empty when I saw it in the summers) and
classrooms below it in the basement. The big, cool dining
room was in the basement, too, with eye-level windows looking across the side yard to the horse chestnut tree.

Food at Piedmont was something I still dream about.
Where it all came from I don't believe anybody quite knows.
"The Lord will provide," said Aunt Lucy, and the Lord sure
did. Spoon bread, Sally Lunn, waffles, muffins and hot rolls,
all these you might meet at a single breakfast, or so my drooling recollection is. And Virginia ham and bacon and kidney
stew, and marmalade and jams and jellies and preserves. . . .
(But no watermelon rind at Piedmont, ever!) All the old
ladies had a sweet tooth, and the desserts were just plain out
of this world. (Each one kept bags of peppermint and lemon
drops, or horehound, in a bureau drawer, too.) God knows
they were poor as church mice, but the table they set groaned
with the fat of the land. I usually left the table feeling a little
groggy and uncommunicative, and as though I would like
to go somewhere and lie down. "Come back and fold your
napkin," Mother would call, and it was an effort to return
and fold and roll the napkin and put it in the ring which
was mine. It was dangerous, too, for there might be a tart,
or a piece of cake, or a bit of sillabub remaining on the table
which I had not noticed. "That boy's got hollow legs, Alice,"
Uncle Bob would laugh, if he were there, "yes, sir, he's got
hollow legs as sure as gun's iron." My plump limbs were
not hollow, I was sure, but still it was a trifle peculiar where
all the food went.

The other side yard, on the opposite side of the house,
screened by walls and evergreens, contained the well and the
outside kitchen where old (colored) Aunt Agnes ruled and

had her way. I was scared of Aunt Agnes, and I would quietly scuttle out of the way when I saw her or heard her coming, as she would have no truck with any small boy fry such as I. She adored Fanny, however, whose "Mammy" she had been. She was big and angular and jutting-jawed, her lower lip sticking out like a shelf, and her white caps and aprons were always snowy and starched as stiff as boards, and her many skirts and petticoats stood out as she lumbered around. She and her helpers lived over the kitchen.

In deference, no doubt, to the modesty of the young ladies of the Institute, the privy—way down in the far corner of the big back yard—seemed unusually far away. It was reached by a long, whitewashed plank corridor, whose pristine walls, I thought, would certainly have been an opportune and fertile field for inscription had the school been for nasty little boys instead of properly brought up and high-minded young ladies. One felt vaguely uncomfortable upon reaching this clean and remote privy, and never tarried long.

Even when I was small, the residential part of the sleepy and slow-moving town had left the old house behind. There were one or two nice places still adjoining, such as Mr. Keller-the-jeweler's, but across the street on one corner was a livery and sales stable, a delightful place, and on the other a printing shop. Both of these enterprises afforded me vast enjoyment, however. Fact is, I thought Piedmont's location ideal, what with the adjacent C. & O. Railroad Station, and the Armory of the Monticello Guards just a half block up the street. From our eminence one looked down across the C. & O. tracks and the narrow little river which ran alongside, to a little plateau which was the circus grounds, and then up the mountain to Monticello. And the trolley tracks were down by the C. & O. Station, too.

I passed by Piedmont not long ago, and remembered all these things. It was always a kind house, and now it shelters orphans. There is a startling structure, a kind of chute, built on the outside wall, down which the orphans can slide to safety in case the old house catches fire.

There was always something doing; Aunt Minnie 'n' Hallie saw to that. Ultimate in stimulation (so refreshing, my mother said) was the long, cool trolley ride, of a summer's evening, to Fry's Spring. Fry's Spring was a sort of picnic ground, a few miles from town, with tables and benches under the trees, and a spring whose waters were good for you, because they contained iron. One was supposed, immediately upon arrival at Fry's Spring, to drink all of this water he could hold. I was always a little skeptical, however, for fear I might begin suddenly to stiffen up. There was a decayed bandstand and a dancing pavilion where people waltzed and two-stepped and the kids stumbled awkwardly around. I believe it was described as an Amusement Park, and it made an objective for the bumpy trolley, which after all had to end somewhere. Mother and my aunts took turns "treating" to trips to Fry's Spring, which was also the only place to go, unless you went to the University and just stood around and looked at it ("Come off that grass, now") or went and saw the room where Edgar Allan Poe lived when he was a student. Whenever I saw that room I always looked around in the corners hoping the raven was still there, for Mother and my aunts started spouting the poem as soon as we arrived. The University had a museum, too, with some skeletons and stuffed things, which was more than we had in Chapel Hill. It wasn't such a bad place. But like ours, their University was deadish and empty in the summers; I'm sure it would have been better with people around. In front of the building which they call the Rotunda, and which Thomas Jefferson built, there was a balustrade with a tin or metal shield on the top to protect it, and this was covered by thousands of names and initials scratched on it. I took out my knife and put mine there, too, one day when my womenfolk were inside the Rotunda. I have always intended to go back and see if the initials are still there. One day we got a carriage from the livery stable across the street, and drove up to Monticello, where Mr. Jefferson lived and invented so many things.

When anybody "treated" to a trip to Fry's Spring it represented considerable outlay, as the trolley ride, round trip, cost ten cents, and there were so many of us. Well, not quite ten cents, either, as street car tickets could be purchased six for a quarter. My aunts spent a lot of time arguing about who owed who a street car ticket. I was always granted the inside-outside seat on one of the long cross-wise benches of the open trolley car. The rest of us usually filled up the balance of the bench. There was a heavy rail there to hold you in, of course, but I was endlessly admonished to keep all my arms and legs inside the car just in case another trolley passed us. When we came home, after drinking the water and listening to the band, and after Aunt Minnie 'n' Hallie had danced sedately together, and then with me, and after I had danced around once with Fanny—and then we'd all drunk more water—I invariably fell asleep, so Mother didn't have to worry so much about my getting dismembered by the passing streetcar.

Mr. Mathews' Candy & Ice Cream store made what we had in Chapel Hill look like snitz. Mr. Mathews was a colorless, dusty-looking little man; I always figured he had a slight coating of powdered sugar which had blown on him. His pièce de résistance was tutti-frutti ice cream, but his candy stock always left you wondering if you had bought the right thing and invested wisely.

In addition to the old standbys like kisses and caramels and gumdrops, there were jaw-breakers which changed color as you sucked them and you were forever taking them out of your mouth to see the new color and getting your hands sticky. There were all-day-suckers which didn't change color, but lasted beautifully. There were sour balls, and candy blackberries and peanut brittle, and lime and horehound drops and rock candy and peach stones and many others. I was never very keen for all this hard stuff—it got your mouth sore from sucking, and also the things lasted so long it postponed your trying something else. I preferred chewy, and to please my fastidious palate there were all kinds of licorice shapes, "Tar Babies," and Teddy bears, and whistles and rope and shoe strings and cigars (which came in chocolate, too, with white stuff inside, and on the tip to look like ash) and plugs of "chewing tobacco" complete to little metal tags, and little barrels and Boston baked beans which were scooped up out of a real little bean pot, and ninepins and little licorice men. There were little maple sugar men, too. Ah, the pure gastronomic ecstasy of a dissolving little maple sugar man! There were all-chocolate cigarettes or cigarettes made of white chewy with a chocolate tip. There were little yellow ears of corn, and "peanuts," which didn't have any particular flavor, only very sweet. Sometimes these were covered with raspberry, or something dark red, anyhow. There was wonderful nougat and Turkish delight and ju-ju paste dusted over with powdered sugar like Mr. Mathews. There were the little hard balls of many colors which came, if you had the dough, in glass pistols or locomotives or lanterns (these last were a great stock-in-trade of the news butchers on the trains, too). There was stick candy in endless variety, of course, and jelly beans and all sorts of flavored "drops." There were green and white and pink wintergreen leaves, and bars of honey comb, and the little mint hearts with mottoes on them —"Will You be my Sweetheart?", "Think of Me," "Oh, You Kid," "Go Way Back and Sit Down." There were little tied up bags of Assorted which had a prize inside, a tiny lead figure or a whistle or a bell, but these cost a nickel. What a time a small boy could have with a nickel . . . I shudder to think what a time he could have had with a dollar! As I see it from here, Mr. Mathews' candy store stands out in a blaze of shining glory.

Charlottesville had everything. Brown's Drug Store was wonderful for limeades, or if you had what it takes you could get ice cream sodas. They had what looked like marble on the floor, and they had even bigger colored urns in the window than Mr. Eubanks'. There were strips of fly paper, however, hanging around—and one day I got messed up in one of these, in my best white suit, too. Another time I knocked a bottle off the counter, and broke it. Mr. Brown wouldn't hear to Mother paying for it, said it was nothing but just a little old bottle of ipecac, but it was most embarrassing. "He's so clumsy, Mr. Brown," Mother said. But such commotions were as nothing compared with the hell I raised the day I sat down on the yellow jacket. It was an extra hot afternoon, and we had walked down to the drugstore, after the ladies had had their naps, to get a cool drink. It was a long, hot walk, but the ladies kept their fans going and touched their faces with their handkerchiefs, and we talked about the delights of Mr. Brown's soda fountain and discussed what we would have. When we got there our favorite table near the front window was empty, and we gratefully sank down anticipating the cool refreshment to come. But I sank down on a yellow jacket on the seat of the chair. My pants were skin tight, and the yellow jacket had no difficulty defending himself. I went straight up in the air, I guess, with an awful scream. All the ladies screamed, too, and Mr. Brown came running. He stepped on the crippled yellow jacket, which had become disengaged and fallen to the floor, and after the nature and location of my injury had been established, I had to go in the back room with Mr. Brown and take my pants down, and he put something on it.

The Armory of the Monticello Guards, the local militia company, was the scene of a weekly drill, and those evenings were thrilling times. You watched the calendar and made sure you wouldn't miss Drill Night. One had to sit, wriggling, on one's chair and watch the Guards march and wheel and halt and port arms and parade rest, and then, "At ease," mop their brows and puff.

A particular Guard whose name, God bless him, has gone along with so much else, used to save empty cartridge shells for me when they went to the rifle range, and by our visit's end I had quite a bagful which I valued no less than my life. Sometimes at the end of the drill the big doors would swing open and there would be shouts for everybody to get out of the way, and the Guards would march out the door and around the block. We always waited until they marched back in, and the ladies and the other onlookers would clap their hands.

"Summer Rest," at Greenwood, was where Uncle George and Aunt Edmonia spent their summers, away from the heat of Richmond, and as Greenwood was only some twenty or thirty miles from Charlottesville we always got on the train and went up there for a visit, too. I think they had owned the place once, and then sold it to one of the big Richmond churches, which turned it into a home and summer resort for Working Girls, Uncle George and Aunt "Monie" continuing to stay there, in the hot months, to run things. It was felt, then, that Working Girls, poor things, needed special protection and supervision, and a lot of missionary work was carried on among them. Those who not only worked but also belonged to the church, were sent up to Summer Rest for their one or two weeks' vacation, if they deserved it. The Working Girls, of course, included females of all ages. A fine, big, hotel-like house had recently been erected for their comfort, and this, in addition to the smaller

Old House, once occupied by Uncle George and Aunt Monie, housed some thirty girls at a time. Their board and keep was on the church.

Summer Rest was a beautiful spot, with great trees sheltering the houses, and rolling meadows surrounding—and the mountains all around. The Girls loved it. The principal diversion, beside sitting on the porch and rocking and waiting for mealtime, was to take walks, and there were many points of interest such as the Bat Cave, the Aquaduct and Lover's Leap. Most of the Working Girls turned out to be good hikers, and after a day of mountain climbing they would come in for supper and eat a meal a horse couldn't jump over. After dinner the "games" were played, Blind Man's Buff and Musical Chairs and Going to Jerusalem. The penalty for being caught or being "It" in one of these games was to get kissed, and this I resented as strongly as the next man would have done, and tried to avoid and wriggle out of it, but they would gang up on me. In fact, I didn't enjoy the preponderantly female element at Summer Rest, and as Uncle George was busy or preoccupied with his responsibility most of the time, smoking his meerschaum pipe and wearing his pith helmet, I enjoyed the society of Ike, the colored man of all work.

Ike was a living example of all the virtues, and many are the contented hours I have spent in his company, while he did everything from butchering pigs to shoeing horses. I used always to accompany him, and Laddie, the Collie, to bring the cows back from the far lot at night, and to the station whenever he had to go to the store or meet a new batch of girls arriving on the train from Richmond. It was always most interesting to look the new arrivals over. We packed them into the big carryall, which held eight or nine, and the city girls would gasp at the beauty of the mountains and the valley as we drove the two miles to Summer Rest. There were so *many* girls, however, it sort of got on my nerves, and I wondered if Uncle Bob felt the same way, entirely surrounded by females at Piedmont. I don't know what Uncle George, or I, would have done without Ike. My first horse-riding was done under Ike's supervision, in my younger years, my fat legs sticking straight out on the broad back of a big farm horse named Boy. Of course I would go on the tramps and hikes with the Girls, too—I didn't just sulk at home with Ike and Laddie—but I have always considered Ike the leading attraction of Summer Rest, and as soon as we would get there on our visits Ike was the first person I would greet.

Conditions were somewhat improved, however, when one summer a cousin of mine, a boy named Donald Powers, came to visit. We hit it off all right except that he was a Virginian and a little inclined to throw off on everything connected with North Carolina. He didn't seem to appreciate what I told him about Chapel Hill. We had a few arguments, and one battle, but after that we ignored the controversial subjects and palled around together.

Mr. Bruce's General Store, at the depot, reminded me of the little store at University Station, in that it was the only building other than the water tank adjacent to the station. But it was a much more complete and fascinating place than the store at University Station, and took a lot of investigation. Mr. Bruce was also the Post Master for Greenwood, and while his duties as such were not heavy he bore himself with official dignity. He had a fine stock of crackers and pickles, and of course all sorts of fruit. For that was a fruit country. Up on the side of the mountain, right by the station, and through which the tunnel passed, there was a small apple orchard of Albemarle Pippins which was known as Queen Victoria's Orchard, because for many years she was annually sent a barrel of the apples. It was assumed that she found them good, for each year she sent back for more, and the orchard was held sacred for her; it would have been quite a transgression to have eaten one of Queen Victoria's pippins.

Sometimes after supper Donald and I would walk the country roads to Mr. Bruce's post office for the late mail, and on one evening a very exciting thing occurred. We were always told very firmly that we must walk around the end of the mountain, on the road (the same mountain which boasted the Queen's Orchard) and never under any circumstances were we to try to walk through the tunnel. This seemed too bad, and a waste of effort, as the tunnel was only a short one and a cutoff which would have saved half a mile of trudging on the road, and one night temptation overcame us and we decided to take the short cut. Besides, it was getting dark and we wanted to get the mail and get on home. So into the gloom of the tunnel we went, as it was long past time for the late train, and we knew we were perfectly safe. But bless Pete, we hadn't gotten more than halfway through the tunnel when around the curve in our rear, and bearing down upon us, came the headlight of the train, the whistle blowing for the station! We lit out and ran as fast as ever we could, floundering from tie to tie in the dark, and scared speechless. I remember falling down once and scrambling up. We fully expected to be ground to bits under the awful wheels of the thundering locomotive, and terror gave wings to our feet. When we dashed safely out the far end we fell on the ground exhausted. But we needn't have worried so much, as we had completely forgotten the lantern which Donald carried, he being the elder by a few months, and it was still swinging from his arm! The engineer had seen the light, of course, bobbing on the track before him, and thinking it a signal of some sort he had stopped the train even before it entered the tunnel, so we never even came close to being ground to bits. He and the conductor and the crewmen had climbed down and walked through the tunnel, to see what the trouble was, until they came upon us, disheveled and panting, at the other end. The conductor put the climax on our fear and trembling. He frightened us' stiff when he ordered us vehemently, "Stay out of this tunnel, you boys! Don't you know it's *against the LAW* to stop a train?" We thought we were going to have to spend the rest of our lives in the penitentiary. We never walked through the tunnel again, and by mutual consent we never mentioned the matter to our mothers or others in authority.

I wonder if Summer Rest is still there? If it is, it could have changed a bit in all these years. Uncle George had a library to interest the Girls on rainy days, and it was mostly made up, as I remember it, of countless old back numbers of *Scribners* and *Harpers* and the *Century Magazine,* going back into the Nineties, and the English *Punch.* The little Old House, down in the side yard, had a bathroom papered with pages from *Punch,* but it had no running water, only a tin tub you had to fill, and empty, yourself. The New House, however, had all the modern conveniences which we did not have, and never did have, in Chapel Hill, with a bathroom containing two of each on each floor, and pull chains and everything. I used to enjoy and marvel at its wonders. There were hammocks and swings around among the trees, and it was so far out in the dead country that there was never a sound, except for the squealing and the chatter of the Girls, beside faraway cowbells and the tinkle of the sheep down in the lower pasture. But the peaceful and bucolic setting held little allure for me, and I was always anxious to get back to the life and color of Charlottesville.

Once, I remember—because we were at Summer Rest —I missed Gentry's Dog and Pony Show, the annual climax, for me, of Charlottesville's summer. I raised an awful rumpus. "I never *heard* such carrying on!" said Mother, "anybody'd think you hadn't seen it, just last summer!" "But Mother,"

I wailed, "you *know* they've got something new; they wouldn't have just the *same show.* . . ."

"Yes it is, too," said Mother, "it's just exactly the same show." But I knew better; to me it was always new, and sometimes they actually did have something they hadn't had before.

Sometimes a little mediocre, half-baked circus came to Charlottesville, but there was never anything half-baked about Gentry's Dog and Pony Show! That was a production! The parade was just like a regular circus, but in miniature. The little gaily painted and gilded cages, which held monkeys or other little trained animals, were scaled down to half-size, but complete in every detail, as was the band wagon. This was occupied by a small band of normal size tootling musicians, however, who looked huge in comparison. How fine it would have been if they could have gotten together a midget band, but then they'd have had to have midget-size instruments and all, and the music would have sounded only midget-size, too. . . . Anyway, they did have a few midgets scattered along the line, and this helped with the illusion. The pony work-teams pulled the wagons and went about their plumed and spangled business with all the seriousness of big horses. The ponies were wonderful, and I almost died of sheer excitement over their grace and beauty. White ponies, black ponies, bay and calico and dappled-gray! Twelve white ponies with red trappings pulled the band wagon. The ring ponies would have monkeys or dogs riding them, even in the parade. There would be dogs riding in little carriages, or pulling a carriage in which a beautiful lady sat. And there was always a monkey fire wagon, drawn by white ponies, and filled with screeching monkeys in little helmets and red shirts. For extra they had a trained seal once, and once there was a baby elephant in the parade. When he came shambling along, just like a big elephant, the people laughed and applauded. The parade

ended with a miniature calliope, too, smoking and screaming
like a real one.

The performance was even more wonderful than the
parade, with monkey acrobats and trapeze artists and eques-
trians, and a tiny little brown bear that rode a tiny unicycle.
The trained dog and pony acts were marvelous, and there
were trained pigs, too, and dog clowns—mostly poodles—
always getting in the way or doing funny things. A monkey
in a little short skirt climbed a pole to a platform at the top
of the tent and then jumped into a net below, while the drum
rolled. The climax of the show was the "fire" in a little house
they would put up in the ring, from which there would suddenly be a red glow and a cloud of smoke—and the monkey
fire engine would come clanging in and the chattering monkeys would scramble off it and squirt water from a hose on
the house and then put up a ladder and rescue a little white
dog, dressed in a long white night gown and night cap, from
an upstairs window. . . .

Once, the day after the show, I sneaked away from
Piedmont and went across the valley and the railroad tracks
to the empty, forlorn little circus lot and walked around in
the deserted ring, and kicked at the sawdust. And I remember the sadness and loneliness that suddenly overcame me,
a strange eerie feeling at being alone there in the stillness
of the sunny, vacant field, where yesterday there had been
so much life. Romance and color had come and touched Charlottesville—and me—and gone and left nothing behind it
but the sawdust. Where the stable tent had been I picked up
a pony shoe, half-buried in the dirty straw, and for a long
time the little plate was one of my most treasured possessions.

The dog and pony show, alas, has passed these many
years. I am sorry, for I should like to see another, and I should
like to take a boy of nine or ten to see one.

CHAPTER TWENTY

THE SECOND affair of my love life involved another blond young lady, one Pearl Mc-- Grew. I have a reason for calling her Pearl McGrew, which was not her name. Like Virginia Taylor, she was beautiful. Come to think of it, all the women I have ever loved were beautiful, and the longer I have loved them the more beautiful have they become. Most of them, at least the early ones, were blondes, too, and fickle. This preference for blondes followed me all the way through business college, and has recurred at intervals ever since.

Pearl, however, was not fickle in her attitude toward me, which was one of complete indifference. The affair, in fact—if it could be called such—was rather mild and temperate on my side, too, as compared with the soul-searing experience I had undergone with Virginia, and I remember little Pearl best for the grim and bloody violence that engulfed her that summer in Charlottesville, and shook that placid old town to its Colonial foundations. It shook me, too, as it was my first contact with melodramatic tragedy.

I had few playmates in Charlottesville, other than the Leigh boys, the minister's sons, that is except for Fanny and my pretty, black-eyed cousin, Sally Nelson. But with all the excitement of dog and pony shows, the Monticello Guards and everything, I didn't especially need them. Little girls came to see Fanny, of course, and we played together in the big back yard, but these as friends I found inadequate and disappointing, until I became enamoured of little Pearl McGrew. The attraction developed, I think—as inevitably it would— because of the fact that she treated me as the dirt beneath her dainty feet. Anyway, I began to moon around her.

She had two brothers, much older than I, whom I hardly knew, and lived in a beautiful house (with a croquet court) on the other side of town. Fanny and I would go there occasionally, and I would wham the croquet balls around and pretend I was "out of practice" when the girls beat me, or had a sore foot, or something. Pearl was nicer to me at her house than she was at ours, feeling the obligation of a hostess, no doubt, but even so her cordiality was not overwhelming. I believe she thought I was just a country bumpkin from North Carolina. Once, in order to correct this impression and show her that I had been around, I asked, "Have you ever seen the Leaning Tower of Pisa?" (I was greatly interested in this strange structure, a picture of which I had seen, and a description of which I had read, in Grandpa's encyclopedia. I didn't intend to say that I had actually seen it, myself, but just to give her the feeling that I was widely traveled.)

"Yes," she said. "Lot's of times." This was disconcerting, and I thought it unlikely, but I skipped it and tried again. "Have you ever been to Wrightsville Beach?" I asked. "Tad Lilly—"

"I'm going in the house," she said. "G'bye."

She had a most disagreeable habit of pretending to ignore me when she came around to Piedmont to see Fanny, and then when I thought I was completely ignored and free to forget about her and put my mind on other things, I'd find her looking at me and she would giggle insultingly and turn her back. It was infuriating. I wasn't all that uncouth and funny, that she would have to laugh at me for no reason at all. I would go hang on the fence and look down toward the station, hoping to see a train come in. Once one did, and I turned around and shouted warmly and invitingly, just as though nothing had happened, "There's a train down at the station," and Pearl and Fanny had disappeared, just like that. I looked all over for them, casually, and finally spotted them in the kitchen with Aunt Agnes. Oh, well—I decided.

Another time, after she had laughed at me, and I had turned my back and gone to the fence, I saw a freight train standing down on the track. "There's a train down at the station," I shouted to her again, just as nicely and politely and in as friendly a fashion as I knew how.

"I don't care," she said, and never even looked.

What can you do with a woman like that?

I got a little revenge and satisfaction one night at Fry's Spring, where she and Sally Nelson had gone with us. We had done all the usual things, drinking the water and listening to the band, and Aunt Minnie 'n' Hallie had danced. I kept wondering if Pearl would dance with me, if I asked her. (I couldn't dance, but that's what I called it.) Finally I screwed up my nerve. She looked mighty pretty, I thought, in a blue sailor dress with white stripes, her golden hair, with a red ribbon, down her back. "Will you dance with me?" I asked, hopefully.

"No," she said.

"Well, I don't care," I said, as significantly as I could. But I did.

Pearl's mother was a quiet, gentle lady, from whom Pearl had got her good looks. She was tall and fair, and she was very nice to me; much nicer than Pearl. Pearl's father was handsome, too, in a dark, stern way, and as he was just about the best known and most highly respected lawyer around those parts, Uncle Bob said, to say nothing of being an F.F.V. and very rich, I stood in great awe of him. Maybe Pearl got her snobbishness from him, for he never paid me the slightest mind, either. I saw him on the street once, and I said, "Good mawnin', Mr. McGrew," and he looked at me and spoke as though he had never seen me before. For some strange reason I remember him distinctly, for all the years between and the fact that I never saw him but two or three times.

All of which brings us to the murder.

I remember that we were sitting, the whole lot of us, on the small front porch that evening, right after supper. Thank Goodness we hadn't gone to Fry's Spring, and that Uncle Bob was home, too!

An old man named Mr. Wingate, who lived down the street and had a peg leg (he had lost it in the War) came stumping hurriedly up the sidewalk and from the gate called to Uncle Bob. "Mr. Bob," he called, "can I see you a minute?" (He never even said "I beg your pardon," or anything.)

This in itself seemed a strange procedure, what with the ladies sitting there, and all, and everybody got curious when Uncle Bob got up and went to the gate (we heard him say *"What"*—like that) and they talked a while in a low tone, Uncle Bob glancing back at us a time or two, and then the two of them walking off down the street. Uncle Bob called something back, and we could see Mr. Wingate talking excitedly and gesticulating with his stick while they walked slowly away. "Well, now, what in the world?" said Aunt Lucy, and everybody had the uneasy feeling that something had happened. We thought that maybe something had happened down at The Mill. We didn't have to wait long to find out.

Uncle Bob came back, very agitated, and stood at the bottom of the steps, and said in a low voice, *"Mrs. McGrew has been murdered!* They don't know who did it, but they've sent for the bloodhounds. The murderer beat Mr. McGrew to a pulp, too!"

The old ladies, of course, after that moment of stunned silence you read about, all began screaming and talking and asking questions at once. You never saw such excitement. I couldn't believe what I had heard Uncle Bob say: *"Mrs. Mc-Grew"* . . . *"MURDER".* . . .

Finally Aunt Lucy made herself heard. "Nonsense," she said. "Mrs. McGrew's in Culpeper; she told me herself she was going, just the other day."

"Mrs. McGrew is not in Culpeper," said Uncle Bob. "I wish to high Heaven she was!"

They forgot all about me, and I heard the whole first report in all its terrible detail. Later on when they discussed the crime (which was practically all the time), everybody lowered their voices and raised their eyebrows and glanced at me, for innocent little children were not supposed to hear of such atrocious things. (The comics, then, comprised nothing more sensational or blood-curdling than "Buster Brown," or "The Katzenjammer Kids," or "The Brownies," and never touched at all upon bloody murder.) However, from what I heard in the beginning, and from what I picked up by hard listening later on, I was able to reconstruct the foul deed in its entirety.

Mrs. McGrew had had the life beaten out of her by a burglar, a tall dark man wearing a handkerchief over his face, and Mr. McGrew, who staggered out for help—while not beaten, to a pulp, as Mr. Wingate told Uncle Bob—did have a lump on his head to prove that he, too, had been attacked and beaten. Mr. McGrew furnished a hazy description of the murderer, and the police and the bloodhounds got to work. They couldn't find a trace of him; it was as though the earth, Uncle Bob said, had swallowed him up. Charlottesville was in a frenzy. People were terrified. Those who had keys to their doors locked them. It was terrible to think of such a fiend at large. I carefully looked under the bed before I blew out the lamp at night, and then lay there in the dark, wondering where the murderer could be, and what he looked like without the handkerchief over his face. Poor Mr. McGrew. . . . There was talk about calling out the Guards. This state of things continued for some days, while the little Charlottesville paper got out extras, and hardly anybody did anything but talk about the murder, and look searchingly at his neighbor, especially if he was tall and dark. . . . And then, slowly, the truth—through a lot of rumor and gossip—began to emerge.

It seems that Mrs. McGrew had had an eye on her eminent husband for some time, and that to settle an ugly situation she had laid a little trap for him. She announced to him, and to various friends, that she was going to Culpeper for a certain number of days, to visit relatives, and to Culpeper she went. Mr. McGrew went with her to the station and put her on the train. However, she came right back to Charlottesville the next day and awaited Mr. McGrew, who—inexplainably—was absent from home when she got back. When he, too, returned, a day or so later, she confronted him with what she knew, and suspected, concerning a Bad Woman in Washington who was the real reason for Mr. McGrew's frequent business trips to that wicked city.

She had the goods on Mr. McGrew, and there was no satisfactory explanation he could offer for his absence, as he was supposed to stay in Charlottesville while she was away and look after the children and the house. Cornered, Mr. McGrew picked up a baseball bat belonging to one of the boys, and with it settled everything. He then gave himself a slight bop on the head and did some shouting and ran out the door, and when the neighbors got there told them his story. It all came out in the trial.

The State of Virginia hanged Mr. McGrew by the neck until dead, and I never saw little Pearl again.

CHAPTER TWENTY-ONE

THE Chapel Hill Volunteer
Fire Department used to "practice" in the cool of early evening, and as the town was very proud of them practically everybody who could wolf his supper and get uptown in time was on hand to watch. In the long summer months, with the University pretty much deserted except for a small summer school made up largely of schoolteachers taking refresher courses, Chapel Hill had little to offer in the way of spectacles, and our daily lives, indolent and easy, might have lacked for colorful excitement except for the terrific vim and vitality of the Volunteers. There was great interest and fierce civic pride in the Fire Department, which, at the end of summer, and following many long weeks of struggle to attain the peak of proficiency, would go forth to the State Tournament in one of the big towns, there to meet the flower of the State's hose reel teams in earnest competition for supremacy and glory. Hose reel teams from all the hamlets and villages and towns in North Carolina (maybe in all the whole country) were likewise busily engaged in drilling all summer long, a covetous eye on the glittering prize at season's end. And proud our town may well have been, for our gallant and fleet-footed fire fighters won both the glory and the supremacy in abundant measure! They were our own, and we were as proud of them

as ever New York City was proud of the Yankees or London of the Royal Family. They belonged exclusively to us, and there was nothing to compare with them anywhere, in all the great, wide world, we thought.

About sundown, while the crowd collected to watch the practice, the young men would appear from various quarters in "gym suits"—the very full and flopping shorts, and shirts with short sleeves, which at that time represented proper athletic costume—and limber up, trotting around and stretching their muscles tenderly and cautiously, as athletes do. Some of the more conservative element of the population sniffed at the shockingly scant apparel, calling it underwear, which it wasn't; the garments were real, genuine gym suits. "It ain't right and it ain't decent for them to run around the public streets in them short pants," I heard an old lady say. "Suppose your house caught on fire; would you like for 'em to come put it out dressed like that?" The old man with her laughed. "Well, Mama," he said, "they'd get there faster than if they was all wrapped up in long pants and overcoats!" But for almost everybody the nakedness of the boys' arms and legs gave the proceedings just the right touch of daring and desperate endeavor, and to us our heroes seemed appropriately clad, and the muscular exposure seemed a symbol of the hardy strength of Chapel Hill.

When the team seemed to feel they were ready, they would slowly make their way up Franklin Street, out of sight, to the starting line which was beyond the end of the long block, the other side of Mr. Emerson's apothecary. You tried to settle down for the interminable period of tense waiting, but patience was difficult, and there was much climbing up on things and craning of necks. You always questioned the delay and wondered what was holding things up and why they didn't come, and people would say "What in the world?" and wonder if the hose reel had broken down, or the wrench was lost, or something. Sheriff Suggs would waddle importantly up and down, keeping people back and the street clear, and even dogs were chased to the sidewalk and caught and held. You listened intently, cocking an ear, and waited. And then finally, when it seemed you couldn't wait another second, you'd hear the pistol shot! *"Here they come!"* you'd scream at the top of your lungs, almost bursting with excitement. The falsetto din of "Here they come!" from all the little boys in town was tremendously exhilarating, and you kept yelling it. You yelled and pushed, and strained the better to see, and here they came! —Doc Pickard and Brack Lloyd and Crook Hutchins and all the rest, tearing break-neck down the street in a cloud of dust, an escaped dog or two flying alongside barking frenziedly, the rubber-tired hose reel swaying and spinning behind them, and it was a fine, fine sight!

They had started a certain distance from the waiting reel, fifty feet, I think it was, grabbed the long rope on the tongue and struggled into their harnesses as they ran. It was a hundred yards to the fire plug by the drugstore. Frenzied moments, those, while the hose was torn free, the reel spinning like mad, connection and coupling made, pressure turned on by the wrenchman, the hose filling and twisting like a snake, and your breath came back only with the water, a fine and rushing torrent which, according to the rules, had to go fifty feet into the air. "Water! Water!" you'd yell, as the foamy stream soared up to spread in a great fan of snowy spray. It seemed as if the whole village was yelling "Water!" such a roar went up. It was the thrilling climax to a great show.

The panting firemen would drop down on the curb to rest before emptying and rolling up their hose, and the people would swarm out into the street and slap them on the back. "You're goin' to win at Asheville," they'd say, or whatever city it was which was to be the scene of the tournament. The firemen would grin and puff, while the younger spectators

would wade and splash around in the puddles left by the hose, getting themselves and innocent bystanders liberally spattered with mud.

The firemen would get over their panting and heaving, and push their hair back and get up and go over to Judge Brockwell, or whoever was the official timekeeper that night, and ask how they had done. "Pretty good tonight," the Judge might say, studying his big silver watch. "I can't tell exactly, got somethin' in my eye; but I think you did pretty good."

As tournament time drew near excitement mounted. Dark rumors, indicating our certain defeat, began to fly: "That crowd in Lumberton, they got a lot of *ringers*," or "Down in Elizabeth City they got a reel with *ball bearings*," but our faith in our Volunteers remained constant, and we knew that only through some sort of skulduggery could they be beaten. Slowly their running time for the test went down, a second now, a second then, and the boys went through their drills with grim determination, knowing that they had the "ringers" and the big city teams, with all their wealth of material, to contend with.

The day the Fire Department left for Asheville the send-off must have warmed their hearts and given them just the little extra something that they needed. "We ain't comin' back with our tails between our legs," said Brack Lloyd, "they've got to go some to beat us!"

The depot and the ground around it was crowded with people and hacks and wagons. The reel was loaded in the special private car—half baggage and half passenger—which was to take our team to its test, and there was great shouting and waving as the Whooper pulled out and chuffed off for University Station, where the car would be hitched onto another train for the trip to Asheville. The Fire Department, in its best clothes, hung out the windows and off the rear end shouting and waving back at us. Everybody stood and waved until the little train crossed the trestle and went around the long curve out of sight.

The suspense of the next two days was terrific, and you thought Saturday would never come. Saturday afternoon half the town was down at the telegraph office, waiting for long hours, for no one knew at just what time our boys would run. It made your heart jump a beat suddenly to think, "Maybe they're running *right now,* maybe they're beating *Lumberton!*" I wandered around in the crowd and asked everybody, "Heard anything yet?"—though I knew mighty well they hadn't. (In my mind's eye I saw a vast field filled with all the hose reel teams of all the towns in all the State of North Carolina lined up in an endless row, waiting for the gun. I saw them break away, as the pistol shot sounded, and the dust swirl about them as they began to thunder toward the far-away finish line. Dust obscured them—shouting, flying feet, confusion—and then from out the melee shoots *Chapel Hill* to take the lead, but *Lumberton*—its team wearing hideous black masks—is pounding just behind them, creeping up on the outside. . . .) And then, suddenly, Mr. Gooch, the telegraph operator, was standing in the door and waving a yellow sheet as he yelled in his cracked voice, *"Chapel Hill the winner! We beat everybody!"* What a mighty roar went up, and back-beating and shaking of hands! Mr. Gooch was holding his hands up, begging for quiet, and finally people stopped yelling to let him speak. "That ain't all," he screeched, "they set a *record!"*

When the boys got back, that was a time! Not only had the Chapel Hill Volunteer Fire Department won the championship, but the record which they set was not just an ordinary one—it was a World's Record! That sounds as though it takes in a lot of territory, but the term was no more loosely applied than in our World's Series baseball games, which

after all only represent this land of the brave. Anyway, the
Chapel Hill Volunteer Fire Department ran a given distance,
dragging the hose reel behind them, connected the hose to the
fire hydrant and "got water" faster than anybody else, anywhere, so far as is known. Of course there was no way of as-
certaining at that time whether the Norwegians or the Chinese
or the Fuzzy-Wuzzies were also dragging hose reels down
their streets and timing themselves—and so, lacking this information the World's Record was properly awarded to
Chapel Hill.

Some people claimed that the moral support given the
team before it went to Asheville had helped its morale. Other
people gave the credit to the testimonial oyster stew supper
tendered the Volunteers the night before they left for the
tournament. But I think it was really neither of these influences, and that it was their own stout hearts and hairy legs
which carried them to victory.

All the hullabaloo before they left was as nothing to what
happened when they got back. It looked as if everybody in the
whole town were out at the depot to meet the train and welcome them, and when the Whooper crawled in, all decorated
with flags and paper streamers, you couldn't hear yourself
think for the noise. The fire laddies fought their way out of
the train, grinning happily but looking very self-conscious,
and some of our more enthusiastic citizens tried to hoist the
boys up on their shoulders, and there was a lot of pawing and
pushing. Ladies stood up in the decorated hacks and waved
their handkerchiefs, and men threw their hats and themselves
around! That's when Chapel Hill needed a band: we had
everything else to welcome the conquering heroes, but we
sure did miss the University Band. We had tried to scrape one
together, but the best we could do was a bass drum and a
couple of horns and a fife. This "band" may not have played
any music, exactly, but it certainly made a lot of noise and

added to the festivity. The hose reel was dragged down out of the baggage car, and as many of the firemen as could be perched on it were made to ride, and the crowd tied a long rope to the reel and pulled it all the way into town. That was a triumphal procession! It strung out behind almost all the way to the depot. Collier and I were up on the box with Poor Dave, riding on his hack, but we decided we couldn't see enough that way and finally got down, halfway uptown, and ran up and down the street so that we could see more of the parade as it passed by. If Chapel Hill had had a museum, I think the town would have liked to hang the hose reel up in it and stuff the members of the team and place them around the walls!

Doc Pickard told me all about the tournament later. He said the boys were mighty nervous, but when the time came they ran the race of their lives. And he was proud to be a member, he said. He said that the teams didn't race against each other, as I thought, but only against the watch, one at a time, and that Lumberton wasn't any good at all and didn't even place. It just goes to show what tricks your imagination can play on you.

In addition to affording us vast and inspiring entertainment, the Volunteers also protected us from the ravages of fire. But—funny thing—I never remember a fire in Chapel Hill. Surely there must have been, with all those stoves and fireplaces and tinder-dry old houses. Mr. Pickard's great, rambling old University Inn burnt down, but that was later and I had gone when that happened. I am sorry I missed it; what a sight that must have been, and what a fine account of themselves our smoke eaters must have given.

Every Chapel Hill boy fully expected to be a member of the Fire Department when he was old and big enough; it was obligatory and certain, an indisputable thing ahead, like military service in some countries, only much more happily anticipated. We began talking about breaking our own World's Record when we grew up. . . .

In addition to the Fire Department, there was another cause of great excitement on Franklin Street, but this occurred at odd and unpredictable hours and was not on schedule like the fire practice drills. There was always an audience, but it was impromptu. This commotion was created by Bruce Strowd's automobile. People said Bruce was a mechanical genius, and he proved it when he was not more than fifteen by building one of the first motor vehicles I ever remember. There had been a few others, of course, strange, high, horseless carriages with doors in the back and horns with rubber bulbs, and lamps which were lighted with a match, but Bruce's is my first definite motor memory because his was such a memorable conveyance. From somewhere he got hold of a little, second-hand, sputtering 1½ horse power engine. As I didn't, and don't, know anything about mechanics, half a horse was hard for me to understand, but he seemed to know what it meant. This engine he mounted on the rear end of the flat bed of an old wagon. His steering wheel was taken from an ancient sewing machine of his mother's, and this was attached to a bicycle chain and sprockets. The motor was not always easy to start—which may be an understatement—and when, after much priming and travail and tribulation, he finally got going, the noise was fearful, as the contraption had no muffler, and the smoke and smell were almost asphyxiating. But it ran! And the horses up and down the street all but climbed the trees. From far away you could hear him coming, usually preceded by a runaway team or two with cursing farmers sawing on the reins, and people hurrying to see him go by. He by no means burned up the highway, and the effort and the tumult seemed excessive for the speed attained. However, if he was going downhill the thing really rolled, and he controlled acceleration by means of a drag brake, a heavy stick bolted to the side of the wagon frame beside his seat in the middle, and which he could drag in the dirt to slow himself up. In case this failed he could always turn into the bank or the ditch.

He was not popular, at this stage. In fact, there is no doubt that he was Chapel Hill's Public Enemy No. 1, and when it was seen that he could be neither controlled nor reformed the town fathers passed an ordinance prohibiting Bruce Strowd from operating any contrivance driven by a gasoline motor upon the streets and byways of Chapel Hill. But that's as far as they went, and Sheriff Suggs never pinched him. He continued happily and freely on his explosive way, went to A. & M. College and studied the theory of combustion and mechanics, and following some postgraduate work in Detroit came back to Chapel Hill and became one of those pillars of America, the Ford dealer.

He has white hair now and a good reputation, an imposing establishment and a new car or so every year. I buy my gasoline from him, and he says that for old times' sake he lets me have it at cost; if this is true it certainly costs him a pretty penny. A few years ago he found and bought back the first Ford he ever sold, in 1914, and polishes and caresses the old crate tenderly. Sometimes he mounts this venerable vehicle and chugs around, to the great amusement and delight of the current generation. As a law breaker he has few equals; the 1907 ordinance, aimed at keeping him off the streets, has never been repealed, and he figures that by now he should have been arrested about one hundred thousand times. But after all, this is a college town, and the Chapel Hill police force, besides being to a certain extent helpless, is tolerant and wise.

An interesting and historic structure stood across the street from the corner now occupied by Bruce Strowd's Ford agency. It was a forlorn and ramshackle wooden building containing the apothecary of Mr. Emerson. It was here that he discovered that boon to mankind, Bromo Seltzer. So much money resulted, via headaches and hangovers, that Mr. Emerson, years later, and after he had removed to Baltimore and made himself and Baltimore famous, presented the University with its first modern athletic stadium—now the baseball field —which bears his name. I have always felt that, as came to be the case in so many big league parks, there should be a heroic Bromo Seltzer bottle in center field. Not a commercial advertisement, of course, but just to honor Mr. Emerson. Or, if this is not feasible, there should be a great monument, of the same design, erected upon the spot once occupied by the apothecary.

Strowd's big, sprawly farm, where Bruce lived, was not too far from town, off the Durham Road, and got closer as your legs lengthened. All of us boys, big and little, used to like to walk out there over the sandy road. Strowd's Creek, a muddy and overgrown waterway, wound through the farm, and from it could be had catfish and suckers and mud turtles and occasional perch, procured by means of a bamboo pole and fishing worms.

The great and mysterious fishing ground, however, was New Hope Creek, which trickled along six miles away, halfway to Durham. Few of us ever fished it, for it was too far to walk, and horses and wagons, like money, didn't grow on trees. In our minds' eye, though, we saw it full of huge and hungry fish who were always waiting for us expectantly, because we never got there. At times, when the Chapel Hill fishing was poor, we conjured up visions of the great strings of gigantic fish we would someday bring back from New Hope Creek, when at last we got there. As a matter of fact, the two little streams were practically identical in everything including their stocks of fish, and we lost nothing by confining, of necessity, our angling to Strowd's Creek. But always the dream persisted.

Bruce had a fine collection of bird eggs, some of which I furnished, as he was a shrewd trader and always got the best of you. One day he came to grief, however, while robbing a buzzard's nest of its big white eggs; the mother buzzard returned to find Bruce despoiling her home and pu—pardon me, vomited on him. All over him. This is what indignant buzzards do.

When I came back to live in Chapel Hill, and he sought to sell me a Ford, I refused to do business with him because of the trimming he had given me so many times so many years ago in the matter of the bird eggs. I think it had an effect on him, too, for shortly thereafter he came around bearing an old mop, handle and all, which had been standing out on his back porch and on top of which a pair of foolish wrens had built a nest and laid two little splotched eggs. He said he hoped this might make amends for anything he had put over on me in the past. He was quite gentlemanly about it, and we shook hands and decided to let bygones be bygones, and I put the mop in the corner of my studio. Something seems to have happened to it, for it is not there any more.

Down in a pasture of Strowd's Farm was a baseball diamond, none too smooth or level, and here most of the more important ball games were staged, as the Strowd boys played on the Big Downtown team (as distinct from Little Downtown, which was my team). Bruce was catcher and Will Tenny pitched. They were a fine battery, and respected by Big Uptown. I can see Bruce squatting behind the plate, barefooted and in ragged, khaki-colored pants. I don't ever remember Bruce as dressed in anything but faded khaki-colored pants, and Will Tenny in faded, ragged blue. The two Venable boys played on Big Downtown, and the two MacRaes and Edwin Tenny, Will's brother, and Doc Pickard and Mr. Patterson's son, Jim. But Big Uptown held the edge, with Bunn Hearn. Bunn was a pitcher par excellence. He was in

Canady's School when I got there (it wasn't called a high school, but it had higher grades than the other little school) and I have even played ball with him—well, catch, anyway. He eventually pitched for several big league teams, including McGraw's Giants, and went on that 'round-the-world trip the Giants and the White Sox made way back yonder. I have known some great and distinguished men in my time.

The Little Downtown baseball (and football) team, however, was the absorbing athletic activity, and we really didn't pay the older boys much attention. (The personnel of our baseball and football teams was exactly the same; the number of players was about the same, too, as we were not overburdened with material and it took our full strength to field a complete team. Our home games were played in the Hertys' side yard—smallish and cramped, but it sufficed—and our games uptown in the Pritchards' pasture. This had some boulders sticking up, as well as souvenirs left by the cows, but was a much larger field than Hertys' and long-hit balls got a fine roll. The games there were always high-scoring affairs.

Once a team of boys from Durham, twelve miles away, drove over to play us. This game had all the flavor of an international contest. We got beaten, but made arrangements for a return game in Durham the following week. We put in hard practice every day, and felt that we were ready for them, this time. Came the great day, and early in the morning we piled into Mr. Pickard's big, straw-filled wagon, boys and bats and lunch boxes and dogs, and were on our way. At noontime we were at the rendezvous, a square with a fountain in it. It was terribly hot, and we drank the water from the fountain and waited in the shade, but the other team didn't show up. Finally we started out in all directions to find them. We did find one or two, but they were not expecting us, due to some misunderstanding, and their team was scattered. (Among ourselves we decided that the reason they hadn't met us was because they were scared of us.) By that time it had got to be so late the colored driver said we had to git goin', so sadly we climbed back in our wagon for the long ride home. Twelve miles behind a plodding team in a crowded wagon, with no ball game played and all the lunch eaten, can be a long way, and the moon was up and shining down through the pine trees when at last we reached the haven of Chapel Hill and disbanded at the livery stable. How beautiful home seemed that night. We claimed the game by forfeit, and never essayed the trip to Durham again.

The pageantry and color of the University athletics, where the players wore uniforms and striped blue and white jerseys and stockings, affected us, naturally, and our own costumes for the diamond or the gridiron seemed drab and uninspiring, and we were considerably put to it to give the appearance of a well uniformed team. My mother made me a baseball suit, I remember, after much coaxing, out of gray cotton flannel, and some of the other boys' mothers made suits for them, too. We cut letters out of felt—LDT—and they were sewed on the shirts. But stockings and jerseys presented a real difficulty, and while we were able in a way to solve the former by strips of red flannel stitched around our black stockings (this made a fine effect, but was not very durable) we had to use our regular old turtle-neck sweaters in lieu of jerseys. Big numerals on jerseys hadn't been thought of then; if they had been necessary, I don't know what we would have done. We got along all right, though, without any of the fancy equipment kids seem to find indispensable now, though sometimes at Christmas you might expect a new rubber nose-guard to replace the one out of which you had chewed the mouthpiece the fall before, or a pair of shin guards. They were made of reeds canvas covered, and did protect your shins from anything but a direct hit, and made you fell really well-dressed for the football field.

Whenever I see little shavers, nowadays, all dressed up in fancy pants, and enormous shoulder harnesses beneath brilliant striped and numbered shirts, and striped stockings and shiny helmets and cleated shoes, playing with a football which they haven't even blown up themselves (they never heard of tying a bladder tube!) I hark back to the under-costumed battles in Pritchards' cow pasture, where the only color came from bloody noses, and you didn't gasp "Down" until you had to. I never had a pair of football pants, or a helmet (which we called a head-gear) until I played at high school in Knoxville, and the helmet, even then, was only a skimpy openwork affair of imitation leather backed by padding.

But we grew up in an athletic tradition and drew our breath and inspiration from our idols, the University players. We were good, too. Why shouldn't we have been? We really learned the games. We were born to them. In place of teething rings we used rubber nose-guards; in place of baby toys we used baseball bats. The boys here still have this tradition to a certain extent, but, poor fellows, they are farther away from the sports and the players than we were and they are diverted by so much else—the radio, the movies, the automobiles—the whole mad scramble and pace of even juvenile life, and considering everything, they do mighty well, or at least it's done for them. Poor little fellows.

Football practice (the Varsity's, not ours) was the highlight around which the autumn days revolved, and if you missed going to practice your day was lost. The team, then, was a valiant handful (shucks, you have more coaches now than we had players!) and the Varsity went in there and played their hearts out for seventy minutes, unless somebody got so badly hurt that he couldn't keep on and was taken out protesting; and then one of the substitutes went in, and you worried. Mostly big, earnest young men they were, with big hands, from the farms and little towns in North Carolina

(this, of course, was before we found out about the Pennsyl-
vania coal fields and other districts productive of football
players) who had never known much about the fine points of
the game until they came to Carolina and were induced to
"come out for" football and the coach taught them something
about it. They learned the hard way. Each of the four undergraduate classes had a team, also, and rivalry and competition
was keen. Even the Freshmen when they played the Sophomores tried their darndest to beat them, regardless of the
reprisals they knew would be forthcoming if they did, in the
form of hazing. Everybody usually beat the Seniors, whose
best players, after two or three years of class football, had
advanced to the Scrubs or even in some cases to the Varsity,
and the Seniors sometimes had a hard time even getting
eleven willing men together. Those class games were battles
royal, hard fought and bitter. The players themselves were a
mixed lot of valorous nondescripts, tall stringy boys and short
fat boys, in a varied assortment of odds and ends of football
equipment, and they looked like anything but football players.
Their hearts were in the right place, though.

But the Varsity . . . There is no adoration which sur-
passes that of a small boy for a football player, and the members of the Varsity, to us, were white knights in shining ar-
mor; they were gods who trod the heights. In addition to the
Varsity and the substitutes, who were in a class by themselves,
there were the Scrubs—a dozen or so hardy, though ill-
assorted, young men in tatterdemalion uniforms, who came
out and gave battle on scrimmage days. I doubt if it was ever
very helpful to the Varsity when they went up against real
competition, but the Scrubs were valiant, too, and the students who came to watch the practice cheered them. Speaking
of equipment, even the Varsity just had cotton batting pads
sewed on the shoulders and elbows of their jerseys, scant protection from the punishment they took.

Among the earliest of my football heroes in the Padded Pants Period was a Chapel Hill boy named Louis Graves. His family home was where the Carolina Inn now stands, his father having been a University professor, and he came of a football-minded family, as both he and his elder brother, Ernest, played on our Varsity. Off the field Louis was quiet and retiring, but once the whistle blew there was nothing shy or modest about him. Sometimes, now, he talks, with a gleam in his eye, of what it was like, half a century ago. "That thick grass in the Stadium looks mighty good," he says wistfully. "Our field had next to no turf on it, by late fall anyway, and the surface was mostly clay with a lot of gravel always coming to the top." The only plumbing in the whole University then were those erratic cold showers in the basement of the Library, and the bruised, sore players would drag themselves thither after practice on chilly autumn days, scratched up and cut by the flinty gravel and clay, and while the icy water splashed down on their bloody abrasions they proved their manhood by trying to imagine it was warm and comforting. I don't remember Ernest as clearly as Louis, for Ernest went on to West Point while Louis was still playing here, and became— as the immortal "Pot" Graves—captain of one of the Army's great teams and All-America tackle (he has been placed on the All Time All-America by many experts). But Louis, willowy and fast, did all his memorable quarterbacking for U.N.C.

In November, 1900, he (and Ernest) took part in one of the most extraordinary exploits in football history, ours or anybody else's. Within the space of five days—and on foreign fields—three games were played against teams at that time among the strongest in the South! It's hard to believe, but there's the record to prove it.

On a Thursday, in Knoxville, they humbled proud Tennessee, 23 to 5. ("We shouldn't have let 'em score," Louis says apologetically.) On Saturday, the boys having got warmed up, they buried Vanderbilt under a 48 to 0 landslide. In Atlanta on Monday, two days later, came a scoreless tie with Sewanee, then the Big Team of the South. It happened, Louis Graves recalls, the day before McKinley defeated William Jennings Bryan (Bryan's second setback) for the Presidency, and while the impending election seemed, at the time, of very minor importance to the football game, it may have been distracting enough to throw the team off its best form. Anyway, it was a hard, tough brawl, with neither side having enough punch to cross the other's goal line. The mere idea of this incredible five-day-three-game performance would put a modern football squad of half a hundred in the infirmary with the shuddering jitters, coaches and all! "Giants in those days," as applied to those valiant pigskinners of Naughty Naught, is no empty phrase!

But that scoreless tie with Sewanee still rankles in Mr. Graves' breast. "I guess the trouble was," he says ruminatively and a trifle morosely, "that by the time we played that game the boys might have been getting just a little bit tired, maybe. . . . I reckon we didn't do ourselves justice. It got so bad before the game was over we even got our signals mixed once, and my brother Ernest, who was our fullback, [Louis never called his brother "Pot,"] couldn't carry more than three or four Sewanee men with him when he bucked the line. Usually, when he was feeling good, he could drag half a dozen. It was bad. . . ."

"What was the matter?" I asked sarcastically, "Did you stay up too late Saturday night after the Vanderbilt game?"

"Maybe we did," he acknowledged, grinning.

"Well, anyway you had Sunday in which to recuperate," I rejoined. "You know, day of rest."

"Day of rest, nothin'!" he snorted. "We had to get from Nashville to Atlanta, and if you don't think that in 1900 that was *some trip* . . . ! We traveled on the only train we could get that Sunday, a local that stopped at every hog path and started up again with a jerk that almost snapped your head off. It was late when we got to Atlanta. I guess that train ride did us in worse than the game with Vanderbilt."

"Why did you ever schedule such a trip as that?" I asked him.

"Oh, the boys just wanted a little fun," Louis said. "We couldn't afford three separate trips away from home just then, either, so we did it all at once."

He said that when it was decided to make the trip, it did seem sort of strenuous, so they took along the whole squad, consisting of nineteen players, in case they got banged around and had to make substitutions. (He admitted that jaunt really must have taken a little out of them after all, however, for on Thanksgiving Day, as usual, Virginia beat them again in the big game of the year.)

Fifty years or so have made a change in Mr. Graves' speed, and I don't believe he could do much in the way of spectacular broken-field running now, even should the opportunity present itself, which isn't likely. He is still a quarterback at heart, however, a white-haired field general, with a fighting face no longer, but a twinkling countenance benign and beaming; and in his newspaper, *The Chapel Hill Weekly,* he always carries interesting football news (and any football news, to Mr. Graves, is interesting) on the front page. When his ball-toting days were over he went to New York and became a star reporter on the *Times,* and a free lance writer of distinction. Years ago, when he got his fill of such, he realized the dream of most newspaper men: he came back to his home town and started publishing his own paper, as Editor, Owner, Editorial Writer, Reporter, Advertising Manager, and probably everything but Printer's Devil. His staff has naturally expanded since then. The *Weekly* has become famous in the world of journalism, and often you see its wise, pithy editorials quoted in the metropolitan press.

Recently a New York newspaper man said to me, "Louis Graves is sort of the William Allen White of Chapel Hill, isn't he?"

"Sir," I replied, with dignity, "down home we have always had the utmost respect and admiration for Mr. White, but we think of him as the Louis Graves of Emporia, Kansas."

Football is big business here now, and the fame of Choo Choo Justice has spread thoroughout the land. Big name coach, big stadium, a Varsity squad of fifty or sixty. The band is even bigger. We had a band then, too, of course —just ten or twelve pieces—but no uniforms or majorettes. I guess this fine and fancy band now would certainly turn up its noses at that tootling little band of the early nineteen hundreds.

I remember with great pride that I was a bandsman, once. No, more than that; it happened on more than one occasion. The snare drummer of the band was absent, or late, and I was allowed to beat his drum! This sounds rather foolhardy on the part of the bandmaster, but I was a fairly big boy then, and the band didn't have any hard and fast rules about playing. Everybody just did the best they could. They said it was all right for me to beat the drum if I just kept time. This I did, I think. Anyway, there were no complaints, and it sounded fine to me. Wonderful, the feeling of well-being you have, beating a drum; even better than pumping an organ, for you know you make the noise! Our band had one piece at the top of its list—Sousa's "Double Eagle March," and they would play that, and "I'm a Tar Heel Born—" several times during a game.

The athletic field sort of sloped down toward the south-west, so that there was quite a dip as you went toward the west goal on the gridiron. There was a little wooden grandstand, way up in one corner back of home plate and the baseball diamond, and a small wooden bleachers near it. The goalposts were saplings from the nearby woods. In the fall a rail fence was put up around the gridiron, and the top rail made a fine perch. The whole was enclosed by a rickety plank fence, with a carriage entrance at one end, but to me that athletic field was the Colosseum and the Field of Glory.

John Abernathy and I used to buy peanuts by the big sack, and roast them and sell them in little bags. We made candy, seafoam and fudge. That candy-making required real strength of character. We mixed and cooked it on his mother's cookstove or mine, whichever one was available, and beat and stirred it, and buttered the pans and poured it out and let it cool and cut it into squares, and hardly ever ate enough to make much difference, for we were in business and the candy was our stock in trade and not to be enjoyed. It was hard, though, to put so much of it into the sacks. We put five or six pieces into a little paper sack and sold them for five cents. We sold grapes, too, scuppernongs and muscadines. Scrimmage days naturally drew the biggest crowds, and we sold a lot of stuff. John was younger than I, and easily influenced and intimidated, and I made him carry the basket and peddle our goods.

The usual practice session, when they weren't scrimmaging, consisted mostly of that wonderful ritual, Running Through Signals, and some kicking, and tackling the dummy. When the kicking practice was going on, two or three of the town boys were granted the privilege of catching, or chasing, the kicks, and getting them back as best we could. I learned something about handling a football that way; it's no mean trick, catching a punt. Watching the ball rise from the kicker's foot, forty-fifty yards away, figuring the wind and the twist, and trying to reach the right spot where it's coming down. Like an outfielder gauging a long fly. But a football may turn and duck in the air, and there are those last few swift steps, as it comes to earth, and the *thunk* of it into your arms and belly is a pretty good feeling. Later on, of course, I learned about a couple of big murderers, practically on top of you, charging in to knock you cold and jar the ball aloose. The ball is different now, slimmer, with pointed ends. In those days the balls got big and fat, like melons. Catching a punt, maybe on the run, and running it back, is a mighty fine thing to watch, and a mighty fine thing to do.

Sometimes during scrimmage I was allowed to carry the water bucket, and it was wonderful to run out on the field with it when play was stopped and the water called for, and to be so close to the panting, perspiring players. There was always a lot of uncooked oatmeal floating around in the water. I asked why this was, and was told, "So you can't drink much of it." Usually the players would take a big mouthful and tilt their heads back and gargle and spit it out.

Practice was hardly ever secret, until maybe the season's last week or so, when the boys might be thinking up something for Virginia. The gates were closed, then, and nobody was admitted; you looked around in the trees for hostile spies. It was maddening to hear the sounds of practice and not be able to watch it, but you knew that whatever was being cooked up behind the plank fence was sacred to our cause, and no eyes could see it until it was sprung upon the unsuspecting Virginians. Of course you were a little bothered by the thought of what the Virginians might be planning for us! Well, anyway, even if you couldn't be a part of the daily practice, and catch punts, you could make yourself mighty useful, and all afternoon you would patrol the woods all around the field just on the chance that somebody from Virginia might be skulking in the underbrush waiting for an opportunity to look through a knothole of the fence.

Off the field, I always tailed a football player, thankful for crumbs of football wisdom. Maybe we boys were an awful nuisance to them, or maybe the players liked it, I don't know. Anyway, they were almost always mighty nice to us; perhaps they liked the unashamed and undisguised worship which we gave them, and they always opened up and talked to us. A teen-age boy can learn a lot of football in Chapel Hill, or could then. I was practically raised, you might say, in the old T Formation. There was none of today's razzle-dazzle ball handling, or scientific, complex formations or plays; they were mostly just end runs and fake kicks and line bucks (if you had a "trick play" your team had a full repertoire), though there was a new fad coming in, the forward pass, which people thought would not amount to much.

There were usually one or two games in Chapel Hill, our opponents being small colleges which were supposed to be pushovers and sometimes were not, but almost all our games were away, so as to draw bigger crowds. These games on foreign soil were always preceded, the night before the team left, by that stirring ceremony, the Mass Meeting. It was held in Gerard Hall, the tiny, ancient one-time Chapel, which nowadays would hardly hold the football squad. But somehow the students packed in. There was a narrow balcony around three sides, and when that was filled, too, they hung on the rafters. I was usually picked up and carried in on some student friend's shoulder. The first two rows of seats were empty, awaiting The Team, and while the mob yelled "Yackety Yack," and "I'm a Tar Heel Born," the air got thick and blue with smoke. The Team filed in, looking pleased and bashful and self-conscious, and the din was deafening. The noise our little band made inside Gerard Hall almost blew the roof off. Then there would be speeches by two or three of the most popular professors, and lastly the coach, all telling what we were going to do to Georgetown, or A. & M., or Virginia, and the crowd went wild.

If we did it, there would be another Mass Meeting when the team got back, and a roaring bonfire in front of the Old Well, with the bell ringing like crazy. Once, I remember, after we'd beaten Virginia in baseball, the students met the train at the station a mile away and tied a hundred feet of rope to a carry-all or station wagon and pulled the team all the way back uptown and to the South Building, just as the villagers had done for the Fire company.

But we didn't often beat Virginia, our great rival then, certainly not in football. They had us jinxed, hexed, buffaloed, beaten almost before we started. But we kept trying. We made "Just Wait 'Til Next Year," our slogan long before Brooklyn and the Dodgers ever thought of it. And sometimes, "next year," we did it! Foy Roberson's team (he was Miss Nellie Roberson-my-schoolteacher's brother) beat Virginia 17 to 0 in 1905 at Norfolk. Because our team was so good that year and it was felt we had a good chance to win, many people from Chapel Hill went to Norfolk to see the game on the excursion train—and Mars' Phil took me.

Being born a Virginian, I suffered greatly. It was a trial and a tribulation, a cross I had to bear, and sometimes the other boys twitted me about my birthplace. I was secretly ashamed of it myself, and on one occasion when I was very young, my mother said, I came to her in tears and asked her if I would always have to be a Virginian. She was greatly shocked, and then proudly, and with hauteur, for she was a true daughter of the Old Dominion, assured me that I couldn't ever be anything else; that I was a very fortunate boy indeed to have such a heritage. But for once, Mother was wrong. I believe I *have* got away from being a Virginian, and now I sing "I'm a Tar Heel Born" as loud as the next man (and we beat Virginia practically every year).

Chapter Twenty-two

THAT 1905 trip to Norfolk with Mars' Phil, when I was twelve years old, stands out in my memory in bold relief because it was the very first time I ever went away from home "on a trip" in strictly male company—and with Mars' Phil as my companion I was as proud as a peacock and keyed to a dizzy height of excitement. "Try not to let him have apoplexy," Grandpa said to Mars' Phil.

The best part of going was the sudden, unexpected way it happened. Great plans had long been made for the excursion, for people thought that maybe this was our year to beat Virginia, and hundreds of people from Chapel Hill were going. Support of our teams was not confined to the students and small fry of the village; the villagers, too, were rabid fans, a condition prevalent even now. All you heard on every side was "See you in Norfolk!" I wanted badly to go, but as usual, my financial condition did not afford me the luxury of paying my own way. I felt lonely and forlorn and out of things, and I had hesitatingly approached Mother just on the bare possibility that my going with the crowd could be arranged. But she said No, it would cost too much. (I *think* it cost six dollars.) I moped miserably around with my tail dragging, even though I tried to make the best of my disappointment at being marooned in a deserted Chapel Hill over Thanksgiving Day.

And then, the day before the excursion train was to leave, Mother called me in and with shining face told me I could go—with Mars' Phil. The wonderfulness of her announcement left me open-mouthed and speechless, but not for long, and I remember letting out a whoop and grabbing Mother and hugging her and dancing her around. Just how my going —and Mars' Phil's—was arranged and accomplished, I never knew exactly, but I think the three of them, Mother, Mars' Phil and Grandpa, put their heads together and dug deep into their pocketbooks.

The train trip to Norfolk is a little blurred in my memory, because, I guess, I was so emotionally exhausted by the time the train pulled out from Chapel Hill that I was in a state of semicollapse and things did not register very clearly. The Southern had put on a real excursion train from Chapel Hill, several coaches (a magnificent long train, I thought) which went right through to Norfolk without any change at University Station or anywhere. The train was packed and jammed, loaded to the gunwales, Mars' Phil said, and full of singing and confusion and tobacco smoke. We left Chapel Hill late in the afternoon and reached Norfolk early the following morning. Everybody took lunches in baskets or shoe boxes to eat that night for supper. I always liked to eat on the train. But after I had eaten, that night, I couldn't stay awake, even with all the noise. I remember waking up in the night, and trying to get more comfortable on the hard coach seat, and Mars' Phil putting his arm around me so that I could lean against him. I went back to sleep picturing the glorious sights I was to see on the morrow.

And I did see glorious sights! Norfolk itself, when we got there next day, was in gala attire (that's what the newspaper said) with banners and streamers of the two Universities' colors everywhere, and pretty girls wearing white or yellow chrysanthemums, with long blue ribbons, waving pennants. I had brought my Carolina pennant, of course, and I made good use of it. Norfolk seemed a mighty metropolis to me—I even saw sailors on the streets—and the streets were jammed with carriages and automobiles and bands and excited, laughing people. At the Monticello Hotel, which was headquarters for both contingents, the excitement and the crowd was terrific. We finally got in the dining room, to eat our dinner, and the waiter called Mars' Phil and me "You Gentlemen!" Mars' Phil knew so many people, and afterwards, out in the lobby, somebody came up every minute and grabbed him and shouted, "Hi, there, Phil, you old buzzard!" or "Hey, there, Phil, I haven't seen you since . . ." and Mars' Phil was mighty happy. Every now and then he would say to me, "Buster, you sit right there. Don't go 'way, now. I'll be back in just a minute," and he and one of the men, or a group of them, would disappear, leaving me sitting in the big chair in the lobby, watching the crowd. But I wasn't the least bit lonely or disturbed; I felt like a seasoned and debonair world traveler, for was I not out on the loose with Mars' Phil?—and anyway the crowd was full of people from Chapel Hill who hailed me, students and townsfolk who had come with us on the excursion train, and bye and bye Mars' Phil would come back, happier than ever.

I began to be afraid, however, that we might be late for the game, and started plucking at Mars' Phil and nagging him to get started for the field. Finally, as I watched the hands of the big clock move closer and closer to kick-off time, I was in an agony of fear that the game might begin and we not there, and Mars' Phil tore himself away from his shouting and back-slapping friends, and we were off. Outside the door of the hotel we fell in with more friends, and we all piled into a carriage and drove out to the field. I waved my pennant and yelled at the

people on the sidewalks and in the street cars and other carriages and automobiles. Ah, it was glorious . . . I wish I could remember more about the game itself, but that's blurred, too. The bleacher seats ran the whole length of the field, and there must have been all of seven or eight thousand people there, Mars' Phil said, you never saw such a crowd. We were way up near the top somewhere, and the field below us seemed far away, and the players pigmies who ran up and down. This was because in the games at Chapel Hill you were so close to what was going on. But I could tell each one of the Carolina players as far as I could see him, even if they didn't wear any numbers, and the identities of the Virginia players didn't matter; all I knew or cared was that they were the enemy in the hated orange and blue.

Virginia never had a chance, the newspaper said next day (though it looked like an awful battle to me, right down to the finish). Foy Roberson, our quarterback and captain, ran Virginia ragged, and three times we went across their goal line for touchdowns, while that great throng of people went crazy—and I the craziest of them all.

One of our backfield, that day, later became United States Senator from North Carolina, if not famous, very well known; but I think he was a better halfback than Senator. Another star for U.N.C. on that great day was a big and burly guard named O. Max Gardner, whose untimely death, just a year or so ago, as he was about to leave for England to become our Ambassador to the Court of St. James's, shocked and saddened so many of us old-timers. Foy Roberson was wonderful, and all the others. The final score was North Carolina 17, Virginia 0, and our tired, happy heroes were carried off the field on the shoulders of their cheering, triumphant followers. Most of the boys, among them Foy Roberson, had played the entire game. Just to show you how much football has changed, even to its figures and specifi-

cations, they played two halves of thirty-five minutes each,
with no break for quarters; the field was 110 yards long,
and a touchdown counted only five points. According to today's scoring, we should have beaten Virginia 20 to 0!

The rest is just a golden, hazy impression of glory
. . . That night we went to the theatre and saw a musical
comedy—my first. The theatre was full of yelling, singing
students of both schools, and you would have thought the
game was still going on. All that I remember of that musical
comedy is the comedian, in white pants and carrying a cane
with a Carolina pennant on it, and a beautiful chorus of ladies,
dressed in Scottish kilts with bare knees, dancing across the
stage and lined up like the Rockettes. And I remember well
the near-riot that ensued when some students (*Virginia* boys,
it was said; certainly they were none of ours) climbed down
out of a box across the theatre and dropped onto the stage
and grabbed at the beauteous kilted girls! (They had had a
Little Too Much, Mars' Phil said.) The curtain came down
in all the confusion, and we heard later that there was a big
fight on the stage, and that the obstreperous students got
thrown out the back door into the alley. We left Norfolk at
midnight, and I remember nothing whatever of the exultant
trip home. But the whole thing was very wonderful, going
with another man, that way.

What is even clearer in my memory than that glorious
victory over Virginia, is a little sequel to it.

Later, in Chapel Hill, I sat one day beside Foy Roberson on the curb in front of the post office. Why he should
have been sitting on the curb, in the early winter sunshine,
flipping pebbles, his feet in the dust of the street, I do not
know. But I remember he was laughing and happy. With the
long, hard grind of the football season behind him, and also
the well-nigh miraculous shutout of Virginia in our big game

—as well as his own personal prize of being named All-Southern Quarterback—well he might have felt happy and relaxed and lazy! Anyway, his high good humor was such that I was emboldened to drop down, and flip pebbles, beside him, and to tell him that I had seen the game in Norfolk and that I thought he had done *"Good Work."* (*"Good Work"* was the accolade, then, if you said it like you meant it.) He seemed to appreciate my compliments, and talked about the game and the winning of it, while I, overcome by suffocating pride that *Foy Roberson* should be talking that way to *me,* hung on his every word. Then (and there is no explanation for the things which make a clear, lasting imprint on a child's recollection) he turned and looked right at me and asked, "Did you really think we would beat Virginia?" I can see him very clearly at this long-after moment. He was grinning, but looking full at me with honest and sincere inquiry in his eyes; he wanted to know, and I was too stunned, I think, to answer immediately. It was the very first time in my life that a grown man, a great one, a celebrity, an exalted being like Foy Roberson, had ever asked me a direct question like that, desiring my answer and opinion. Man to man . . . just like that. I believe that was the moment I first felt I was growing up.

Dr. Roberson is not so young any more. He is a distinguished and renowned surgeon who does his skilled and merciful cutting in the Durham hospitals. I have never told him what a terrific thing he did for me, so many years ago, and I know he will think I have a long, long memory. I have.

CHAPTER TWENTY-THREE

PEOPLE (that is, the human beings among them) can do such wonderful things to and for boys—small and impulsive things, perhaps, to which they themselves never give a second thought, but which to the boys are epic, unforgettable, treasures to be stored away in their hearts for all their lives. The littlest things may assume utmost importance when you are young. Boys, of course, are given to black despair at times, like everybody else, and go moping around feeling sure the end of their world has come, but they can know high ecstasy and exaltation, too . . . and almost always either of these extremes of emotion is at the hands of one of their various gods or goddesses. For empty is the boyhood which isn't packed with hero-worship and idolatry.

In the imperishable and friendly frieze of my memory there are many handsome and heroic figures, varied, vivid. They parade forever past me; beings I have loved and worshiped. This bright and beautiful frieze is conveniently portable, accompanying me and furnishing delightful decoration wherever I go. In addition to the humans of assorted ages, my gods and friends, it also includes a few horses and of course many dogs. But in this gay and golden frieze of recollection it is the grown-ups who for no especial reason were kind to me when I was a kid who head the parade, and ride the horses. People like Foy Roberson, who asked me a question, and Miss Nellie, his sister, who went with me to a ball game.

The fact that I have always thought of Miss Nellie as My Schoolteacher speaks for itself. Of course I have had many other schoolteachers (some of whom I detested)— male and female, young and old and middle-aged, crabbed and kindly, helpful and discouraging—but while I was only under Miss Nellie's beautiful eye and thumb for a comparatively short period, she has always remained to me a symbolic figure, on a pedestal, of what a boy's schoolteacher should be, and was. I adored her with all the intensity of my early teens; I endowed her with all the virtues human and divine; the dusty earth o'er which she dragged her skirts was holy ground.

When I got "kept in" after school, because of my dumbness or my deplorable deportment, it was a pleasure, for was I not alone in the big room with Miss Nellie? When she got me started in Latin (and little farther, at that!) it was with "Amo, Amas, Amat," and it was wonderful and thrilling to be speaking with Miss Nellie of *love,* even if the class was listening and it was only in Latin. When I recited "Amo—I love," I'd always add, to myself, *"you!"* and my heart would bump! Please don't remind me that everybody at one time or another, has a crush on his schoolteacher; mine was no crush, it was a Grand Passion, and it reached a great climax. Even if impersonal, Miss Nellie was sweet and kind and generous, and because of the goodness of her heart she went with me to a ball game!

Going to the ball games, for myself and the other boys, depended largely upon the most coveted job in Chapel Hill, that of Tacking Up Signs, and proud and swaggerful were we who won the honor and distinction of this well-rewarded work. The signs were small, cheap throwaways printed on the hand presses of the *Tar Heel,* the student newspaper (and the only one, then, in Chapel Hill), announcing a baseball game or other athletic event. We had many ball games in the early spring, when northern college teams came south on training trips, and on through to commencement time. The securing of the contract, or commission, or gentlemen's agreement to pick up an armful of these signs, and, armed with a hammer and a pocketful of tacks, cover the town, was eagerly sought, of course, by practically all the boys in the village. Two or three of us, thus honored, shared the work. The job was had only after much flattery, bootlicking and cajolery of the team manager. You became the abject slave of this august being, and gladly did his bidding in all sorts of extraneous endeavor. You invested much time hanging around the frat house where he lived, during that season of the year when the awarding of the contract was in doubt, just in the hope and on the chance that he might ask you to do something for him. I made it very much my business to stand in the managers' good graces, and almost always it paid off, and I jockeyed myself into the juicy job.

You tacked the sheets to poles and trees and fences and almost any vacant surface (except the Church bulletin board). Rashly, I did this once; the board was entirely empty, and it was hard to pass an empty space. I remember that when Grandpa saw it, after church that Sunday, he read it all the way through. It announced a game with Guilford. Then he looked at me over his spectacles. "Did you put this here?" he asked.

"Yessuh," I said, red faced.

"Well, take it down," he said patiently, "and pull out all the tacks."

But all you had to do, when your work was properly done, was to go up to the field on the exciting day of the game (of course you got there very early, sometimes before The Man on the Gate did) and say to this Man on the Gate, "I Tacked Up Signs," and he, knowing you spoke truly, would always pass you right in, usually with a friendly slap on the rump. Just the other day I was looking at some photographs of old-time Chapel Hill, and there in the foreground, on a telephone post, was a well-remembered sign which said "BASEBALL," in very large letters—"Lehigh vs U.N.C." —and pride and nostalgia welled within me at the thought that in all likelihood I myself had tacked it there.

That's how come I could ask Miss Nellie to go to the ball game, and pay her way, for I got in free! I had conceived and nurtured the daring idea quite a while before our home game with Virginia, carefully assembling my resources to make certain I would have the necessary fifty cents. I decided to ask her in plenty of time, too, fearful that she would accompany some other beau should I delay too long. All the while, however, grave doubt as to her acceptance persisted in my mind. "Maybe she will," I'd tell myself, trying to bolster my courage and determination; but then I'd think despondently, "No, she won't." It got to be like tearing up a daisy: "Maybe she will. No, she won't. Maybe she will. No, she won't" . . . and on the day I asked her, after school, I was not over-confident.

I delayed getting my things together, my breath getting shorter and shorter, and then—when everybody else had gone —I walked up to her desk. "Miss Nellie," I asked (as the schoolroom up-ended and began whirling around me), "May I have the great pleasure of seeing you to the ball game next Sad'dy?" (I put it that way because of a story I had read in which the suitor had inquired of the beautiful heroine if he might have the great pleasure of seeing her home, and it seemed to me that if it was in print, in a story, like that, a proper invitation should be thus phrased.) I had carefully rehearsed the

line, saying it over and over to myself for days, and I had
kept repeating it soundlessly all that day, to the detriment
of my lessons. When the moment came I delivered it well,
however, with never a mistake or a stammer, and I remember standing there with thankful pride, and gazing at her in
embarrassed adoration, while I awaited her answer.

Miss Nellie smiled, and then she said, "Why, yes. That
would be very nice." That's what I mean about high exaltation.

The ensuing week, while a long one, was a period of
delightful anticipation. With the dawning of the great day I
attempted to clothe myself appropriately. I felt that I should
have had a new suit, or something, but the old one had to do.
However, a spanking clean white blouse, with a blue and
white necktie Mars' Phil had given me the preceding Christmas knotted tightly around my neck, made me look a little
better than usual, and with freshly blackened shoes and my
hair well plastered down with water, I did not present too
ruffianly an appearance, I thought, and my well-scrubbed
face, at least, must have been shining like the sun. Anyway,
when she saw me, Miss Nellie said, "Well!" That was it, I
thought exultantly. "Well!" *All was well.* She couldn't have
said anything more beautiful.

When we started out, I her escort, her protector, Miss
Nellie didn't take my arm or anything, but I imagined her
hand resting there, and was content. The late May afternoon was hot, and Miss Nellie looked particularly lovely in
a light, summery dress with ruffles, and a picture hat. She
carried a parasol, and I wondered uneasily whether I ought
not to offer to open it and hold it over her. Other ladies,
accompanied by their swains, wore similar costumes, and
all over the Campus, as we walked toward the baseball field,
you could see them coming, couples and quartettes and groups,
laughing and fanning. I wasn't walking, exactly, either—I

was floating—and I couldn't have been prouder had I been a plumed and armored knight astride a dapple-gray charger, with my lady, clinging frail and vinelike, behind me. Miss Nellie chatted gaily, about what I do not know, but it was beautiful. We passed signs I had tacked up, but of course I ignored them; it did not seem suitable to the occasion to mention that I had put them there. I naturally assumed an austere and dignified savoir faire when we encountered boys I knew, even though I could almost feel their insulting jeers and sniggers behind my back.

I had one really horrible moment, however, when we reached the field and I approached, importantly, the ticket window and took my place in line to buy Miss Nellie's ticket. All the way, I had fingered the change in my pocket, amounting to fifty cents, and I knew there was no hole there and that I had the fifty cents safely, but when the time came to use it and I pulled it forth and started to shove it across the shelf, the sum, incredibly, was only forty. I died a thousand deaths of shame during that horrified instant. The preposterous and desperate thought came to me that in my extremity I might say to The Man on the Gate, "I Tacked Up Signs; *She* Tacked Up Signs, too." But instantly I rejected the idea not only as unworthy, but also because I realized I wouldn't stand a Chinaman's chance of getting away with it. And then, pulling all the stuff out of my pocket, I found the missing dime. It had slipped in between the blades of my pocket knife, and with a surge of relief and joy I handed it over to the man and clutched my ticket—Miss Nellie's ticket!—and in we sailed, as I whispered to the grinning gateman, behind Miss Nellie's back, *"I Tacked Up Signs!"*

It was one of my great days. We beat Virginia, 6 to 1. Of the game I remember, now, not a detail except one; a Virginia man named Pollard who, late in the game, got a walk, stole second, third, and *home!* He was fast as a greased

streak of lightning, Mars' Phil said later. I can see him now,
sliding across the plate in a cloud of dust, and the umpire calling him safe. (He later became a distinguished judge, I understand, and I have sometimes wondered about his judicial
attitude toward theft.) The only sour note of the day was
that I lacked a nickel with which to buy Miss Nellie a bag of
peanuts, and I have always reproached myself bitterly. It is
small comfort to think that perhaps she didn't like peanuts
(some people don't) ; I should have been in a position to
offer them to her.

I do not believe, in retrospect, that Miss Nellie was what
you might call a rabid baseball fan, but she was no dumb-
bell about it, either : she knew a double play when she saw
one, and you weren't bothered by the silly questions most
women ask. We stayed until the last man was out in the ninth
inning, too, and as our band joyfully played "I'm a Tar Heel
Born," I took Miss Nellie's elbow and helped her climb down
the grandstand. I don't remember the long trudge back across
the Campus to Miss Nellie's house, because my ambition had
been realized, my dream had come true—I had taken Miss
Nellie to the ball game!—and I was triumphantly tired and
happily spent.

Smilingly and sweetly, she thanked me, and I said,
"You're welcome; thank *you*. Goodbye, Miss Nellie." In the
story I had read, in which the hero craved the great pleasure
of seeing the heroine home, he had asked, after he saw her
there, "When may I hope to see you again?" I had pondered
this question and said it over to myself several times, but
somehow, with Miss Nellie, it didn't seem just the thing,
and I decided against using it. It was enough that she, divine
being that she was, had, figuratively speaking, put her hand
in mine and gone with me where I willed; best not to try my
wonderful good fortune too far. Shucks, I knew I'd see her
again, all right!

I carefully carved the score of the game, the date, and Miss Nellie's initials on the arm of The Bishop's Residence. This was an ancient seat, out in our front yard, a chair which had belonged to my great-great-grandfather, and upon which he is supposed to have written the sermons, tracts, essays and ecclesiastical and genealogical history which made him famous in our part of the country. It was a heavy Windsor

with a writing arm, and was always referred to as The Bishop's Residence, unless the term That Old White Elephant was used. (He was the first of a three-generation string of clerics, to which it was hoped, I believe, my name would add a fourth, alas, alack.) Anyway, it stood outdoors, under a big tree, and took the weather. The ravages of time and sun and rain did it no good, and its feet gradually rotted off, in the damp grass, until it rested upon the braces, or stretchers, between its hickory legs. However, this served to make it lower and more comfortable, and as the family didn't seem to really give a hoot about it, other than hanging onto it though some vague sentiment, it became a sort of throne for me, on which, with my jackknife, I inscribed and recorded things. (Antiques, then, what with beautiful Bird's Eye

Maple and Mission furniture coming in, were of small account, and all you did with an antique was to nail or wire it
together and hope it would last until you could get something better.) The big writing arm was covered with carved
initials, designs and dates, data I wished to perpetuate. Somehow, and even through all the later vicissitudes of the family,
our moving around and all, we held onto the whittled-up old
Bishop's Residence, and ultimately it was discovered that it
was not only an interesting heirloom but a unique antique,
worth, in the eyes of the Wallace Nutting nuts, a small or
minor king's ransom! My wife, bless her thrifty heart, has
had the old chair restored, and the broad writing arm, planed
down, now shows no evidence of the time and loving labor I
put in decorating it. One of my best jobs was the N.R. under
that Virginia game score.

As a complement to my Chapel Hill schooling, Miss
Nellie stands out in crystal clarity. Most everything else relating to school is blank in my memory, or at best very foggy
—and there are occasions, as for instance when I attempt to
add a column of figures or name the chief exports of Nicaragua, when I wonder whether or not I ever really went to
school. But I must have; there is Miss Nellie to prove it. In
any event, and even with her help and inspiration, my early
scholastic training must have been pretty sketchy. Or rather,
my ability to appreciate and absorb the subjects taught me
must have been inadequate. Only a pitiful smattering of this
and that remains—such as in Latin, for example (which at
that period was stuffed down the throats of helpless juveniles
because it was Classical), where I learned only two items of
any importance; the fact that Amo means I love (Miss
Nellie) and the information that All Gaul is divided into
Three Parts. The relative significance of these two bits of
knowledge is ridiculous, of course, and I don't know why I

should have remembered about Gaul, or what good it ever did me. Enlightenment in even the supposedly simple things like readin', writin' and 'rithmetic was shed by me as a duck sheds water, and my happy and unconscious refusal to accept education must have been a sore trial to Grandpa, who was the only erudite member of my family I can think of at the moment.

For Grandpa knew a lot. The simplest and easiest thing to do was just to go to Grandpa when you needed the answer to something. He was a Greek scholar (not that I anticipated ever reading the Old Testament in Greek, and even in the Greek restaurant in Greensboro, where I went once with my father, the bill of fare was in English) and in addition to the little gold cross on his watch chain he wore a key which I understand was given him long ago in college because he was so smart. It had a Greek name. Also, he was a brother in a Greek fraternity, the Beta Theta Pi (but all the members in Chapel Hill were only American boys from North Carolina). He never hung around the Beta House, as I did (for it seemed to be an accepted fact that if and when I got to college I would be a Beta, too, because of Grandpa), but once a year, at least, he would join the brothers for a group photograph to be printed in the *Yackety Yack*. He was listed on the *Yackety Yack* page as Frater in Urbe, which meant, if you knew your Latin, that he was a brother living down on Rosemary Street rather than up on the Campus in the frat house. This posed a question which even Grandpa found it difficult to answer. Why, I asked him once, if it was a real Greek fraternity, was he and other brothers (Frater in Facultate, Frater in Universitate, etc.), designated that way in *Latin?* Why not in Greek? Latin was Italian, early Italian. "You and Dr. Wheeler, you aren't *Italians,* are you?" I queried.

"Hmmmm," he said. He put down the book he was read-

ing and looked at me. "Why'd you think of that?" he asked.
(I figured maybe he was stalling for time.)

"Well, if you're real Greeks," I said, "why do they talk
about you like that in *Latin?*"

"You know," he said, "I'll have to find out. It never came
up before."

"Yessuh," I said, and waited, while he knocked out his
pipe.

"Of course," he said, "Greece and Rome had a lot in
common. Early civilization and culture. . . . Besides, most
people couldn't read it if it was in Greek; I suppose it just
looks better in Latin."

But it did seem funny. Rome, Greece, Italian, Latin; it
was all too much for me, and I let it lie. I figured right then
and there I didn't want to be a Beta Theta Pi; it involved too
much study and knowledge (even Grandpa wasn't any too
sure about it, himself). It would be a lot simpler just to join
an American club, or something.

The brothers around the Beta House were mighty nice
to me, however, whenever I happened around and sat on the
edge of the porch or in the swing, even though they never let
me in on any of the handshakes or passwords or initiations.
(One of the brothers, a fellow named Leonard Blackburn,
told me once that when they initiated new members they took
all their money and then skinned 'em alive. They may have
taken all their money, but I never saw any evidences of skin-
ning, and I think he probably exaggerated.)

This contact is about as far as I ever got in Greek, or in
Latin, for that matter. I've never really needed either of them;
while I have never sojourned in the Beautiful Isles of Greece,
I have been to Rome, and all you have to do there is go around
to the American Express and get an interpreter and a car;
saves a lot of time and bother. It's likely the same way in
Greece.

The first school that I remember was Mrs. Cranmer's,

and except for its location, I swear the only thing I recall about it is the fact that I wheedled my mother into embroidering a big yellow C on my blue cap so that it might look a little more like a baseball cap. I was very proud of it. Then there was the other little school, name forgotten, but it was where Cobb Terrace is now, and all I remember about that is the climb I had to make up the side of a deep ravine to get to the little plateau on which the schoolhouse stood, and that the schoolhouse itself was red (red like the barns in Connecticut) just as they always are in old-time pictures. Then I went to Canady's, the "upper" school, and the fog gets lighter there and I remember things, because of Miss Nellie, I guess. I remember very well big Bunn Hearn, the pitcher, and I remember a pimply-faced boy named McMillan who seemed to feel it his duty to teach us younger ones a lot of stuff nobody would approve of; and I remember struggling with Algebra and English. I was in Miss Nellie's room a year, and then in Mr. Holloman's room, 'though I still had some classes under Miss Nellie, thank goodness. William Pritchard and I had a desk together in the rear of Mr. Holloman's room, and I remember a lot of chalk and spitball throwing, and that I would draw cartoons of Mr. Holoman, who was the Principal, and bald, and pass them around. My only defense in all this, and it's a lame one, I know, is that there were so many charming things to think about and do that I just couldn't get interested and absorbed in the dryness of organized study. But even if I emerged an ignoramus, I enjoyed school; and somehow or other, and by the grace of God, I passed my grades, and that seemed to be all that was necessary. Well, not quite all, either, for I did have to be tutored (I preferred the word "coached") occasionally by a student protégé of Grandpa's, or by Mars' Phil, and this at least shows that my family had some concern for my book-learning, and didn't want me to disgrace them.

Perhaps my shortcomings in scholarship should not be

censured too severely. The atmosphere of a college town—the grim battle of life far away—was not altogether conducive to sober study, and even in those days I formed a suspicion, later confirmed, that students, even University ones, do not necessarily study. Among my academic aquaintances were many gay blades who spent happy and carefree lives without ever making the Dean's list, and who seemed to be convinced that higher education includes many things not found in books. The term playboy is fairly modern, I believe, but we had plenty of them who fitted into this category in spirit, if not the letter, and the shining example of these may have influenced me more toward the pursuits of pleasure than of pedantry.

Even if my family may have been discouraged about my intellectual future they nevertheless saw to it that I got a little polish in the social graces, and about this time Mother sent me to Jake Morehead's dancing class. Jake Morehead, whose first name was really James, was a law student who had graduated from the University a few years before, and then had been around a bit before coming back to Chapel Hill to study the statutes. He was one of the most extraordinary physical contradictions I ever saw. Handicapped by a short and withered leg (we hadn't heard of infantile paralysis then but likely that is what had done it) he nevertheless got gaily and expertly about in activities in which sounder men seldom excel. He was one of the most beautiful dancers I ever saw; he was an elusive and artful boxer; and to cap it all he was an extremely good catcher, for four years, on his class baseball team and the Scrubs. What a man! His proficiency was such that he taught very popular classes in the first of these two arts, and in both of them I was an enthusiastic pupil. The boxing part of my education was unknown to and unpaid for by my mother or grandfather, and was just handed me, gratis, by Jake. (He could really hand it to you, too.)

Often when I was supposedly attending dancing class, I was in reality—my fists encased in pillowlike and too-large boxing gloves—being energetically cuffed around in Jake's boxing class despite my best efforts in the manly art of self defense.

But those all-male dancing classes must have been something for an impartial observer to behold! The entrance fee to these classes was low: there was nothing commercial about Jake, and besides, the money just wasn't there, so, like most great teachers, he taught almost purely for the love of it. If I wasn't one of the clumsiest of his pupils it was because I was the smallest; some of the six-foot-plus farm boys, agonized and perspiring, were really awesome in their awkwardness. After we had learned, alone, the simple footwork of the waltz and two-step, or at least been given every opportunity so to do, we were divided into two groups, Girls and Boys. This occasioned a great deal of tittering, ribald remarking and horseplay, but was done for the sake of trying to impress upon us the customary approach of polite society to the Dance. The "Girls" sat along the wall, and the "Boys" would approach and bow, and say "How do you *do*, Miss Guzzle? May I have the pleasure of the next dance?" And "Miss Guzzle" would probably kick at him and roar with laughter, and then rise and mincingly give him her hand, and melt into his arms, and off they'd go, struggling and lumbering through the crowd on the gym floor, bumping and bulling their way along and trampling down all opposition, while somebody banged out "The Blue Danube" on the tinny piano and Jake glided gracefully and effortlessly in and out the melee, marking time and shouting *"One*-two-three! *One*-two-three!" When the dance ended the boy was instructed to offer his arm to the gasping Girl and lead her back to her seat and bow again and thank her very much (and in theory open her fan and fan her. What he usually did was to take a poke at his partner and say "Damn your soul, can't you keep off my

feet?"). Everybody wanted to lead, of course, and be a domi-
nating male—and the Girls' revenge came when the sexes
were switched and they themselves assumed the offensive.
There was a lot of shoving and hauling, however, for everybody—whether theoretically male or female—wanted and
tried to guide the other fellow. Even when I was supposedly
given the privilege of leading, I would likely as not find myself paired up with some big gorilla I couldn't possibly push
around to save my life, and he'd take the lead away from me.
At such times I would think back to the slender frailty of
Virginia Taylor or Pearl McGrew and bet myself I could lead
them, by golly, or know the reason why! Anyway, and in
spite of injustice and my mashed and maimed feet, I learned;
and with my skill safely secured for future use when there
were really girls, I thought of myself as quite a Dog and accomplished Man-About-Town.

This "May-I-have-the-next-dance?" instruction applied
merely to informal affairs. Jake lectured to us on the cus-
toms of the formal terpsichore, most important of which was
to get your girl's program filled (with prominent and impressive names) as far ahead as possible. This redounded to
your own prestige as well as to that of the young lady. Of
course, you reserved for yourself a certain number of dances,
not too many, not too few, all depending on the girl. Just in
case the girl was a horse, or not very pretty, or something,
and you might have trouble, when the time came, exchang-
ing dances (and this was one of the many invaluable tips he
gave us) you did a lot of advance selling among the numerous stags who would attend the ball ladyless, and painted the
charms of your date in glowing colors; for regardless of what
the girl was like you had to present her with a full card, and if
she was, well, not the knockout you had hoped for, you of
course didn't want to get stuck for too many dances yourself. He said you ought to be very careful about agreeing to

squire somebody's sister, or a friend of his sister, who was just dying to come up to Chapel Hill, even though the girl was guaranteed. You could get into a lot of trouble that way. In some ways it was better to be a stag, he said. He said that if you were really serious about this dancing business you ought to begin planning, right now, to get into the German Club, but that inasmuch as this required a tail coat, the pros and cons of the question should be carefully weighed. Even the rental of a dress suit went into money, and made you wonder sometimes if it was worth while. On the other side of the picture, a life in Society—where you could hold your own on the ballroom floor—held many advantages, and some of the contacts you made might prove very enjoyable and valuable. He said it was a Great Asset.

Anyway, he said, a man ought to think it over very carefully. We all did, sitting there—and afterwards, I'm sure. I believe the tail coat feature must have frightened some of the fainter-hearted ones, for they dropped out. Jake was fair and square about it, warning us like that, and he certainly knew his stuff. Inasmuch as I was still in short pants I wasn't particularly worried by the dress suit hazard because I felt I wouldn't be expected to wear a tail coat with knickerbockers; the evening clothes would come in time, I thought, everything else always had. And I determined upon a full and abundant life in Society.

The balls and germans at the University were glittering and glamorous affairs. To my eager eyes they seemed the ultimate in romance. And beautiful they really were, especially the daytime germans at commencement. The village overflowed then with sweethearts and sisters and fiancées who came in droves, and families bent on watching their pride step up in cap and gown to claim his sheepskin, and for three or four days there was a gay whirl of dances and dates and ball games and buggy rides for belles and beaux. Boys moved out

of fraternity houses and girls and their chaperons moved in.
Mrs. MacRae's and other boarding places bulged at the seams,
and Mr. Pickard's Inn all but had a S.R.O. sign out. Tradi-
tionally, Commencement Week is one of the hottest of the
year, and while the June sun glared down the Campus came to
life with pretty, frilly frocks like pastel flowers blooming everywhere, and parasols and fans, and creased and gleaming peg-
top pants of snowy flannel, where before there had been only
the drabness of the boys' everyday attire. Even the air was
stimulating, and song and laughter filled it.

The focal point for the climax of celebration was Com-
mons Hall, the large and dingy structure which was the students' dining hall. Its exterior was of a depressing dreariness,
but for those dances it was transformed, within, into what was
for me a gorgeous palace from the Arabian Nights. The
faculty and the townspeople, old and young (if these latter
behaved themselves), were welcome to come and watch, and
of course everybody came. The beauty and grace of the girls,
and the marches and the intricate and elaborate figures of the
german impressed me very much, and I eagerly looked forward to my tail coat days, when I, too, could belong to the
German Club and have a beautiful young lady on my arm, and
wear an imposing ribbon sash, with rosette, such as identified
the marshals and leaders of the german.

But even if I then couldn't take part in the dances, there
was one thing, exciting and almost as popular, I could do—
and I did it. I took a good-looking girl buggy riding! Her
name was Thelma Johnson. This could not be compared in
any respect with the achievement of taking Miss Nellie to the
ball game, for my heart was in no way involved; I only did it
as a gesture.

Thelma Johnson was a girl I knew—and, I must admit,
liked—at Canady's; a large and voluptuous and perfectly beautiful creature, with black hair and high color, a couple of years

(at least) my senior. She was friendly and fresh and wholesome, and our relationship was purely Platonic. Just because, once or twice, I chose to walk along with her leaving school, there was Talk; and I was enraged to hear, upon one occasion, that final and unforgivable taunt being chanted by some derisive and despicable characters among my contemporaries:

> "Billy's mad, and I am glad,
> And I know what will *please* him!
> A bottle of wine to make him shine
> And Thelma Johnson to *sque-e-e-ze* him!"

It wasn't that way at all. I never squeezed or was squeezed by Thelma Johnson, and never had any ideas or desires along that line. But there's no denying that perhaps I was becoming just a mite girl-conscious, and I *used* Thelma, and her good nature, not only because she was very decorative, but also to further my own ego. Because everybody else, it seemed to me, took a pretty girl buggy riding at Commencement, and because I wanted to appear grown-up and socially successful too, I took Thelma Johnson!

That also cost me fifty cents, but the self-esteem I gained thereby was worth it. Mr. Pickard charged fifty cents an hour for a horse and buggy, and of course when the University gallants and their girls took a rig out they usually were gone some hours. Mr. Pickard seemed a little surprised, but understanding, too, when I asked him if I could have a buggy and Floss, his roan mare, for just an hour. (I think Thelma was surprised, too, but then she was surprised, and pleased, that I even asked her, so that was all right.)

When I drove around to get her, right on time, she was not quite ready (*why* are girls that way?) and I suffered considerably while I waited, thinking of the valuable time a-wasting. But she wasn't long, and when she came she looked beautiful, with a yellow Leghorn hat with flowers on it. I helped her in the buggy while she giggled and chattered, and then I touched Floss with the whip and clucked, and off we trotted down Franklin Street. It was wonderful. I held the reins in my left hand, and sat up straight, and when we passed people on the sidewalk, or in other buggies, I touched my cap with the whip in salute, just as the more debonnaire student drivers did, and felt, jubilantly, that I must look pretty fine driving that buggy down Franklin Street with Thelma, and that I was greatly impressing those who ordinarily just took me for granted.

I drove out to Strowd's Creek, and stopped in the ford so that Floss could put her head down and get a drink. It was cool and quiet and shady there, with the water purling around us—darned romantic, I thought—and I visualized a picture of Thelma and me and Floss and the buggy standing there in the stream. On the other side I turned around, as I was keeping a watchful and necessary eye on the time (having borrowed Billy Cobb's Ingersol "dollar biscuit" for the occasion).

"What's the matter?" asked Thelma. "What time is it?"

"We got to get back," I said. "I gott'n engagement."

"You *have?*" she said. "Well—that's all right. So've I."

So we splashed back through the Creek and started up the long grade to Chapel Hill, Floss stepping out a little because she was headed for home . . . and then trouble overtook us in the form and sound of Dr. Herty's automobile! Floss was usually pretty good about automobiles; she was getting used to them, Mr. Pickard said; but as Dr. Herty's red Reo chugged up behind us, and I was pulling off the road to let him go by, it gave an extra-loud explosion, and Floss shied. One wheel went in the ditch, and I thought we were gone: Dr. Herty shouted and Thelma screamed! And then Floss dragged us out of the ditch and took off up the hill. Thank Heaven she was headed up the hill and not down! I sawed on the reins and kept them tight, just as Poor Dave had taught me (I wished frantically that he was driving then, for I was scared). Thelma hung on and didn't make a sound after that first squeal, and by the time we got to the top of the steep hill Floss was winded and slowed down to her customary bumpy trot. "You're just wonderful," Thelma said. And I said, with a deprecating gesture, "Oh, that's nothin'. That happens lots of times."

So we trotted back up Franklin Street, and lots more people saw us.

"It was a wonderful ride," Thelma said. "I had a wonderful time. And you were just *wonderful* . . ."

I helped her out, and she stood at her gate and smiled and waved while I drove off down the street to Mr. Pickard's.

When he saw Floss sort of lathered up he said, "You ain't been running this mare, have you?"

And I said, "No, suh. It's justa nawfully hot day."

One of the people I saw on that occasion, and the one I impressed the most, I think, was Mars' Phil. When we passed the post office on our way home he was standing on the sidewalk talking to somebody, and when he recognized me I saw his eyes pop. He waved, and I saluted him with the whip. Later he added the final, glorious touch to my pride and satisfaction: *"WELL!"* he said, when I came in that night (and the word carried astonishment and admiration as well as a sly male understanding). Grinningly, he gave me a leer and a knowing wink. *"Lady-killer!"* he said.

My cup was full.

CHAPTER TWENTY-FOUR

IF THERE is really any such thing as celestial music (and I am sure I have heard it), it does not come from harps, but from guitars.

I fully realize that I may be going out on a limb, as it were, and inviting a lot of argument by coming out with such a flat and unqualified statement, because most people simply accept and believe what all their lives they have been told, and follow unquestioningly the ancient theory that the melodies of Heaven are produced by gilded harps in angels' hands. On whose authority, say I? To my mind this is pure legend, unfounded, with no basis in fact. Also, most people are inattentive or inexpert listeners, and if the music is good (as Heavenly music always is) they are not prone to analyse the orchestration or the instrumentality, and they never note the subtle but powerful difference between harps and guitars. For it is *guitars* the angels play. That is, when they really go to town on something. Of course I grant you that in Grade B work the angels may use harps, or anything they wish, but for their top drawer music, produced on Sundays and moonlight nights, they only use guitars.

I have a feeling of absolute knowledge and certainty in making the above declaration. So would have any man of sensitivity who in his early youth and that of the century has heard the sound. To hear it he must have drifted down a shadowy Southern village street on moonlight nights in summer, with the scent of honeysuckle heavy on the air-waveless air—for no radios blared at him from brightly lighted picture windows, no full volume record-players dinned their dance tunes in his ears, no jukebox at the neoned tavern on the corner made turmoil of the night. No, there would only have been the warm darkness and the silence. There must have been, for him, only peace and stillness, with the faraway baying of a hound, perhaps, and here and there a yellow lighted lamp to cut the moonlight's checkers, and the sound of gentle voices and soft laughter from a shadowed lawn, and, from some dark porch he couldn't see, the golden sound of a guitar. I have been there, and I know whereof I speak.

The man—or the boy of Then—was never quite sure whether the music he heard was human or divine. He may have thought the little breeze was made by angels' wings. Or he may have thought Miss Etty Mangum made the music. Perhaps she did, but if so her delicate white fingers, strumming the responsive strings, were guided by the angels; that I know.

I don't mean to get too lyrical about Miss Etty Mangum, or the dark village street of a summer's night—but there she was, in the shadows, and you can draw your own conclusions and figure out for yourself what it must have sounded like. She, Miss Etty, was my pal Charles's aunt, an Old Maid, they said (not the angels; they would never have said anything unkind about Miss Etty). Sometimes in the evening, resting in the hammock on the darkened porch of the beautiful old house on Rosemary Street, she would bring out and play her big, silver-trimmed guitar, or sometimes, sitting on the corner of the broad front step, strum it tenderly and seductively the while she looked up at the moonlit sky. Miss Etty wasn't really old, you understand—in fact, by today's standards her years would not be questioned and she would be considered only of

an interesting and maturely attractive age—but any girl who went through her twenties unmarried, back in the time when Teddy Roosevelt rode the range, risked the awful and humiliating designation of Old Maid.

Miss Etty was pale and slender, not beautiful, but sweet and gentle. She wore soft white dresses, and bangs, with a fascinator sometimes over her head or shoulders. Her eyes occasionally looked red and unhappy, as though she wept in secret. I somehow understood that she had been Disappointed in Love, and even though I may not have fully appreciated what this represented I thought it a most interesting condition, and my heart went out to Miss Etty.

Her lonely music, when she could not longer bear her

loneliness, almost tore the heart from your bosom, melodies
like "Long, Long Ago," and "In the Gloaming (Oh, my
Darling . . .)," and "The Rosary," softly plunked out on the
summer air. Miss Etty did not sing, thank goodness; I don't
believe I or anyone could have borne that. There was only the
simple tune of the aching little love song, strummed by her
empty hands upon the guitar held in her empty arms. I used
to feel all this keenly, for I was reaching a very sentimental
and emotional age.

I used to speculate pleasurably upon Miss Etty's past,
and her Broken Heart. I thought her a most enchanting and
romantic figure, draped in melancholy mystery. I wondered
about her Faithless Lover, whether he had jilted her at the
altar, or whether he had been killed in the War, as the lovers
of so many Southern girls, I read, had been. No, of course not;
Miss Etty wasn't old enough for that. Unless it was the
Spanish war, there was a thought! Perhaps he had been mor-
tally wounded charging up San Juan Hill with the Rough
Riders, and died there on the battlefield all alone. Or maybe
it was nothing so heroic as that, just a train wreck, maybe, or
something fell on him. Another delightful idea was that Miss
Etty's Lover might have fought a duel over her, like the one
at Piney Prospect—and I wondered which of the antagonists
she loved—the one who got killed, or the handsome, fiery-
tempered one who pulled his hat down over his eyes and
mounted his horse and spurred away, like Peter Dromgoole.
It was all very stimulating.

I asked Mother, once, tentatively, what happened to Miss
Etty.

"What? When?" Mother asked.

"Why didn't she get married?" I asked, to clear the situation up.

"Oh," said Mother, and laughed. "I don't know; maybe
just because she didn't want to."

"Why not?" I inquired.

"Oh, just because," said Mother.

But I was doubtful. "Do you reckon her Lover got killed?" I persisted.

"*No,*" Mother said, smiling. "She just never found the Right Man."

"The Right Man?" I asked. "Did she look for him?"

"I don't know about that," Mother laughed, "I reckon she did."

That was all the satisfaction I could get. But that gave me a slightly different train of thought, and I began to think about and wonder what the Right Man for Miss Etty would have looked like, if she could have found him. I felt that he would have been very handsome and dashing and romantic. I wished I could have found him for her, but I didn't know where to look.

Having been somewhat disappointed in love myself, I felt a slight bond between us, and I looked forward to the time when I could have a guitar, too, and cloak myself in an atmosphere of sweet and lonely sadness, like Miss Etty. I wondered just how one secured a broken heart . . . The porch is gone, and the steps where she sat in the moonlight, but now, whenever I go to Betty Smith's (who, according to her deed, is now the owner of the house), I always find Miss Etty there with her guitar. No one else sees or hears her, I believe, so I've never mentioned it.

Mars' Phil had been disappointed in love. It was never talked about, until later, but somehow I understood this, too. But he didn't pine away, or look sad and romantic. (He looked romantic, all right, to me, but not the disappointed-in-love way.) He seemed to me to be very cheerful, most of the time, and sometimes I wondered if he had really been very much

disappointed, until I found out, later, how badly disappointed
he had been.

Back in the gay and early days of our residence in Chapel
Hill, Mother had had Mars' Phil's and Mars' Pike's "fiancées"
come, one summer, to visit us. It was a happy time. The girls
stayed in my uncles' room, while they bunked next door at
the Abernathys'. There was a Kodak picture, once, of the
four of them—I wish I had it now. It showed them stretched
out on the grass of our front yard, the little cottage in the
background. They were pretending, coy and kittenish, to
drink from the bird water stone, their heads touching—a very
daring photograph. Almost risqué. The girls, big-sleeved,
laughed up at you from beneath their pompadours, and the
boys were all dressed up, their straw boaters beside them on
the grass. There was a lot of singing and laughter around the
house those days. There were parties at other peoples' houses,
as well as ours, for the girls immediately became very popular;
and there were picnics in the woods or at the mill pond or on
the Creek. Sometimes, gala occasions, there were buggy rides;
but I was seldom allowed to accompany either of the couples
on these, because "Three's a crowd," Mother said. She was
not quite accurate in this, because when she and Dad and I
went anyhere in a buggy there was always plenty of room. On
rainy days there were hot games of Flinch or Authors or car-
roms. Sometimes everybody would get down on the floor (I
had to be careful not to get my feet on the girls' skirts which
were spread out around them) and we played tiddlywinks on
the carpet, or mumblepeg outdoors on the grass. But I liked
the Flinch games in the study best, and it was great fun to
shout "Flinch!" suddenly, and scare the girls, when you made
one.

Once Mars' Phil and Mars' Pike got a team and a surrey
from Mr. Pickard, and they and the girls drove to Durham

and took me along, and I didn't crowd them at all. They drew
the line at taking Duke, however; I can still see him standing
on the sidewalk, looking after us—Grandpa holding his collar
—as we drove away. The girls and my uncles sang all the way
to Durham, "Oh, Susanna," and "There is a Tavern in the
Town," and "The Spanish Cavalier," and "Daisies Won't
Tell," and lots of other songs. The trip took us all day
(Mother had packed a fine lunch basket for us, and we had a
picnic on New Hope Creek). Coming home they didn't sing
so much, but I do remember Mars' Phil singing a solo, in his
rich bass voice, and they joining in the chorus of "Seeing
Nellie Home." When we got home, and Mars' Phil and I took
the team back to Mr. Pickard's and walked home to the
rectory, it was suppertime. Everybody said it had been a fine
day.

It was considered great fun to eat your slice of watermelon without benefit of fork or spoon, and it was understood
that in so doing you were fair game and might get your face
pushed into it. The boys did this to the girls, and there would
be hilarious laughing and squealing. Both girls were pretty
as peaches, even with watermelon juice and pulp streaming
down their faces. Mars' Phil's fiancée, Miss Floy, was really
very beautiful, a tall and striking brunette with wonderful
black hair and eyes, and flashing white teeth, and Mars' Pike's,
Carolisa, was blondish, maybe not quite so beautiful as Floy,
but beautiful enough to satisfy any man.

Of course I could go along (also Duke) when the four
of them went for walks in Battle's Park, which they did quite
often, but this was not any too much fun because they wanted
to sit down so much. They really didn't see much of Battle's
Park, and I don't think they ever did go to Piney Prospect.
Mother didn't come with us on these walks, even though she
was the chaperon. "I know when I'm not wanted," she would
say, archly and significantly, "I can take a hint," and the girls

would blush and laugh, and Mars' Phil and Mars' Pike would guffaw and beam on the girls. I never saw anything out of the way, however, on these walks without Mother, except that once I saw Mars' Phil try to put his arm around Aunt Floy's waist, and she made him take it away, right off.

Both the girls made me call them "Aunt"—Aunt Floy and Aunt Carolisa—which shows how far along things were. Mars' Phil had known Aunt Floy back in Roanoke—they'd been sweethearts since they were little—whereas Mars' Pike hadn't known Aunt Carolisa but just a few years. She came from down in the eastern part of North Carolina. All four of them seemed very much in love, "regular love birds," Mother said, and when Dad came I heard him say something about "billing and cooing," and that Mars' Phil "looked like a dying calf" when he looked at Aunt Floy. He didn't at all! and Dad shouldn't have said it. Both the girls called Grandpa "Father," just as my uncles did. Everybody was mighty happy that summer.

Mars' Pike married his fiancée, a little later, and went in the tobacco business down at Kinston, but Aunt Floy, just before she was to have married Mars' Phil, ran off and married a Congressman with a lot of money. I had not the faintest idea what a Congressman might be, but I felt instinctively, when I learned of this shocking elopement, that a Congressman must be a black villain, a snake-in-the-grass. I may not have been so far wrong: mine is not an uncommon estimate, even to this day.

It was rough on Mars' Phil, I know now (he had got a new suit and some beautiful new golden oak furniture for the back bedroom), but not as rough as it got to be later on. Even then I knew that something was wrong (this was before I really understood about the elopement) and I felt vaguely unhappy about it. He didn't turn to a guitar for solace, like Miss Etty Mangum. He took to disappearing for days at a

time, and rumors of evil companions registered on my consciousness. There was a fellow named Sweeney, whom Mars'
Phil knocked around with . . . Mars' Phil was the first
person I ever heard referred to as a black sheep. I heard somebody say something, once, very significantly, about " 'A minister's son'—*you* know," and "professional baseball," and of
course I knew it could only mean Mars' Phil. It was hard to
understand, and it troubled me. There were times when
Mother was very sad, and Grandpa was even more silent and
preoccupied than usual. Everybody loved Mars' Phil, they
couldn't help it. He was so big and good-looking, and so gay
and kind. I didn't love him; I worshiped him.

He had wanted to be a doctor, but somehow it didn't
come off. I don't know why, but looking back now, I think
that after he finished Episcopal High School, in Alexandria
(where he was a star athlete), there wasn't the money to support the long years of medical training, and likely he went into
baseball to make some. Maybe it wasn't easy to save. You
know how it is, traveling around with a baseball team. Maybe,
because he loved the game, he stayed in it longer than he
should. Then he really fell in love with Aunt Floy, even deeper
than he had been as a boy, and—well, that's the way things go,
sometimes. So he gave up the idea of medicine, and took whatever jobs seemed promising. Where he has been buried for so
long, in the little old Cemetery so closely pressed by the growing University, seems to me an ideal spot. Mr. Emerson's
baseball field is just a couple of hundred yards away from his
grave. I'm sure it must be pleasing to him to hear the crack of
a bat and the yelling, in the spring.

After the bad time, when Aunt Floy jilted him, he began
losing his jobs. He went away for a while, up in Maryland
somewhere, and taught at a boy's school. When he came back
to Chapel Hill he had nothing to do, and that's when he helped
with the University team. He picked up a little, here and

there, umpiring ball games, too. Then he was express agent in
Chapel Hill, and this went fine for a long time. People would
say "Phil Meade's himself again; isn't it fine?" But after a
while, suddenly, he didn't have that, either. He tutored me
that summer, because he didn't seem to want to do anything
else, and he was a good teacher; he made you *want* to know.
The interest he gave me in history has always stayed with me.
That's the only schooling I ever really enjoyed, I guess. He
used to play catch with me a lot, too, and we would go to the
town ball games together.

Then Mother got her legacy, and Dad went in the chicken
business, and Mars' Phil pitched in to help him!

Raising chickens was a popular ambition then, a sort of
golden dream of Utopia, to many men the Ultimate Goal. It
was something like the little-place-in-the-country-and-your-
own-car the insurance ads promise you now, the shining
vision at the end of the trail of hard work. To anybody like
Dad, who had spent his life in the smoke and cinders of railroad trains, or cold or stifling warehouses, or in the dry
monotony of a railroad office, with nothing much to do at
night but walk around, alone, on hot city pavements, the idea
must have been particularly alluring. Not only could he be
with Mother and the rest of us in the fresh air and beauty of
Chapel Hill, in the country, in a way, but he could be His Own
Boss, he said, and not dependent on the Southern Railway,
even though he loved it. Dad would cuss the Southern Railway at times, but he wouldn't let anyone else do it.

He had talked about raising chickens, off and on; it had
always been in the back of his mind, ever since I first knew
him. But he could never do anything about it. It took capital,
he said. He couldn't pass anybody's chicken yard without
stopping to look. "Um-m-m," he'd say, "Wyndottes. Now
aren't they pretty?" Once I remember him going to the door

of a little Negro house down on Windy Hill and telling the
man to give his chickens, in the little yard up by the road, some
water, as their pan was empty and the chickens were walking
around with their tongues out. He spent a lot of time fussing
with our few chickens, when he was in Chapel Hill, even my
bantams. "Chickens need a lot of care," he said, "you can't
just leave 'em alone." 'Way back there he used to say "When
I get my chicken farm . . ." but that got to be "If I get my
chicken farm . . . " and I guess the idea got to be a beautiful
mirage ahead of him and which he never really expected to
reach. But still he talked about it a lot . . . And then my
Great-aunt Anna died.

When my Great-aunt Anna died she left my mother *five
hundred dollars!* When the unexpected news came, Mother
almost fainted, then she cried, she couldn't take it in. She
didn't know what to do, she just laughed and cried! Grandpa
walked around, grinning through his whiskers like a Cheshire
cat, and patted her on the back. "Well, well," he said, "I declare!" I was sent running uptown to find Mars' Phil and tell
him about the letter from the lawyer, and he came running
home with me, laughing and shouting. He pummeled me and
knocked me around, and threw his arms around Mother and
kissed her, the happy tears streaming down her face. "Oh,
won't Dad be happy!" she'd say, and then start crying again!
The excitement around our house was terrific. Even Viola,
her eyes popping and her grin spread all over her face, couldn't
quite believe it; she kept saying, "My, My! What y'all go'n do
wid all dat money?" Old Uncle John Atwater didn't cut much
wood that day. I doubt that any member of the family had
ever conceived of five hundred dollars all in one lump. We
were rich! The world was ours! Dad's chicken farm was his!

No one had known, apparently, that good old Aunt Anna
was in the chips, and we were very proud of her and thankful.
Everybody in the family began calling her Dear Aunt Anna
instead of Aunt Anna. I had known her only as legend, a name

who lived remotely in Virginia, but instantly she turned into a good fairy with wings and a magic wand, the most beautiful fairy I ever saw. The legacy came as a complete surprise to Mother (the wording in the will said the bequest was to Aunt Anna's favorite niece), and this made it all the better. If I won the Irish Sweepstakes now, there couldn't be more jubilation! Five hundred dollars all at once was hard to take in; you'll understand when I tell you that my grandfather's salary as rector of the Chapel of the Cross was six hundred dollars a year, and Dad's, I'm sure, even though he was working for the Southern, little more. Money was worth something then, and five hundred dollars was a lot of it!

Mother sent Dad a telegram. I know, because I went up to the telegraph office with her and she gave it to Mr. Gooch and paid for it. The telegram said "Have received large inheritance Aunt Anna can you come love Alice." She and Grandpa had written it, pondering and scratching out and writing again; what they finally settled on seemed to cover everything, and was very good, I thought. I asked Mother couldn't I take it to the telegraph office and send it, but she said No, she would go with me so that there couldn't possibly be any mistakes. When he read the message Mr. Gooch pushed his glasses up and smiled all over himself at Mother. "Well, now, isn't that fine?" he said. *"Large,* eh?"

"Well—yes," said Mother.

Of course the news was all over town in no time, once Mr. Gooch knew it, and people began coming to the rectory to congratulate us and try to find out all about it. People would congratulate Mother on the street, and even me. Mr. Rob MacRae said, "That's just wonderful, Miss Alice; I'm cert'ny mighty glad to hear it . . . I'll bet you're going to buy an *automobile!"*

I sure did prick up my ears at that, but Mother said, "Oh, no, I'm not!" and I knew she meant it.

But *five hundred dollars,* maybe that would buy an automobile, *too.* There were three or four in Chapel Hill by that time, and the thought of a family automobile, for our family (which had not occurred to me until Mr. MacRae suggested it), was dazzling. I was thirteen years old at that time, and beginning to get some advanced ideas. But I knew the money was going into Dad's chicken farm, and so did everybody else.

I made the most of reflected glory. In fact, in one or two instances, and of course in strict confidence, I told some of the boys that Aunt Anna had left the money to Mother and me. Some of the younger ones believed it. "You're *rich,*" said little Arthur Bruner. "Yes," I said, modestly. I know that Bruce Strowd and Collier and some of the others like the Venable boys didn't think I really had all that money, but they did seem to treat me with a little more respect and consideration. I remember Collier suggesting that I "set him up" at the drug store, a proposal which under ordinary conditions he knew would be quite useless.

"Oh, the money's in the bank," I said.

"Haven't you got *any* of it?" he asked.

"No," I said, importantly, "It's in the bank—for safe-keeping."

Dad gave up his position with the Southern, along with his passes and the attendant prestige, and beat it for Chapel Hill, just as fast as he could, he said, to plunge into the long-awaited and hoped-for and almost-despaired-of venture. "Just goes to show," he said proudly, "that all things come to him who waits!"

"Well, you cert'ny have waited, Dad," Mother said, "and now you've got the money! It's just a *miracle,* that's what it is! Bless Dear Aunt Anna's heart."

Dad hadn't cried as Mother did, when he got home, but you could tell he was mighty happy.

"Well, sir," he'd say, "you know, I don't hardly know where to begin!"

The first thing that he and Mother did, though, was to take care of the only other thing, along with the chickens, Dad had ever wanted for himself—a gold watch. (Mother said she didn't want a thing in the world.) I'll never forget the day we bought that watch! Dad got a rig with yellow wheels and a high-stepping bay from Mr. Pickard (he tipped the colored boy who brought it around to the rectory ten cents), and the three of us drove to Durham and picked it out. It took all day. And it cost fifty dollars! We had a fine dinner at the hotel; Mother said the strawberry ice cream was the best part of it. I remember Dad was almost speechless on the way home, overcome, probably, by what had happened to him. But he'd take the watch out of his pocket (we'd bought him a chain, too, with a seal on it which he could use on a fob if he wanted, and later his initials were engraved on the seal), and snap it open and look at the time and grin at Mother, foolishly, and flick the horse. Boy, was he happy! All of us tried to listen to the watch, but it ticked so softly you could hardly hear it. I tried singing "Seeing Nellie Home," on the way back, but it didn't sound as good as Mars' Phil's rendition.

This watch was a thin Hamilton, beloved of generations of railroad men, with a hunting case, a stem wind, and a queer little contraption on the side. Dad said all railroad mens' watches should have them, but why he had to have a railroad man's watch then, I couldn't understand; he wasn't a railroad man any longer, he was a chicken farmer, or, as he said proudly, a poultry breeder. Anyway, railroad men's watches were not supposed to be set by a free stem, he said, because it used to be common practice for an engineer, or somebody— if he was having a beer and wanted an extra minute or two— to set his watch back and then claim that the stem wind must have caught on his pocket when he pulled the watch out, and done him dirt. So railroad men's watches were made special, with a little tongue or lever on the side which you had to pull out first before you could set the hands. This prevented any alibis, Dad said.

Dad didn't know a thing about raising chickens, really, but he thought he knew everything, and if confidence and joy, and enthusiasm and energy count for anything he had what it takes. We were going to make a million dollars, he said, well, maybe not a million, but a lot anyway. He had lived for so long with chickens in his heart and his head—fine, fat, healthy, productive chickens—that he had gradually developed and evolved a whole set of theories for taking care of these dream birds, and in his mind's eye he never saw a hen which hadn't a bright red comb and a yellow bill, and wasn't laying an egg.

Every time Dad heard a hen "sing"—that little, monotonous, almost songbirdlike noise they make, which corresponds to a kitten's purring—he'd smile indulgently, and say, "Hear that? That hen's happy. Yes, siree, that's a mighty happy hen." Whenever he saw a hen all spread out on the ground, stretching luxuriously and dusting herself, he'd say, "Now, just look at that hen! Isn't that wonderful? She knows just what to do to get rid of those lice, by *instinct;* I tell you, you can't beat *instinct*. Or Nature." He was strong for Nature. "Nature knows a lot more than we do," he said, "just leave it up to Nature."

I don't know whether he was too close to his subject or too far away from it. Nevertheless our chickens thrived on his doctrines. "Chickens are just like human beings," he'd say, "yes, sir—all you have to do is treat 'em kind and keep 'em clean. Of course," he would add, mysteriously (leaving himself an opening, as all expert theorists do), "you've got to know *how* to do this. It's not as simple as some people think."

He redoubled his efforts in the gathering of information. He read everything pertaining to poultry he could get his hands on, whether or not it had to do with developing the color and the extra-long tails of Chinese Chickens—though he knew

mighty well we'd never have a Chinese chicken—or How to Keep Eggs Through the Winter in Manitoba. There wasn't much in the way of poultry or farm journals then, but there was one published up North—*The Rural New Yorker,* I think it was called—which Dad subscribed to and read as avidly as ever I did the *American Boy.* "You never can tell where you're going to pick up something," he said," even if those Yankees up there don't know much." All his life, of course, he had been talking chickens with any kindred soul he happened to meet, and he had gradually accumulated a tremendous store of information and misinformation, theories, both untried and proven, old-wives' tales, superstitions, "home remedies" and methods handed down from generation to generation. He talked a lot with the local farmers, and even went over to Raleigh to A. & M. College and talked with the people there (he snorted when he got back and said they were a bunch of college professors who didn't know their way around a real chicken yard, with their new-fangled notions, and all) and thought most of their methods and manners were wrong. He'd show 'em!

"Of course Modern Science knows a lot," he'd say, "but not about chickens!" (He always spoke of Modern Science as though it were a person.) "Now, I remember, when I was a boy at Petersburg, my father . . . " or "A man whose judgment I respect, down in Alabama, told me . . ." Such persons as the man in Alabama gave Dad a lot of wild stuff, some strong medicine, but he said you had to take everything "with a grain of salt." He'd say, "Just pick out what you know is right, and leave the rest to Nature."

Our money was in the bank, and Dad used to spend a lot of time at night, that spring, going over his accounts and figuring his balance, Mother leaning over his shoulder. Mother didn't know a thing in the world about banks, she said (and I don't think she altogether trusted them; "*every*body makes

mistakes," she said, "even Banks"), and when she endorsed
the lawyer's check over to Dad she wrote on the back of it
"Please pay this money to Mr. Robert Watson Prince, Mrs.
Robert Watson Prince, Rosemary Street (the Rectory)
Chapel Hill, N.C." She wasn't taking any chances. Mr. Jim
Taylor, the bank president, said, "Just write "Alice Meade
Prince" under that, Miss Alice; that's the way the check is
made out."

"Will Mr. Prince get the money all right?" Mother
asked anxiously. (As was the fashion then, she always referred to Dad as Mr. Prince, though she never addressed him
as "Mister," as some of the older ladies called their husbands.)

"He's got it already," Mr. Jim smiled, "you'd better
watch him!" as he entered the amount in Dad's bankbook and
handed it to him. Because Dad already had a bank account!
It contained our nest egg, and amounted to practically *one
hundred dollars*. This nest egg was what Dad and Mother had
been slowly saving and adding to, for the rainy day, and was
under no conditions to be touched until the rainy day came.
The legacy and the nest egg together really amounted to something! Dad said that the chicken farm was going to cost a lot
of money by the time we got everything we had to have—and
even though he didn't intend, "under any conditions," to use
the nest egg, still it made you feel good to know it was there
if you really needed it. I remember Grandpa smiled and said
he couldn't think of a better place to put a nest egg than in a
chicken farm. When Dad ordered the incubator he sent a
check with his order. He showed it to us. "I'll owe no man,"
he said. He never did. He didn't believe in charge accounts,
and if we couldn't pay spot cash we went without.

While we waited for the incubator and all the other stuff
that Dad and Mars' Phil had decided on and ordered, the
hammers—Mars' Phil's and Dad's—were ringing in the back
yard. A high fence of chicken wire began to creep around the

big lot where our cornfield had been, an acre or two of it, for
"free range." That was mighty tough work, with Mars' Phil
and Dad digging all those post holes and setting the 4 x 4s.
Wagons from the lumber yard and the sawmill and Mr. Herndon's hardware store rolled up and dumped timbers and planks
and siding and shingles and tarpaper and wire and staples and
nails, and then went back for more. Dad and Mars' Phil
labored all day and sometimes until after dark. Most of the
time I was helping them.

Like a lot of men who never had much experience, Dad
fancied himself as a carpenter ("I was always mighty handy
around the house," he would say, and nobody could dispute
this because he hadn't been around the house enough to prove
himself otherwise), but as a carpenter he was something less
than brilliant. What he put together, however, even if it looked
a little cockeyed and crude, hardly any man could put asunder
—I'll say that for him. "There, now!" he'd say, as he finished
putting in three or four superfluous nails, "That'll stay! Of
course it's not like a regular carpenter might have done it, but
it'll stay; so much of the work you get done nowadays is just
jerrybuilt." He, and his office-soft hands, took a beating, but
Mother would dress the wounds and stick the blisters, and at
night rub him with witch hazel. He might mash his fingers or
cut his hands or strain his back, but she'd always fix him up
and send him back again. Every morning he was up before
day and back at it! Mars' Phil—so much younger and bigger
and stronger than Dad—did most of the really hard sawing
and lifting, even if it was over Dad's protests. "I'm just as
good a man as you are!" Dad would say to him (and I believe
he thought it).

"Go on," Mars' Phil would answer. "Go 'way back and
sit down. You've already got one foot in the grave!" Then
they'd both laugh, and Mars' Phil would do the sawing, or
dig the hole.

The main house was a fine affair, about forty feet long by twelve wide, the siding-covered walls sealed with tarpaper to keep out the drafts; drafts were mighty bad for chickens, Dad said, you never knew what drafts might lead to. Two points Dad was sure of: you had to keep chickens dry—and warm. The house may have been a trifle off-center and -level, in spots, but it sure looked substantial by the time we got the last shingles nailed on the roof. "This house is going to be here when we're all dead and gone," said Dad.

Inside we built a long, sloping shelf of boards under the tiers of roosts, on one side, to catch the droppings. Later, when we got into operation, it was part of my job to keep this shelf clean, every day, with a hoe and a broom and buckets of water. Along the other side wall were the rows of nest boxes, two deep. Nothing was ever built with so much joyful anticipation as those nest boxes! Dad said he could just see 'em full of eggs, and he tenderly shaped the fresh, clean straw he put in them, so that the hens would be as comfortable as possible.

There was one regular size main door, of course, for us to use, down at the end, and several little doors, for the chickens, with the prettiest little ramps leading up to them, with cleats nailed across so that the chickens could walk up easily. When it began to get dark and the chickens went to bed these little ramps really got jammed, sometimes, with traffic, and it was wonderful to see the chickens walk up them: *instinct,* Dad said. Inside the house the windows over the nest boxes were in little tracks, and you could slide them back and forth. It was the best chicken house I ever saw.

Outside, and joined onto the big house, we built several "runs," or smaller yards, with smaller houses in them, for special purposes such as the "breaking up" of hens who wanted to set, or for fryers or broilers we wanted to fatten up, or just for any kind of segregation or experimentation Dad wanted to carry out. He was always experimenting. Then there were the separate pens, covered over the top with wire, where the little chicks were to be kept (so that the big chickens couldn't hop in and hurt them, or eat their food). Then there were the brooder pens, for the very little just-hatched chicks; and lots of little houses for this and that.

Dad and Mars' Phil pored over catalogues and papers by the hour, at night, and we ordered more stuff than you could shake a stick at. We had to have at least three brooders, they decided, because the hatchings would be coming along so fast. (There was a time when they got so enthusiastic they even thought of buying another incubator.) These brooders were imposing pharaphernalia, when they arrived, with huge metal "shades"—like a lamp shade but more flattened out and spreading—for the chicks to huddle under at night, in lieu of a real warm and protecting mama, and flannel curtains around the bottom which the chicks could push aside to get in or out. The brooders were kept warm by a hot water container inside, protected by a cover so that the chicks couldn't burn themselves, and this hot water was heated by a kerosene burner on the outside of the brooder. A wonderful piece of machinery, Dad said. Wonderful what people can think up. And I wish you might have seen what-all we had for the chickens, big and little, to eat and drink out of. We got flat feeders that sat on the ground, and couldn't be turned over, with divisions in them so that one greedy chicken couldn't hog everything, and feeders that hung on the wall, divided the same way, and round water containers and fountains with rows of holes around the bottom where the chickens drank, and we had hoppers which let the stuff inside down as the chickens ate it. We had boxes and hoppers for charcoal and ground-up oyster shell and limestone grit—"roughage," Dad said, for the chickens' craws—and he explained, learnedly, how a chicken had to grind up what he ate, like in a mill. We had beautiful little drinking fountains (all this stuff was galvanized steel, so that it would last a long, long time—with care) for the little chicks, so that they couldn't fall into their drinking water and get drowned. We bought a bone cutter, which fastened on the edge of the work bench and had a big wheel which you turned to grind up the fresh bones which Dad would get from the butcher shops uptown. I tell you, it all looked wonderful after we got it assembled and everything was done, and then when our first chickens, the grown ones we'd ordered, came, it just looked exactly like the picture you might see in an advertisement of a chicken farm! Mars' Phil and Dad and I used to sit down on the top step of the back porch, and look at it . . .

That was when we got the bulldog. Dad said a man would be a fool to have that many chickens and no watch dog. Especially in Chapel Hill. And as Duke knew and liked everybody in town, white and black, he wasn't any good that way, and so we got Spot. Spot was a sort of bull terrier, but he had a corkscrew tail and a terrifyingly fierce face, although he turned out to be very amiable and never bit anybody. He was not a thoroughbred bulldog, but the man we got him from said his mother had a pedigree. He was all-over brindle, but as Dad said he had always wanted a dog named Spot, Spot we named him. He and Duke had some arguments, and once or twice Duke put Spot in his place and gave him a good thrashing, "boxing" him, Mars' Phil said, like Jim Corbett. Duke was a wise old battler, and he had had a lot of experience, and Spot hadn't. We built Spot a fine kennel in the chicken yard, and he stayed there o' nights, protecting our investment.

And of course a heavy investment it got to be. We spent all Aunt Anna's legacy, and as Grandpa had suggested, we threw in the nest egg.

Dad bought two hundred Leghorn pullets to get started with, a hundred brown and a hundred white, because they were the best layers. He couldn't decide between the breeds;

"I believe maybe the Brown Leghorns are the best layers," he said, "but those White Leghorns are so dog-gone pretty!" They were, too, 'way off across the big field. We ordered these from one of the big breeders whose farm, Dad said, was highly recommended. I'll never forget the day they came, by express, in their big crates. They were the gladdest chickens to get out you ever saw, and it was wonderful to see them stretch and look around at their new home and then begin exploring and eating. We had to handle each one to see if it's wing was clipped, so that it wouldn't go over the fence and far away. We always had to clip one wing of all our own chickens which we hatched, as they grew up, too. Those Leghorns fly like birds.

We also had a couple of dozen Black Minorcas, beautiful chickens with huge red combs which flopped down across their faces. This was a new breed which Dad wanted to experiment with; they were fine layers and their eggs were large, and white as milk, would bring fancy prices, we thought. The Minorcas were a little larger but a trifle more delicate than the wiry Leghorns. We kept them in one of the smaller runs, with their own house, and Dad used to go in the yard and catch the rooster, a beautiful big bird with silky, iridescent plumage and his great red comb, and hold him, fighting and squawking, on his lap while he stroked him lovingly.

For incubation we ordered Leghorn eggs, for our future laying stock, and Rhode Island Red eggs for the chickens we would sell to market. The Reds were big, fat fowl, fast growers. These eggs we ordered from a place in Mississippi which Dad said was tops. Dad and Mars' Phil pondered and worked out formulas and put together sure-fire laying mashes and grain diets and chick feeds, and bone builders and conditioners. Our birds had to have a lot of green stuff, too—that's where the free range came in—but after a while they picked the big lot clean, and we had to give them lettuce and cabbage, all we could get.

Dad was the happiest man in the world when feeding time came up, and he could stand in the big yard with a huge can of grain, in a sea of hungry chickens who climbed all over each other trying to get to him, and toss the feed around in great sweeps and yell, "Ch-h-h-ick, chick, chick, chick!" But you should have seen him the first time our incubator "came off." Of course it didn't "come off" like a hen, but this was the term we applied on that twenty-first day, when the eggs hatched. The incubator, a beautiful, big, 250-egg affair, was in a little room off the kitchen, and its care and temperature supervision was a matter of prime importance for three weeks. Like the brooders, the actual heat came from hot water, which, in turn, was heated by kerosene. It was, I believe, the first incubator seen around Chapel Hill, and many people came for a look at the new-fangled contraption. Dad would drop whatever he was doing and come running to display it, proudly. He couldn't open it, to show its works, like a clock —because that would have disturbed the temperature—but he would explain how it operated in great detail, and display at length its various gadgets and devices as though he had invented it.

The night the eggs hatched, Dad didn't go to bed at all! As the chicks broke their shells and got free, they'd slowly work their way forward toward a little glass window in the front. I'll never forget how those first chicks looked, through that little glass window. Brown Leghorn chicks look like little Bob White quail. Hardly any of the eggs failed to hatch; we had candle-tested them for fertility before we started the incubation, and they came all guaranteed.

That incubator never got cold! By the time we cleared out one batch of newly hatched chicks, and got them safely in their brooder, there would be another big shipment of eggs from the farm in Mississippi, and off we would go on another setting. Mars' Phil and Dad took turns getting up at night to check the thermometer; I wasn't called on for this,

I guess they knew I couldn't be waked up. At 250 eggs a throw, you can get a lot of little chicks in one summer, and they thrived and prospered. The place was lousy with chickens, big and little, and medium sized. Our brooder pens and our other runs were loaded to capacity.

Right from the start, the pullets layed; every minute of the day you'd hear their cackling, the proud and excited announcement of accomplishment. And the nest boxes looked just as Dad had said they would, full of eggs. Twice a day it was my job to gather the eggs in big water buckets. That was as thrilling a job as I've ever had to do (though sometimes Dad couldn't resist the temptation and he'd gather them himself. "Just wanted to see how many we got today," he'd say.) And how the eggs rolled in, or rather, out; those Leghorns were good! Some of the eggs we sold to the stores uptown, and some we crated and shipped away to a wholesaler in Greensboro. Mars' Phil and Dad would stagger uptown carrying great loads of eggs, and never fall down. They even began talking about buying a horse and wagon, as the business grew, as sometimes we had to hire one to carry the eggs, or the crates of frying-size chickens, uptown. Mars' Phil seemed mighty happy, too, and he whistled and sang as he used to. Life was good, and we had fried chicken all the time.

And then, that winter, when the goose hung the highest, catastrophe came.

Roup is a loathesome, deadly affliction of poultry, and that's what hit our flock. It spreads like a prairie fire, with just as terrible effect; you fight it just as hard and desperately, but there's no stopping it, or wasn't then, so far as we could find. Roup is catarrhal, respiratory, akin to membranous croup in humans. Membranous croup is what had killed my little brother and sister, and this made it even harder on Mother and Dad. Roup strikes just as suddenly and with just as much vicious power . . . and our wonderful, beautiful chickens just choked to death.

Dr. Merritt couldn't do much for us, try as he might; we tried all his suggestions and prescriptions. He'd come down and work with the sick chickens by the hour. We swabbed out their throats, we put Roup Remedy and other patent medicine preparations in their water and their food, which they couldn't eat, we burned sulphur, and brown sugar, and turpentine, we used creosote and lye and lime, we sprayed the whitewashed walls and the roost poles and the floors with strong antiseptic solutions doped up by Dr. Merritt, but nothing stopped it. It was a terrible, a ghastly time, with the collecting and the carting off of the dead ones every morning, more and more each day. It was an awful sight, to push open the door of the chicken house in the dark before dawn in the cold mornings, and see, in the fantastic, flickery lantern light, the poor dead birds everywhere on the shelf and on the floor, the ones who were still alive huddled together and gasping for breath. And even the little ones in the brooder pens.

Somebody was always digging a hole. Mars' Phil and Dad went around with a shovel in one hand and a bucket of creosote solution in the other, their faces drawn and grim. I never felt so sorry for men in all my life. Every afternoon when I got home from school I'd go out there immediately, and neither Mars' Phil or Dad could even smile or say anything; they were too tired and bewildered. Neither could I; big boy as I was, I couldn't keep the tears back, sometimes, at what I saw, but I'd get a shovel and start in, silently, to help them. The scourge, the epidemic, went through us so fast you couldn't believe it; it wasn't possible that we were being cleaned out. And then suddenly we were through. There was nothing left but the big, empty yards and the houses and pens, and the red mounds of earth where the chickens were.

It must have been a bitter pill for Dad, but he swallowed

it. He had been so happy; it had all been so beautiful; he had been so sure he couldn't fail . . . And now the chickens were gone, the money was gone, his job was gone, and his dream was ended. He and Mars' Phil hitched up their pants and talked about tearing down the houses and selling the lumber and the equipment for whatever little it would bring, but nobody wanted it for fear of germs of the deadly roup. Dad said he felt like a leper, and that his chicken farm was a pest house. Mother always put her arm around him when he said this. So there it all stood and began slowly to go to pot, and the drinking fountains and the hoppers rusted, and the grass and weeds began to grow again in the big field.

Everybody was mighty sad, but everybody tried hard to be cheerful, too. "You just weren't cut out for a chicken farmer, Bob," Mars' Phil said, "you're a city slicker."

"Yes, I was, too," Dad answered, doggedly. "Next time . . ." But he knew there wouldn't be any next time.

Mother was wonderful. "Yes, sir," she'd say, "*next* time, everything is going to be fine! I think it was just those *Leghorns;* next time we'll get some other kind of chickens!"

"Well—maybe . . ." Dad would say.

I heard Grandpa talking to Dad, once. He said, "It's just like everything else in life, Robert; the Lord giveth and the Lord taketh away. It wasn't your fault, boy."

After a while, Dad brushed up his old clothes and his derby hat, and went off to Washington to see the powers that were, and he got his old job back, and went out settling claims again. The Lord may have given Dad this interlude, which even with its tragic ending was wonderful, but Dear Aunt Anna helped in the giving, too, and the Lord didn't take everything away from us, either, for there was still Dad's gold watch—and this was fine and fitting, for he was a railroad man again.

William Meade Prince had the great good sense to be a boy at the turn of the century —in that nostalgic period before World War I when peace was something that was always there and small boys could have a good time in an American small town. He was lucky in the place he was brought up in, Chapel Hill, North Carolina, where he had everything that makes for the good life for a small boy—a loving family, two young and friendly uncles, a faithful dog, a host of good friends, and his developing talent as an artist. Like any real boy, he enjoyed them and made the most of his luck. He grew up to become one of this country's best-known book illustrators, whose drawings add an unforgettable savor to these memoirs.

At that time Chapel Hill was a small college town of 1,200 inhabitants, including 600 students of the University of North Carolina. It had all the advantages—football and baseball stars for hero worship, young and pretty teachers, volunteer firemen, penny candy, the town's first automobile—and, of course, the infectious good feeling Chapel Hill felt for itself and its college. First published in 1950, *The Southern Part of Heaven* has become a classic of growing up in the older America.